"Dr. David Gill reveals for us the c
the home, office, or field, and for
of dignity in the eyes of God. Thr
to deliver impact and leave this world a better place. Many books talk about discipleship and our mission as Christians, but how does this translate into what we say and do in the workplace? Now we know! Thank you, Dr. Gill."

—Catherine B. Blake, Founder, Institute for Executive Women
CEO, Sales Protocol International

"*Workplace Discipleship 101* contains a wealth of encouragement and practical advice for Christians who are serious about living out their faith in their daily work lives. It led me to take a serious look at the ways I was (and was not) effectively expressing my faith in the workplace. I felt both convicted and encouraged."

—Clay Collins, Public High School English Teacher
Author, *Tethered: Technology, Faith, and the Illusion of Self-Sufficiency*

"I wish this book had been published when I first entered the workplace. David has infused such wisdom from years of teaching workplace theology that this very practical manual should be carefully studied by any believer who wants to have joy and satisfaction while glorifying God at work."

—Ernest Liang, Director, Center for Christianity in Business
Editor, *Christian Business Review*
Associate Professor of Finance, Houston Baptist University

"Few people I know have thought more deeply and practically about the integration of the Christian faith in the workplace than David Gill. In *Workplace Discipleship 101*, David Gill's keen intellect, ethical clarity, and encouraging heart frame a persuasive and practical guide for all apprentices of Jesus who long to embrace an integral faith. This book is an invaluable resource I have been waiting for a long time. I highly recommend it!"

—Tom Nelson, Lead Senior Pastor, Christ Church, Kansas City, Missouri
President, Made to Flourish
Author, *Work Matters: Connecting Sunday Worship to Monday Work*

"David Gill has produced a significant, biblically based, practical introduction for those who care about faith in the workplace. With clarity, crisp categories, and memorable stories, Gill provides a realist's view of the workplace's opportunities and challenges. Pragmatic suggestions and provocative questions for reflection punctuate each chapter. *Workplace Discipleship 101* will be relevant for anyone who works for many years, serving as a guide and foundation by which to live 'full-faithed' at work."

—Mark Washington, National Director of MBA Ministry
InterVarsity Christian Fellowship/USA

"*Workplace Discipleship 101* is a powerful primer for activating Christian faith in the work lives of believers. This book is packed with simple, practical suggestions, all organized in an intuitive format with straight-forward language. If everyday working Christians applied everything in this book, we would transform the entire workplace. I pray that the common sense of *Workplace Discipleship 101* becomes common practice!"

—Chuck Proudfit, Founder and President, At Work on Purpose, Cincinnati

"Discipleship is about following Jesus, but it's important to have an experienced guide like David Gill charting the way. He's packed decades of trail-savvy wisdom into *Workplace Discipleship 101*. If you want to live a God-honoring life at work, grab a copy of this book, recruit a posse of fellow followers, and hit the road. You'll be outfitted and ready for the toughest trails."

—Bill Peel, Executive Director
Center for Faith & Work, LeTourneau University

"As someone who works with those in the trenches trying to figure out 'how' to do faith and work day to day, this book fills a gap in the available resources. It enables a senior leader, a middle manager, or a blue-collar worker to gain practical implementable next steps toward a more integrated life. Kudos to Dr. Gill for bringing his academic and corporate consulting learnings together to embolden believers to move closer to Christ on Monday—this Monday in fact."

—Missy Wallace, Executive Director
Nashville Institute for Faith and Work

"Given David Gill's impressive academic pedigree and decades addressing issues related to faith and work, I expected *Workplace Discipleship 101* to be rock solid biblically—and I got what I expected! But I was struck by just how down-to-earth it is. While there is plenty here for pastors and scholars, David speaks plainly, persuasively, and passionately to a broad range of people, addressing the real challenges they face in their daily work, with dozens of wise 'to do' suggestions that can be put into practice right away. I am delighted to recommend this book enthusiastically to all who seek to grow as workplace disciples of Jesus."

—Mark D. Roberts, Executive Director
Max DePree Center for Leadership, Fuller Theological Seminary

"Dr. David Gill's book *Workplace Discipleship 101* goes straight to the heart of what it means to be a workplace disciple. The principles contained in each chapter are sure to give a follower of Jesus the tools they need to make a difference in the workplace. I've known Dr. Gill as a passionate leader and a disciple of Jesus Christ in the capacities of professor, mentor, and friend."

—Larry Ward, Senior Pastor
Abundant Life Church, Cambridge, Massachusetts

"For me as a Chinese reader, *Workplace Discipleship 101* opens a new horizon to see how my faith can have a much deeper and more practical impact on a central part of my life. Even if the verbal proclamation of the gospel is prohibited, living a Christ-centered life still speaks powerfully!"

—Rachel Tang, English Teacher, China

"David Gill draws on his diverse, unique experience (seminary and business school professor of ethics; pastor; business consultant; and community organizer) to guide Christians through a foundation for integrating their faith and their work. Thoughtful, practical, and helpful."

—Albert Erisman, Director of Technology, Boeing Company (retired)
Editor, *Ethix Magazine*; Co-chair, Theology of Work Project
Author, *The ServiceMaster Story: Navigating Tension Between People and Profit* and *The Accidental Executive: Lessons on Business, Faith, and Calling from the Life of Joseph*

"*Workplace Discipleship 101* is a pragmatic and applicable teaching on allowing one's faith to inform and positively affect one's work life. Dr. David Gill expands the reader's notion of calling beyond preaching and pastoral ministry by presenting a clear linkage between calling and general vocation. Then he describes what that looks like in the daily work life of believers at the office, factory, and boardroom. This book is a must-read for laypersons, as well as pastors."

—Gina Casey, AME Zion Pastor and Chaplain

"David Gill's *Workplace Discipleship 101* is the culmination of a lifetime dedicated to supporting Christians in the workplace. The clear and straightforward organization focused on preparation, presence, and post-work is must-read material for followers of Christ interested in a 24/7 application of their faith!"

—Tom Cowley, Former VP, American Hospital Supply
Director, DMin Program, Olivet University, Mill Valley, California

"*Workplace Discipleship 101* is a truly practical primer for living out one's faith at work; about reforming Christian workers, not economic systems or companies."

—Buddy Childress, Founder and Executive Director
Needle's Eye Ministries, Richmond, Virginia

"*Workplace Discipleship 101* is an excellent collection of wisdom for Christians who want to live their faith effectively outside the walls of the church and inside their workplace. David Gill calls upon his vast knowledge of faith, Scripture, and life experiences to create a clear, well-organized, practical guide for workplace disciples."

—Paul Figueroa, Police Officer

"Reading David Gill's *Workplace Discipleship 101* took me on a very immersive and rich journey. It is a practical roadmap for anyone who wants to explore a new approach to their work, where Jesus is truly Lord. This is a must-read for all Christians who want to share their faith and see God transform their work."

—Fernando Tamara, Made to Flourish City
Network Leader, Hispanic Los Angeles

Other Books by David W. Gill

The Word of God in the Ethics of Jacques Ellul (1984)

Peter the Rock: Extraordinary Insights from an Ordinary Man (1986)

The Opening of the Christian Mind (1989)

Should God Get Tenure? Essays on Religion and Higher Education (editor, 1997)

Becoming Good: Building Moral Character (2000)

Doing Right: Practicing Ethical Principles (2004)

It's About Excellence: Building Ethically Healthy Organizations (2008/2011)

Political Illusion & Reality: Engaging the Prophetic Insights of Jacques Ellul (coeditor, 2018)

Workplace Discipleship 101

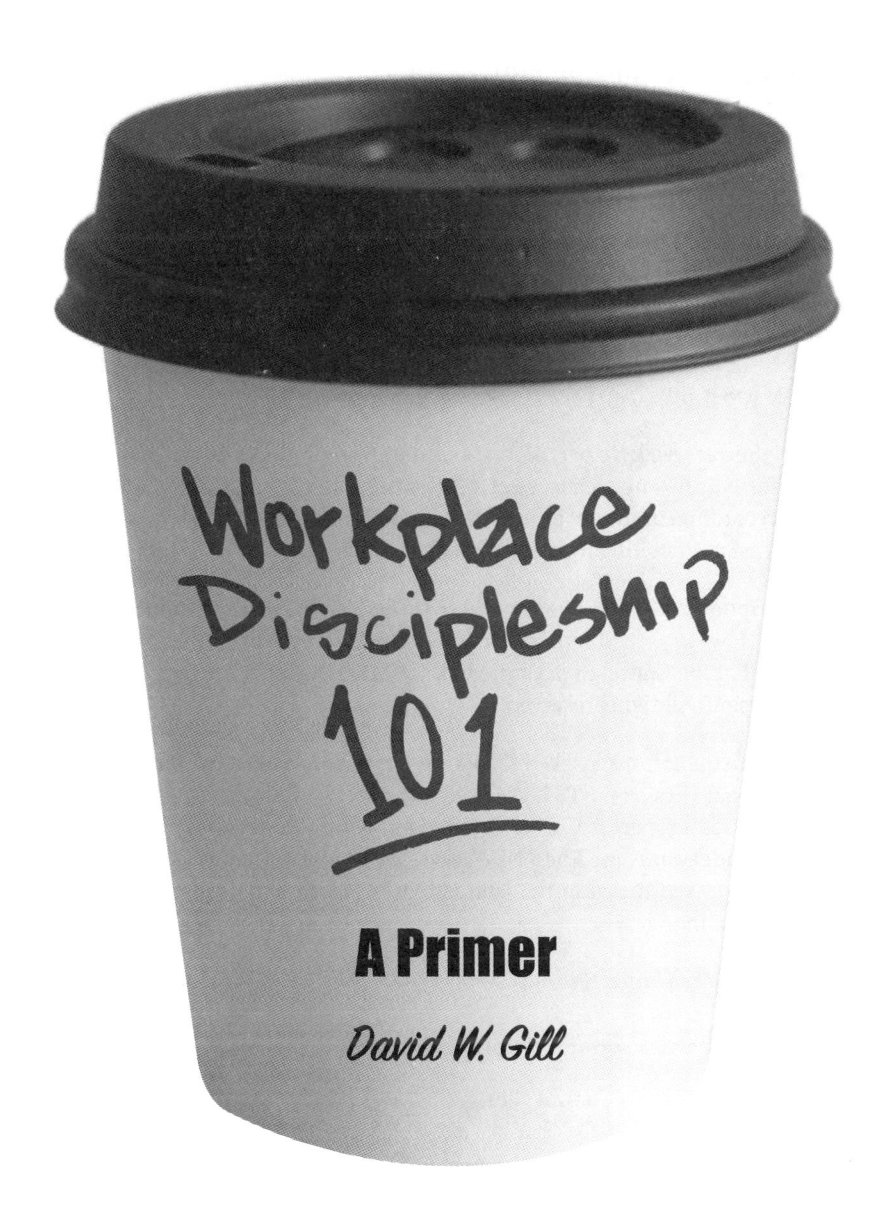

an imprint of Hendrickson Publishing Group

THEOLOGY OF WORK PROJECT

Workplace Discipleship 101: A Primer

Published by Hendrickson Publishers
an imprint of Hendrickson Publishing Group
Hendrickson Publishers, LLC
P. O. Box 3473
Peabody, Massachusetts 01961-3473
www.hendricksonpublishinggroup.com

ISBN 978-1-68307-311-6

Printed in the United States of America

First Printing — October 2020

Library of Congress Control Number: 2020941698

For

John & Marj Erisman
Al & Nancy Erisman

Lifetime friends and coworkers
for workplace discipleship

Contents

Preface

Workplace Discipleship 101 is a basic introduction to what biblical Christianity means for our work lives. While there are many books today on various aspects of this topic, we still need a primer—a simple, straightforward, basic, practical guide for workers. That's what this book is. It is not an argument about economic theory or reality. It is not much about organizations (businesses, schools, factories, etc.) as such. It is about *workers*, men and women at work. It is a kind of curriculum, a study and action plan for Christians who really want Jesus to be Lord of their work. In school we might call it "Course 101"—the introduction—not "201" or something more advanced or specialized.

Think about this: Christians who go into traditional pastoral or missionary callings and jobs receive lots of help and affirmation along the way. There are numerous books, training programs, and specialized schools (such as seminaries and Bible schools) that are ready and eager to train people for church ministry and work. Graduates are usually commissioned, ordained, commended, or affirmed in public ceremonies for choosing to serve God in these vocations and for completing educational programs in preparation. (For that matter, elders, deacons, and other church workers are often recognized and commissioned in church services.)

That's all fine and good, and these folks are doing good and important work. But what is missing is for non-church-based *working people* to see clearly and profoundly that *their* work is also all about service to God. In this perspective, *every* Christian is involved in "full-time ministry"—not just pastors. Our work (whatever it may be) ought to be seen as *ministry* ("service") to God. Remember what Paul wrote, "Whatever your task, put yourselves into it, as done for the Lord and not for your masters" (Col. 3:23).[1] That's what this little book is about: doing our work heartily for our Lord, wherever and whatever that work may be.

This book is about the "workplace" rather than (just) the "marketplace." You may have heard of "marketplace ministry" and "Christianity in the marketplace." But the term "marketplace" puts the focus on *markets*, on the exchange of goods and services. Of course, marketing is work, but it is only one kind of work. "Work" (in an accurate, inclusive sense) is a broad term. (Work, by the way, is not defined by the fact that you are paid for it. A lot of our human work is uncompensated financially, sometimes even voluntary.)

My own definition of "work" is as follows: "effort in thought, word, and deed to provide needed and wanted products and services." It is about *effort*—exerting ourselves to provide something that people (including ourselves) need or want—from the thinking and planning phase to the exertion and effort of turning those ideas into products and services. If we are not exerting ourselves, then we are *resting* or kicking back. "Labor" is a synonym for this core aspect of work. Some of our work is about making material *things* such as food, shelter, and equipment, but other work is providing *services* such as hospitality, medical, teaching, caring, organizing, or driving. Some of this exertion is in our minds as we think, analyze, and invent; some exertion is in communication ("word") and some is physical ("deed"). Most of our

---

1. Biblical quotations are from the New Revised Standard Version unless otherwise indicated. Any words or phrases in brackets indicate my own translation.

work on the planet is about survival, meeting the most basic of needs. Some work is more about satisfying people's wants, luxuries beyond mere survival.

We can understand work better by comparing it to *rest* and *play*. "Rest" is "not-work." Rest is when we cease from our work. "Play" is about voluntary effort that is not about meeting needs (unless we want to say that we *need* to play some in this life—to which I agree). Play can become an obligation, even a job or profession—but at that point it has become work. The distinction isn't just about being lighthearted or having fun—we can experience that at work and not just while pursuing our personal hobbies and games. A key aspect of work is that we need to do it or somebody else needs us to do it. It is, however, complex: some of our work can almost feel like rest or play . . . and some of our attempts to rest can feel like work . . . and our play can evolve into work. While all three are to some extent interwoven into the reality of daily life, the distinctions are important.

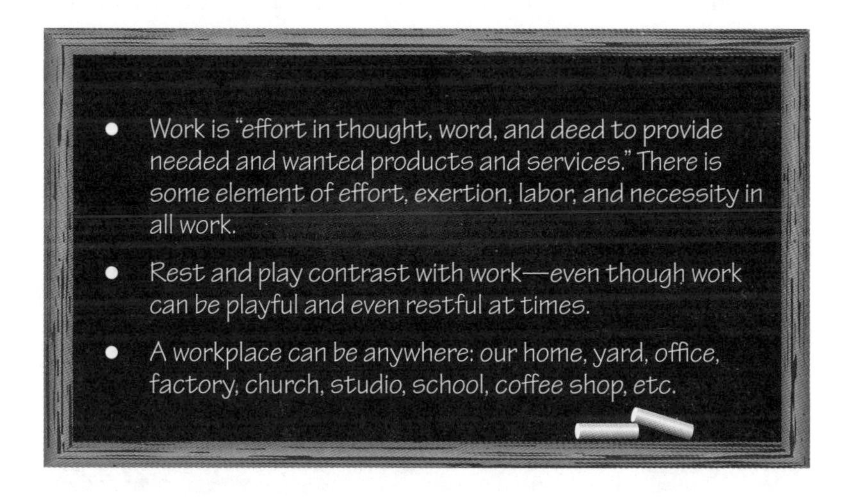

Everybody works (or should work) at all ages, whether paid or not. We are made in the image and likeness of a working God (and, we should add, a resting God). It is part of our human nature as created by God. People from every continent and nation—east and west, north and south—need to work. They need work to put food on the table and meet basic needs. But they also need to recover their dignity and meaning in life as part of their identity, made in the image and likeness of a working God. Kids should work while growing up, and retired people should take on some meaningful work even as they get old. Wherever we work (office complex, factory, home, church, campus, laboratory, studio, farm, etc.) is our workplace. One of the most misguided and insulting questions is when a mother is asked "Do you work?" Come on! "Every mother is a working mother" insists a bumper sticker.

So, the *workplace* is the territory, the location addressed by this book. This book is also about *discipleship*, which I mean in the most basic sense: "learning from and following after Jesus Christ." In recent decades, you may have heard the phrase "faith at work," which usually means something like "the implications of the Christian faith for our work." "Faith at work" is a good label, but I prefer the more explicitly activist tone of "workplace discipleship." By this, I mean how we think and act, how we believe and behave, as we follow Jesus as our Lord in our workplace, wherever it may be.

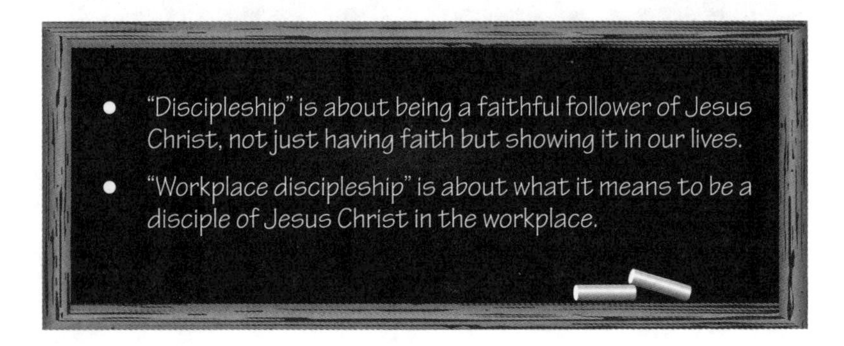

There is a ton of literature on marriage and family discipleship in the "home place," and a ton on discovering our spiritual gifts for the "church place." There is also a lot of help for the *inner life* of devotion and spiritual growth, and even some on the *afterlife* in a place called heaven. But "workplace discipleship" is often neglected. Think about this: we spend roughly one-third of our lives (eight hours of every twenty-four, if we're lucky!) in bed sleeping, another one-third working, and the final one-third for everything else (family, church, recreation, etc.). That final third receives almost all of our theological attention. As for the other two-thirds, the implications are that (1) we should spare no expense in buying a good mattress (I write tongue-in-cheek, but we do spend one-third of our lives there!), and (2) we should commit to a radical upgrade of our workplace discipleship.

I would argue that the basic lessons of *Workplace Discipleship 101* apply to all workers in all workplaces, in all economies and cultures, anywhere in the world. My examples and applications come out of my experience, and I do not expect them to relate easily or exactly to working Christians in other vocational, economic, and cultural contexts. But I believe we human beings have a lot in comon, especially when it comes to our human nature—all of us made in the image of God. Let us not forget that we Christians believe in one God, the creator and redeemer of the whole world, not just our tribe or nation. I would therefore argue that the basics of workplace discipleship are the same everywhere and at all times. Again, I am writing about the discipleship of workers, not about reforming economies (capitalist or socialist) or companies and organizations. This book is about reforming workers and then trusting God to work in and through them on their organizations, cultures, and economies.[2]

2. My book *It's About Excellence: Building Ethically Healthy Organizations* (Eugene, OR: Wipf & Stock, 2011) is a practical road map to organizational reform and strength in companies, schools, hospitals, businesses, and other organizations. It is written for a general market but is

Where I Am Coming From

I grew up in a family and church setting where we really believed Jesus Christ is Lord of all, all the time, not just in our personal and church lives. And we believed the Bible was God's word guiding all of life.

In the fall of 1966, when I was a junior studying history at the University of California, Berkeley, I vividly recall a day when it struck me that God (or religion, for that matter) was never a factor in any historical study, lecture, or explanation delivered by my famous Pulitzer-Prize-winning professors (not even in a course I took on the Reformation!). In one sense that was no problem, because I didn't go to Berkeley to learn about God.[3] But I had a dilemma: in my personal and church life, I thought God was definitely (although mysteriously most of the time) involved in human history. My

---

based on biblical perspectives. As for economic systems, I get impatient with all the debates about capitalism and socialism, especially when we have little chance of actually impacting things on a systemic, economic level. Rather than getting lost in theoretical debates about economic labels and systems I urge all Christians, anywhere and everywhere in the world, to practice and advocate what we could call "steward-ism"—*everything* belongs to God (not ultimately to the state or private owners). No matter our laws or structures, and whatever power and responsibility we have, let us work as good stewards, managing and caring for God's property, as God wills. Michael Barram's *Missional Economics: Biblical Justice and Christian Formation* (Grand Rapids: Eerdmans, 2018) describes the kind of biblically organic thinking about economics workplace disciples need, in my view.

3. The only academic advice my non-college dad gave me as I went off to Berkeley was, "Remember, David, your mind belongs to Christ." It would have been unimaginable for us to gripe that Berkeley didn't teach me a Christian perspective—just as it would never have occurred to us to wish that my public school teachers and principals growing up would lead us in some (probably) wimpy official prayer! The integration of faith and learning had to happen, but we never expected—or wanted—public, secular institutions or leaders to try to do that for us.

career plan was to graduate and become a public high school history teacher. But what was I going to do once I had this job? Could I maintain a divided mind in which God was part of one side but not the other? Or was there a way in which I could integrate these two perspectives that would do justice to both? Furthermore, my concern was not just how to *think* about God and *history*, but also how to *do* God-honoring *teaching* in a public school.

Christian friends of mine, who were studying banking and finance at the time, wondered the same thing about how to integrate biblical teaching on money, debt, and property with their own "secular" business studies. Likewise, those studying law wondered what to do with the massive biblical teaching on law, justice, and righteousness, and on Jesus Christ as Advocate, alongside their "secular" legal studies. I decided to push this agenda in my own studies by doing a master of arts degree at San Francisco State University with a thesis on "Contemporary Christian Philosophies of History: The Problem of God's Role in Human History" (which I submitted in 1971).

Throughout the 1970s, my concerns evolved from intellectual integration to ethical demonstration. I became convinced that the major challenge to the Christian witness in our world was to *demonstrate* the truth and reality of the faith—not just argue for it intellectually. My quest became overcoming any division between a public, secular education and career (in which God was silent, excluded, or ignored) and a more private theological view of life and work. Sometimes this is called the "sacred/secular" divide. But Jesus is Lord of all, so what does that mean?

What I am sharing in this book is the product of fifty years of thought, prayer, study, reading, conversation, and teaching in schools, colleges, churches, and other contexts. But my views on our topic are also shaped by my work experiences, which began as a kid selling my car-washing and lawn-mowing services to neighbors . . . then four or five years as a newspaper delivery boy every morning before school . . . then eight to ten hours a week as a gas station attendant all through high school . . . then forty to seventy hours a week doing hard physical labor in a noisy factory during every summer and academic break of my four years as an undergraduate. After that my career as a teacher began, briefly in junior and senior high school . . . then decades in college, seminary, and graduate business school settings . . . with some years as a dean or president . . . countless committee and project initiatives . . . and a couple interim pastorates and several grassroots entrepreneurial ventures outside the academy. I've had good bosses and horrible ones, great coworkers and a few scoundrels, physically exhausting work and mentally or relationally stressful labor, and some amazing generosity along with being exploited and mistreated at times.

I mention all this only to explain that my book is not about some theoretical or academic project created in an ivory tower, but part of my life in the work trenches of different kinds. While, of course, I hope you will find my personal suggestions and examples helpful, all of the ideas in this book need to be applied in your own context and supplemented by your own study and reflection. My views and experiences are illustrative, not normative!

If you happen to pick up this book and you are not a Christian, then welcome to the discussion! You might find it most interesting to read Parts Two and Three first so you can see where this is going, what kinds of impacts Christians could and should be making in our workplaces. Or maybe this book will help you see the Christian faith in a more holistic and positive way than you have up to now. That would be my hope for you.

The Approach in This Book

Workplace Discipleship 101 is a summary of what I believe makes for a faithful and wise workplace disciple who is (1) blessed personally, (2) a huge blessing to others in the workplace, and (3) whose life and career bring glory to God. The real heart of the book is Part Two (chapters 6 through 10) which describes five key aspects of Christian presence in the workplace: "Impacting Our Workplace.." This is what we are and do in the workplace; it is our distinctive contribution as disciples of Christ. Sharing our gospel faith is one, but only one, of five important pieces.

To use an athletic analogy, we can't compete well in the game if we are not trained and conditioned. That is what Part One, "Getting Ready for Our Work," is about: five things we do to be prepared for faithful and effective presence in the workplace. It just can't and won't happen otherwise. And this is not a one-time sequential operation. Throughout our whole careers, we repeatedly need to do all the things in both Parts One and Two. It's like going to the gym and trying to get fit. It must be a lifetime habit. We work out and practice, and then we get in the game. After that, we rest up, work out, practice some more—and then it's game time again.

Part Three, "Moving Beyond Our Workplace," takes us outside our primary workplace with reminders to contribute not just money but also our work skills back to our church and community. In this section, we are reminded that healthy and faithful workplace discipleship must be balanced with rest, worship, and play. Work is important, but it must not become an idol or obsession. The book concludes with a "Postscript to Pastors," outlining a few basic steps they can take to support the workplace disciples in their congregations (which means *most* of their congregants).

Each chapter concludes with a couple of action points to put on your to-do list to help you follow up on the reading. There are also questions for personal reflection and group discussion ending each chapter. In your book "class sessions," you will find old-fashioned "chalkboards" along the way with (hopefully!) helpful summaries of key points, which should help you stay focused on the main idea. (Of course, if you are terribly busy, you can just read the chalkboards to grasp the summary message in short order!)

Finally, since this is an "introductory course," I purposefully avoid my professorial tendency to load up either the text or the footnotes with academic discussion and references. I think, however, that you will find the footnotes that I did include provide some suggestions for further study of the topics—in case you wish to advance to the next level in your learning about being a workplace disciple. School is now in session!

PART ONE

Getting Ready for Our Work

In Part One, we will look at five steps that workplace disciples need to take to prepare for faithful and effective presence in the workplace. Although some of these steps may seem obvious at first, they are often overlooked and undervalued. When we really start to think about it, it's actually not so obvious how we should pray about our work or study our Bible regarding that work. In this case, we should view these steps not as five one-time activities but as five life *habits*.

1

Commit

Be Intentional, Not Just Casual, about the Workplace Adventure

Who then is the faithful and wise workplace disciple? What does it take to get there from here? The first critical move is to understand the basic meaning and importance of workplace discipleship—and to make a firm and bold commitment to the adventure of making Jesus Lord and Master of our work. This is really just a subset of making Jesus Lord of our whole life.

The Christian life begins when we receive and confess Jesus as our Savior and Lord. We make a conscious commitment. It is not just an inherited or casual thing. From that point on, when we are "born again" into God's family, we are challenged (and expected) to grow into mature men and women of God. The whole Christian life is about this pilgrimage, this growth in grace and faithfulness. The apostle Paul described it to some fairly new Christians):

> In our prayers for you we always thank God, the Father of our Lord Jesus Christ, for we have heard of your faith in Christ Jesus and of the love that you have for all the saints, because of the hope laid up for you in heaven. You have heard of this hope before in the word of the truth, the gospel that has come to you. . . . For this reason, since the day we heard it, we have not ceased praying for you and asking that you may be filled with the

> knowledge of God's will in all spiritual wisdom and understanding, so that you may lead lives worthy of the Lord, fully pleasing to him, as you bear fruit in every good work and as you grow in the knowledge of God. (Col. 1:3–6, 9–10)

While these people had heard the gospel, responded in faith, and were already manifesting the virtues of faith, hope, and love, they were now being challenged to be "filled with the knowledge of God's will" so they could lead lives pleasing to the Lord in every good work. The Christian adventure is the pursuit of being *filled* with God's knowledge (not just knowing a few basics), in order to please God in every aspect of our lives (not just some aspects). Some wise wordsmith once said, "If Jesus is Lord *at all*, he is Lord *of all*."

"Why do you call me 'Lord, Lord,' and do not do what I tell you?" Jesus once scolded his disciples (Luke 6:46). Jesus has not just provided his followers with a ticket to forgiveness, heaven, and eternal life. He has not just come to transform our Sundays or our life at home and church. I have sometimes, tongue-in-cheek, preached a sermon titled "Jesus Rose on Monday" to startle people into the realization that Jesus' resurrection happened on the morning of the first day of the workweek of that era—not on the Jewish Sabbath, which was their day of religious observance. The resurrected Christ shows up on what (in that era) was "Monday morning" of the workweek.

Workplace discipleship begins when we truly understand this truth and reality: Jesus Christ wants to be Lord and Master of our whole existence, including that huge chunk we call "work." We need to bow before him and commit our work lives to his Lordship. I mean that literally: We need to commit our education and career to our Lord in prayer. I would further urge that we make that commitment public by sharing it with others. Workplace discipleship is not about a casual, occasional tip of our hat to God—or an emergency-only practice. It is a conscious, deliberate, serious, daily, yearly, lifetime commitment, an "I surrender all" experience.

Workplace discipleship is hard work, and it has its share of sacrifice and struggle. In his classic book *The Cost of Discipleship*, Dietrich Bonhoeffer compared "cheap grace" and "costly grace"; "cheap grace" is grace without discipleship, without the cross.[1] Although workplace discipleship is not easy, it also brings a level of meaning and purpose far above any alternative, because now at work we are "on a mission from God!"[2] Workplace discipleship is about bringing our work into alignment with the work of the creator, sustainer, and redeemer, the Alpha and Omega of human history. It is visionary, often joyful, and usually in meaningful community with others committed to the adventure.

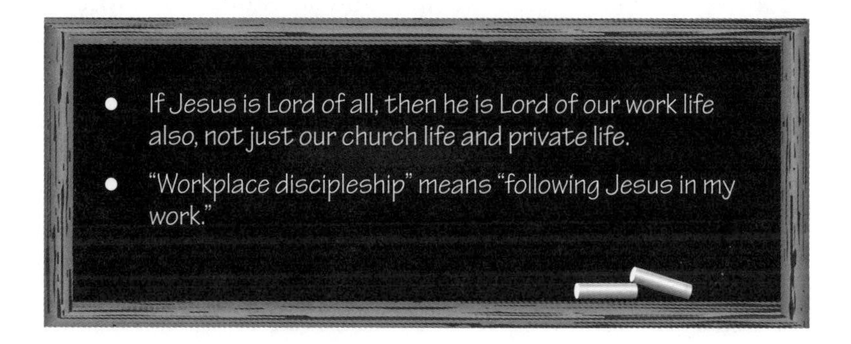

Saying No to the Bad Stuff

Let's begin thinking about this commitment as something entailing a no and a yes. The faithful and wise workplace disciple needs to learn how to say no to certain things and yes to others. Our world—including our world of work—has a

1. Dietrich Bonhoeffer, *The Cost of Discipleship* (Munich: Kaiser Verlag, 1937; English translation by R. H. Fuller, 1949).

2. With a grateful nod to the Blues Brothers for rendering this line into an iconic phrase in pop culture!

great deal of beauty and excellence in it. But it is also messed up and unacceptable in many ways. That is why workplace discipleship must begin by saying no to the bad side of work and to the bad side of our own history and performance. Paul wrote to Titus, “The grace of God has appeared that offers salvation to all people. It teaches us to say ‘No’ to ungodliness” (Titus 2:11–12 NIV). Jacques Ellul often said that the first act of freedom is to say no.[3] For example, an alcoholic is not truly free until he can say no when faced with the possibility of having another drink. Likewise, our freedom in the workplace begins when we say no to bad workplace behavior.

This point is so important. When people hear the gospel, the “good news”) of the kingdom of God, their first action step is to *repent*—to turn around, to renounce their sinful past lives. Even the great symbol and sacrament of baptism begins with being submersed in water. The old life is symbolically buried, before one is lifted up to newness of life. So, too, Jesus told his disciples that although they would be sent into the world, they must be nonconformists: they will be *in* the world but *not of* it (see John 17:11, 14).

Paul’s powerful statement of ethics in Romans 12–13 begins, “Do not be conformed to this world, but be transformed by the renewing of your minds” (12:2). Christians are strangers and pilgrims traveling through this world toward a city with foundations, whose builder and maker is God (Heb. 11:10; 1 Pet. 2:11).

---

3. Jacques Ellul (1912–94), whose name will appear a few times in this book, was a professor at the University of Bordeaux (France) who is best known for his critique of our technological society, but who also wrote many books on Christian topics. The best introductions are Jacques Ellul, *Presence in the Modern World*, trans. Lisa Richmond (Eugene, OR: Cascade, 2016), and Patrick Troude-Chastenet, *Jacques Ellul on Politics, Technology, and Christianity: Conversations with Patrick Troude-Chastenet* (Eugene, OR: Wipf & Stock, 2005).

Workplace discipleship starts with a critique of "business as usual" and a resolute commitment not to be simple-mindedly conformed to our workplace context. We need to think differently about our work: what it is, why we do it, how we choose it, and the meaning of our career. We need to work, manage, and lead differently. We pursue a different purpose. We are not just going along for the ride with others. We don't just roll over in front of every workplace trend. We raise questions—or more precisely, we ask God to raise questions about virtually every aspect of our work. We are not satisfied with the status quo. We are not going to slink along quietly through our work life. This point just cannot be stressed enough: Be a nonconformist! Question authority! Do not just submit to the "everybody-else-is-doing-it" way.

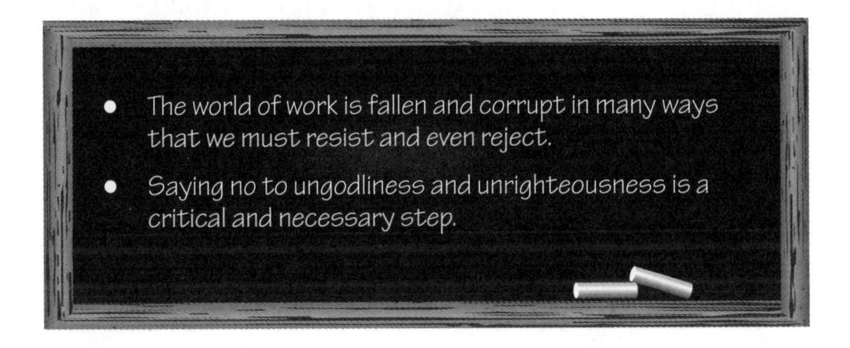

Of course, we do not say no to everything. Not everything in the workplace is objectionable or evil! Much of it is wonderful and we should cheer it, support it, and thank God for it. If we measure our workplace context by the Ten Commandments or other clear biblical expressions of God's standards, however, then we will understand that it is the idolatry and worship of money or profits to which we must say no. While money and profits are not necessarily bad (in fact, they can prove most helpful!), we must say no to turning them into idols we worship.

We must also say no to 24/7 workaholism. Working hard for six days is good, but working seven out of seven is bad. We must also say no to dishonesty or false witness in our advertising and product testing, accounting and tax returns, employee evaluations, or personal résumés. The point is to be aware, to be resolute in our commitment to God's standards and values, and say no when they are clearly violated. Workplace disciples embrace God's standards and say no to their violation.

Saying Yes to the Workplace Discipleship Adventure

We are not, however, trying to be randomly eccentric—or grumpy, judgmental naysayers. Saying no is the first step, not the last; it is a way station, not a destination. We may not be "of" the world, but we are definitely going "into" the world. We refuse to be *conformed* to this world, but that's not the end of the story. We also seek to be *transformed* so we can discover and then carry out the will of God, which is "what is good and [pleasing] and perfect" (Rom. 12:2). The grace of God teaches us to say no to ungodliness, but also to "live" in this world; to say yes to godliness while we wait for the blessed hope: the appearing of the glory of God in our history (Titus 2:11–14). Right now, although we live in a cultural nighttime, Paul says that we are to "live honorably *as in the day*" (Rom. 13:11–14; emphasis mine). This is a powerful metaphor.

While we start with a no, we must move on to the yes. We are not just pilgrims and strangers; we are also *ambassadors* from another country, the kingdom of God (2 Cor. 5:20). We must not just be the "religion of no" in our world of work. We must not just curse the darkness but also light some candles. Remember the old folk wisdom: We can't get an old bone out of a big dog's mouth just by pulling on it; we do it by throwing down a steak. "Overcome evil with good," urges Paul (Rom. 12:21).

So how do we figure out the yes—the good—of workplace discipleship? While God has shone his light and truth in many different ways and at different times throughout human history—and we want to learn from all possible sources of God's truth—we Christians believe that in a unique and extraordinary way, God came into our history in Jesus Christ, who is "the exact representation of [God's] being" in human flesh (Heb 1:3. NIV). Jesus was fully human and tested and tried in every respect like other humans but without ever sinning (Heb. 4:15). "In him the whole fullness of deity dwells bodily" (Col. 2:9). Jesus Christ brought into our human view the very Creator, Sustainer, and Redeemer of the universe. Jesus was God himself in human form. He was the one truly and wholly Spirit-filled human being on the planet. He was the Teacher; the one who, far from abolishing God's law given to Israel, lived and explained its fulfillment in the gospel (Matt. 5:17–20).

Jesus had more to say about money, property, and wealth than he did about heaven and hell, gay and straight marriage, or any number of other hot topics. Not that those (and other) controversial topics are unimportant or unaddressed by Jesus, but we need to recapture the great emphases Jesus placed on work and economic life. The fact that God was incarnate in a carpenter's son, not a rabbi, and that his earliest followers were drawn from the ranks of fishermen, tax collectors, and physicians—not from rabbinic scholars—says a lot. Jesus' miracles often occurred in the workplace, his parables dealt with workplace imagery, and his miraculous activities brought food to the hungry and healing to the sick and injured, not just theological insights. This is a workplace Lord.

In short, Christians are called first to resist any kind of simple-minded conformity to the workplace culture in which we find ourselves. We need to take a step back and say, "Wait a minute, let me think about that." Then, second, we need to have a much bigger and fuller understanding of Jesus Christ our Lord. It is by drawing close to Jesus Christ, understanding his teaching, and following his example that we will be transformed in our approach to our work.

What is the difference Jesus wants to bring to our work? Jesus taught us to pray, "Your kingdom come. Your will be done, on earth as it is in heaven" (Matt. 6:10). Jesus himself could say "not what I want but what you want" to his Father in heaven (Matt. 26:39). He could say, "I always do what is pleasing to him" (John 8:29). That is what we are after: the will of God (that is, what God wants done—the God of all people, in all of the world, not just our tribe or nation). What does God want me to do in my work? How can Jesus' life and teaching help me figure that out?

Our guidance, while centered on Jesus Christ, will of course come from the entire Bible, not just the Gospel stories of Jesus. "All scripture is inspired by God and is useful for teaching, for reproof, for correction, and for training in righteousness, so that everyone who belongs to God may be proficient, equipped for every good work" (2 Tim. 3:16–17). The whole of the Bible, therefore, will be important in guiding our workplace discipleship. While God can guide us through nature and other people in history, it is the Bible, with Jesus at the center, that will always be our main, ultimately authoritative textbook on workplace discipleship.

This is the adventure of workplace discipleship, the no and the yes. It is a lifetime of going beyond business-as-usual in favor of the constant search for work according to God's will, bearing witness to the coming day, not the passing night.

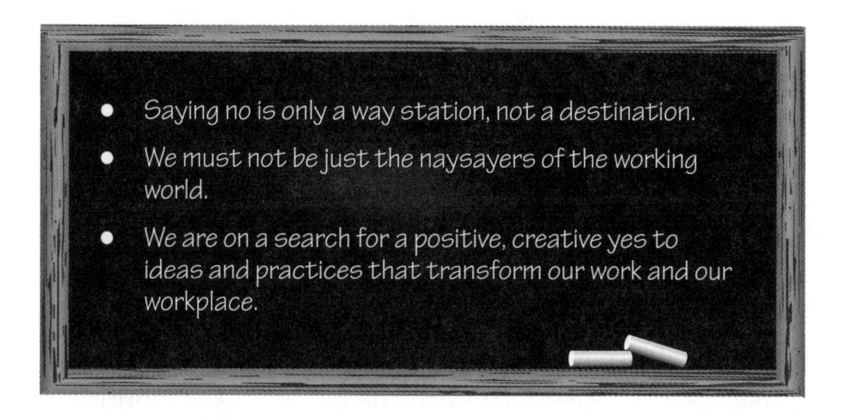

Workplace Discipleship Is Good for Us

If we follow this call to a no and then a yes, what are the results and impacts of faithful and wise workplace discipleship? The Bible teaches that there will be three results. First of all, it will be *good for us*—that is, good for the workplace disciple. The wild "health and wealth" promises of some televangelists are pretty bogus, of course; the Bible itself is full of examples of good people of faith who suffered deeply and unjustly. There are no guarantees that life in this broken world will be smooth sailing. But even on our worst day, it is better to be a faithful disciple than not. Better to have the Lord walk with us through the valley of the shadow of death than to walk it alone. "Blessed are those who are persecuted for righteousness' sake, for theirs is the kingdom of heaven" (Matt. 5:10). This Beatitude promises that even (or especially) in the horrible circumstance of being persecuted unjustly, we can be blessed by the experience of having God our king right beside us.

But it is usually better than that. It is interesting how Paul argues that people who serve Christ with lives of righteousness, peace, and joy in the Holy Spirit will not only be pleasing to God but will also be approved by those around them (Rom. 14:17–18). Normally, people like, welcome, and approve those with strong convictions and commitments to righteousness and justice, if they are also peace-making team/community builders and are full of joy. And each of the Beatitudes promises that practitioners will be "blessed" (Greek, *makarios*), which means "well-being," something that is objectively "good for you," not just some kind of subjective happiness or feeling good.

Generally speaking, we do feel better about our lives and ourselves when we reach out and help others. And more often than not, being an honest, diligent, responsible, and agreeable worker wins us praise and approval. Bringing creative and redemptive ideas to our work teams is often appreciated and rewarded. Workplace discipleship is also about purpose and meaning. It inserts our daily work into the grand cosmic story of God and humanity. We see our work in the light of God's work. When so much of today's work can seem meaningless, Christian discipleship brings powerful purpose and adventure. On the whole, at least, we see that faithful workplace discipleship is good for its practitioners.

It's *Good* for Others

Second, our workplace discipleship is *good for others*. Remember that the Christian life is not just about loving God. It is also about loving your neighbor as yourself. This means loving the "neighbor" working near us, the neighbor buying our stuff or hiring us, the neighbor in our supply chain anywhere in the world, the neighbor affected by our work and our company even if they are not customers.

Jesus told his disciples that they would be the "salt of the earth" and the "light of the world" (Matt. 5:13–14). Not just more earth and more world, but salt and light. "Salt" was a metaphor referring to preservation from rotting or spoiling, an agent that retards deterioration. "Light" provides the conditions and capacity for growth and for truly seeing reality. Retarding evil and enabling good: that is the impact of disciples who live Beatitude-shaped lives in the workplace.

Our workplaces badly need people who are not just in it for themselves—and not just in it for the stockholders. We are in it for God and our neighbors as well, for all of the "stakeholders" in what we do.[4] Our workplaces need people who bring their best selves to work, ready to contribute great effort and good ideas, and who can strengthen teams and build good relationships. Workplace disciples are on their way to that kind of impact capability.

It's *Good for God*

Finally, workplace discipleship is *good for God*. It is interesting that the Hebrew word *avodah* in the Old Testament had an interchangeable meaning of "work" and "worship." The point is that our work is one form of our worship of God. People will "see your good works and give glory to your Father in heaven," Jesus says in his Sermon on the Mount (Matt. 5:16).

As Christians, we want to show love back to God. After all, we love because he first loved us. He gave his all for us, so we want to give our all back to him. We want to live lives that are pleasing to God. I love how Jesus prayed to his Father just before he was put on trial and put to death, "I glorified you on earth by finishing the work that you gave me to do" (John 17:4). That is what we want to do: bring glory to God by finishing well whatever work he has given us to do.

---

4. The usual term is "stakeholder," which refers to anyone with a "stake" or interest in our work (and company), anyone impacted by our presence and activities.

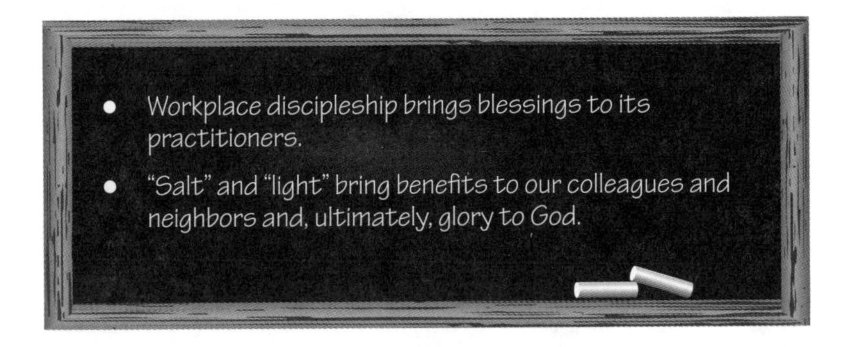

Commit to Being a Workplace Disciple

I want to challenge and encourage all of us to make a conscious, deliberate commitment to the task and the adventure of workplace discipleship. Wherever we live and work on our planet, whatever our age, whatever kind of work we do, whatever kind of culture or economy surrounds us, we can make this commitment. So let's make the commitment to God—and reinforce it by sharing it with others. Think about how difficult it is to lose weight or get fit if we don't make a commitment and resolve to get it done. Likewise, let's put our commitment out there to others to help reinforce it (and we will feel guilty if we bail out; a little guilt is good sometimes). Having people around us make the same commitment strengthens us for the challenge. No commitment and no plan mean no progress. The coming chapters will lay out the plan to which we commit ourselves. Just as Alcoholics Anonymous has a twelve-step program, so workplace discipleship is also a twelve-step plan. Step One is to *commit* to the adventure! Are we "fired up and ready to go"?

One final note: Workplace discipleship is never *only* about our commitment and effort. While it is that, of course, at the same time "we are [God's] workmanship" (Eph. 2:10 KJV). And while we must "work out [our] own salvation with fear and trembling . . . it is God who is at work in [us], enabling [us] both to will and to work for his good pleasure" (Phil. 2:12–13). "Not by might, nor by power, but by my spirit, says the LORD of hosts" (Zech. 4:6). This is the paradox or dialectic of the Christian life. Fundamentally, we want to yield ourselves to God and to his power and guidance. We pray that he will fill us with his Spirit. While we are not doing this on our own, we are called to cooperate with God's work in us, to "put off" some attitudes and behaviors and "put on" others (Eph. 4:22–24). We are not on our own in the adventure of workplace discipleship. We are welcoming God's Spirit and his work within us.

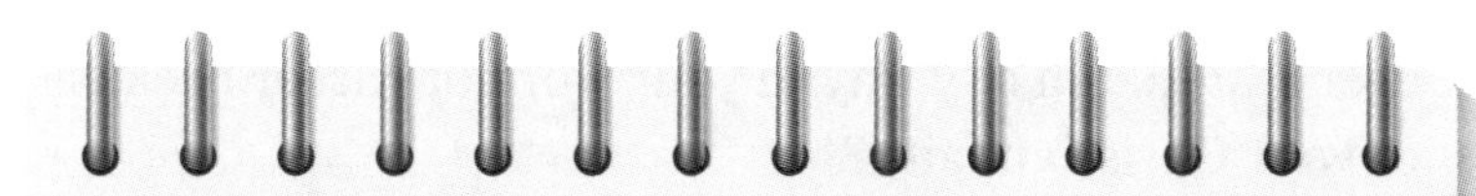

To Do

- ✓ Understand the argument: Why Jesus should be Lord of our education, work, and career.
- ✓ Make a serious, radical commitment to God in prayer, yielding control of our work to him.
- ✓ Reinforce this commitment by sharing it with others.

For Reflection & Discussion

1. What are some of the negative aspects about many of today's workplaces and work practices that you would like to see resisted and rejected? If God were to speak up, what do you think he would most strongly object to in today's world of work?

2. Have you ever had an experience where your Christian commitments helped you in your work? And have you ever suffered in any way in your work or career because of your Christian faith?

2

Pray

Talk to God, Not Just When in Crisis, but Proactively and Daily

A commitment to workplace discipleship leads right away to prayer. Jacques Ellul once wrote a little book on prayer in which he described prayer as a kind of "wrestling with God"—like Jacob wrestling with the angel and refusing to let him go until he blessed Jacob.[1] Even if it's not quite wrestling all the time, prayer is sometimes a bit like work: it takes effort and discipline. But if there is a God, if God is alive, if God is capable of caring for each of his creatures anytime, anywhere, 24/7, if God loves us, knows our name, and has adopted us into his eternal family as sons and daughters . . . then prayer not only makes sense but is a daily necessity in our life and our work.

Let's stick with a simple definition: prayer is talking to God. If workplace discipleship is about following Jesus as Lord of our work lives, then a basic and critical step is to ask for his help and guidance in this adventure. We want God to be involved! We can't do this on our own. "You do not have because you do not ask," wrote James (4:2). My friend and former seminary student and assistant, Andrew

---

1. Jacques Ellul, *Prayer and Modern Man*, trans. C. Edward Hopkin (Eugene, OR: Wipf & Stock, 2012); the Jacob story is in Genesis 32:22–32.

James, used to work with Christians in business and often used a little book called *Monday Morning Atheist*. The not-so-subtle message was that we might be fervent believers on Sunday, but then think and act like *atheists* when we go to work on Monday. "Atheists in practice"—though obviously not in theory—we just leave God out of our workplace lives.[2]

The Bible is full, cover-to-cover, with recorded prayers of all kinds, and with teaching and encouragement about prayer. The Psalms especially are a book of prayers for all kinds of circumstances: celebration, mourning, remembering, repenting of mistakes, begging for help, and so on. And think about the famous stories of prayerful individuals in the Bible. Working in Babylon's administration, "Daniel . . . continued to go to his house, which had windows in its upper room open toward Jerusalem, and to get down on his knees three times a day to pray to his God and praise him, just as he had done previously" (Dan. 6:10). "Pray without ceasing," wrote Saint Paul (1 Thess. 5:17). The book of Acts is also full of references to prayers, such as, "When they had prayed, the place . . . was shaken" (Acts 4:31). When I was young, one of my pastors, Clarence Mayo, urged me to go through Acts and circle every mention of the words *prayer* and *power* just to see their close relationship—which I did!

Jesus told a famous parable about an "importunate widow" who badgered a judge for justice so relentlessly that he finally helped her out just to get rid of her (Luke 18:1–8). Jesus told that story to encourage his followers to be relentless in their prayers to God. Jesus himself (and Paul and other early church leaders) showed us an amazing example of a life of prayer. And, of course, Jesus gave us a recommended pattern for prayer—the Lord's Prayer—to which we

2. Doug Spada, *Monday Morning Atheist: Why We Switch God Off at Work and How You Can Fix It* (Cumming, GA: Worklife Press, 2012).

will return below. But let's think about three kinds of prayers, three kinds of talking to God about our work, which I will describe as (1) emergency, crisis prayers; (2) proactive, holistic, proactive prayers; and (3) conversational, "chat" prayers.

Emergency, Crisis Prayers

We are often pretty good already at what I call "emergency prayers" or "crisis prayers." "Oh God, please help me get that job!" "Lord, don't let me get fired for missing that meeting when I overslept." "God, please help me figure out this computer problem, which is my responsibility." "Lord, please give me the courage to speak up and blow the whistle on my boss who keeps touching and grabbing me." And so on. You know what I mean. Sometimes we might feel hesitant to ask for help, because we think God may be busy with more important matters and our problems seem trivial or of our own making. Sometimes we might just forge ahead on our own strength and try to get through our crises on our own. Wrong on both counts: God is all-powerful, and God is all-caring. Jesus reassured his disciples: "Are not five sparrows sold for two pennies? Yet not one of them is forgotten in God's sight. But even the hairs of your head are all counted. Do not be afraid; you are of more value than many sparrows" (Luke 12:6–7). So, the smallest details of our life can be brought to God in our prayers. We should never hesitate to bring our emergency or crisis prayers to God. "Call on me in the day of trouble," he says. "I will deliver you" (Ps. 50:15).

But here is a qualification. Let's think about our other relationships. What if the only time we spoke to our spouse or best friend was when we were in crisis and needed something from them? What would that do to our relationships—coming and speaking to them only when we wanted or urgently needed their help? Isn't that kind of an insult? How do you think God feels, then, when most prayers are desperate pleas for help? Certainly, God is patient and forgiving, but our relationship is personal, not mechanical. God should not be treated as a rescue-machine, but as a loving parent.

Wouldn't it be a better idea to add into our talk to God some requests for help *before* we get into trouble? There used to be times when I begged my wife for last-minute help in the kitchen when I volunteered to cook for our guests. "The main dish in the oven isn't heating up right!" "My Volcano Cake dessert looks like a LaBrea Tar Pits disaster! Help!" But I learned over the years that if I asked her for some advice in advance, I radically reduced the need for emergency help (the marriage also went better).

This is a huge lesson for our workplace discipleship prayers: that is, be *proactive* rather than just *reactive*. Pray in advance and ask for guidance—don't just pray for help once the disaster has occurred. Pray while situations and circumstances are still relatively fluid—not just after circumstances have hardened and options have narrowed. Pray, asking for God to reveal his agenda, rather than barging ahead on your own agenda and then needing God's rescue. Let's keep on with those emergency or crisis prayers. But let's not have our prayers be limited to pleas for help alone.

- Yes to emergency, crisis prayers: "Call upon me in the day of trouble!"
- But our relationship with God (and with people) will become impoverished if our only communication is, "Help me, please!"

Proactive, Holistic Workplace Prayer

How can we move beyond our tendency to talk to God about our work only when we are in crisis mode? How can we pray in a more proactive, holistic way about our work? Here are some examples or models I have found helpful. For sure, these are not the only models of how to do it, but maybe they will inspire you to figure it out for your own context.

An Anonymous Worker's Prayer

I found this nice prayer online recently. Nobody was listed as the author, but it is a beautiful prayer for the start of a day at work:

> My heavenly Father, as I enter this workplace I bring your presence with me. I speak your peace, your grace, your mercy, and your perfect order into the atmosphere of my workplace. I acknowledge your Lordship over all that will be spoken, thought, decided, and accomplished this day.
>
> Lord, I thank you for the gifts and skills you have blessed me with. I commit to using them responsibly in your honor. Give me a fresh supply of strength to do my job. I do not take them lightly, but commit to using them responsibly and well. Give me a fresh supply of truth and beauty on which to draw as I do my job today. Bless my creativity, my ideas, my energy so that even my smallest task may bring you honor.
>
> Lord, when I am confused, guide me. When I'm weary, energize me. When I am burned out, infuse me with the light of your Holy Spirit. May the work that I do and the way I do it bring hope, life, and joy to all that I come in contact with today. And, Lord, even in this day's most stressful moments, may I rest in you. In the name of Jesus, I pray. Amen.[3]

---

3. An unattributed version of this workplace prayer can be found at http://www.beliefnet.com/Prayers/Christian/Work/Workplace-Prayer.aspx#ixzz1VtRohL2r.

The Teacher and the Students

Several years ago, I got a chance to hear a talk from America's "National Teacher of the Year," Guy Doud.[4] I was totally mesmerized by his autobiography and testimony. I never forgot his story of how before the school day began, he would arrive at his classroom early, go around and sit in each chair, and pray for the particular student who would shortly be sitting there. What a wonderful, proactive way of asking God to be involved in his work with each individual student with his or her special potential, value, and challenges. We can easily imagine doing something similar in other work settings—a parent going to where each child sleeps, a restaurant manager saying a prayer in each part of the restaurant, from the kitchen and supply room to the reception desk, and so on.

Working in the Presence of God

Denise Daniels and Shannon Vandewarker coauthored a wonderful guidebook for a prayer-saturated workplace discipleship attuned to God's constant presence. In their book, they describe three stages:

1. "Orienting to Work"—Prayers and meditation related to our preparation for and commuting to work and to the spaces within which we will be working.

2. "Engaging in Work"—Prayers of gratitude, celebration, confession, and lament while we are at work.

3. "Reflecting on Work"—Getting alone with God after work, reflecting on our experiences with the help of the traditional "Examen" and Sabbath practices.

---

4. Guy Rice Doud, *Moulder of Dreams* (Colorado Springs: Focus on the Family, 1990).

Their approach might be called "the contemplative Christian at work." Highly recommended![5]

A Relationship-building Model

Think about any relationship, such as with your spouse, kids, or close friends. (Remember: we are all made in the image and likeness of God, so learning to talk to God is going to have some parallels to our communication with people.) In this perspective, I think we can appreciate four important themes in our talking to these others: (1) praise you, (2) thank you, (3) I apologize, and (4) help me. (Of course, we will also want to ask "How are you doing?" "What's on your mind?" and so on—but here, we are confining ourselves to what we would want to say to them.)

First, it is important to praise our conversation partners (our family members, friends, students, and so on) to compliment them when they do something praiseworthy or for the admirable traits we see in them. How much more might this be true of our talking to God? "God, you are so good!" "God, it is amazing what you have done and how your glory and compassion have been shown in this industry (or company or market or technology, etc.).

Second, let's say "thank you" to God for his past help, for the skills and education he has given us, for our colleagues and customers, for freedom and opportunity. I once preached a sermon titled "Lord, Help Me Be in the 10 Percent." Remember the story of the ten lepers Jesus healed, and how only one came back and thanked him? (Luke 17:11–19). I think "one out of ten" is pretty much normal for our human race when it comes to gratitude—but that's pathetic. I want to be in the 10 percent who express gratitude to God (and to

---

5. Denise Daniels and Shannon Vandewarker, *Working in the Presence of God: Spiritual Practices for Work* (Peabody, MA: Hendrickson, 2019).

people) for blessings received. If we don't learn to say "thank you" and verbalize our gratitude to others for their kindness and help, our relationships will suffer. So, we don't just praise God ("You are so great"), we also thank him ("You have been so good to me"). Thank God for the work we have, for the opportunities we have, and for help given in our work lives.

Third, we apologize and ask for forgiveness. The statistics here are a lot like gratitude: maybe one person in ten thinks to apologize for mistakes, injuries, and failures, and ask for forgiveness. In my prayers to God—just as in my conversations with my family and friends—I want to be regular in apologizing for my failures and shortcomings, known and unknown to me, in my work and career as in other parts of my life.

Finally, we bring our requests to God (just like we do to our family, friends, and colleagues). But notice that we don't just ask for crisis help—we ask for guidance, ideas, wisdom, and growth. This is proactive, rather than just a reactive prayer for help. It is broad not narrow. It is mission-focused, not crisis-focused. This is true in our human relationships as well as our God-relationship. We don't just ask for help to survive a narrow and immediate problem. We listen to longer, broader counsel for our work as for all other aspects of our life.

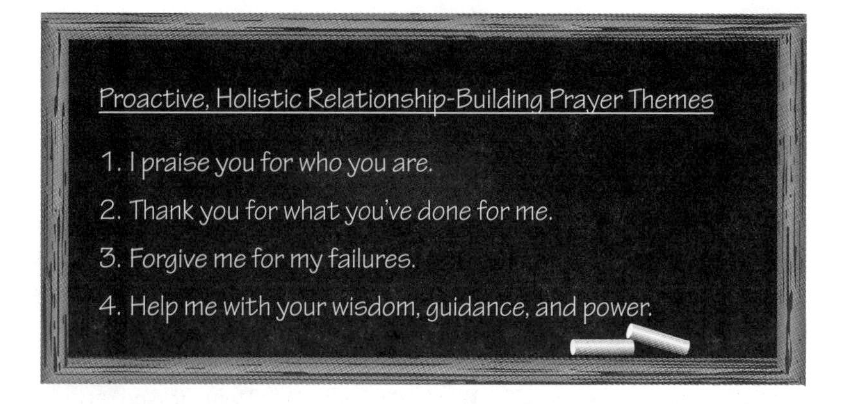

Using the Lord's Prayer as a Model for Workplace Prayer

As a final model for our workplace prayers, consider the pattern of the Lord's Prayer given in the Sermon on the Mount (Matt. 6:5–15). In preliminary remarks, Jesus says: (1) "Do not be like the hypocrites," who are praying not in order to talk to God but to be seen as pious by others. No, go pray quietly in a more private way and focus on God. And (2), "do not heap up empty phrases, babbling away endlessly. No, keep it simple and straightforward. Then (3), Jesus says, "Pray in this way" and gives what we call the Lord's Prayer. I have been using this prayer as a kind of template for many years, and I highly recommend it. Below is how I implement it in my own life.

On Mondays, traditionally the first day of the workweek, I use the Lord's Prayer as a template for a workplace emphasis, illustrated below. On Tuesdays, I use it as a template for a prayer focus on my marriage and family. On Wednesday, I focus on my church. Thursday is "friend" day. Friday is "world" day, and I use this template to pray for my neighborhood, city, and the world. Saturday is "me" day. "Sunday is "God" day. In this way, I cover all the main arenas of my life in my conversations with God. Sometimes I miss a day because of a crazy schedule, but I always default back to this pattern. Of course, the urgent and emergency issues (about work, money, health, family, etc.) get into my prayers as needed. But using the Lord's Prayer in this way ensures that I pray regularly, proactively, and holistically about my work, as well as my family, church, and world.

To give you a bit more detail, which I hope you will find helpful, my Monday workplace discipleship "Lord's Prayer" goes something like this:

Our Father in heaven, hallowed be your name.

You are so good and you have been so good to me, Lord. Thank you for my job and for my education and the experiences you have led me through.

May your name and the name of Jesus be honored and viewed positively through my life and my work this week.

Your kingdom come. Your will be done, on earth as it is in heaven.

Lord, I want you to be king and boss over my work this week. I don't just want to do what I want or what my company wants but what you want. (I then mention to God the specific projects and challenges I will face the coming week).

Give us this day our daily bread.

Lord, you know we need more funding and a couple key additions to our team to really do the job right.

Lord, would you help me find the right resources to sharpen my capacity to do a great job here?

Lord, help my boss to be patient, and help our customers to understand.

God, I am really hoping I can get that raise in salary after my annual review so I can take better care of my family and be a more generous steward of your planet and church.

Forgive us our debts, as we also have forgiven our debtors.

Lord, help me to avoid making any serious or costly mistakes this week in my work and in my relations with coworkers But if and when I do fall short of the excellence to which you call me, I ask you to forgive me.

Help me, Lord, to have a forgiving attitude toward others, my bosses, colleagues, and customers, when they make mistakes or step on my toes.

Deliver me, Lord, from any kind of vengeful attitude or action.

And do not bring us to the time of trial, but rescue us from the evil one.

Lord, help me stay focused on serving you with excellence in my work. Please help me not to be tempted toward laziness or toward dangerous shortcuts.

Lord, help me not become arrogant or overconfident, but stay humble and teachable. Help me in my relationships to support and care for those with whom I work, and keep me from any inappropriate talk, action, or thought.

Lord, protect me from any temptation to remain silent and comfortable when I see wrongdoing among my colleagues, bosses, or customers.

Lord, keep me from any temptation to forget you and your constant presence by my side at work.

Yours is the kingdom, the power, and the glory forever. Amen.

Lord, go with me to my place of work, and may you be the king I serve, may your power and strength be with me, and may you receive glory and praise for anything positive I accomplish this week. Amen.

We have now looked at five approaches to proactive, holistic workplace-oriented prayer. All workplace disciples need to decide on some plan for regular, dedicated prayer concerning their work. We need and want God's help and presence. Yes, he will show up and will often save us even when we ignore him, but that is a pathetic and wimpy approach to our workplace life when what we have available is the living God in conversation by our side.

The Lord's Prayer: Workplace Edition

Our Father in heaven, thank you so much for adopting me into your family forever. May your name be glorified in my work today and this week. May you be the king of my work this week, and may your will, not mine, be done in my daily work. I want to do what you want me to do. Lord, I need your help and your resources every day this week. Help me have a forgiving attitude toward the people I encounter in my work—just as you are so forgiving to me, Lord. And Lord, please protect me from the snares of the devil; keep me from pride and arrogance, and from temptation of any kind. You are the king, Lord, and I want all the glory and power to be yours in my work this week. Amen.

"Chat" Prayers through the Day

Finally, I think there is also a third way of praying about our work. When Paul tells us to "pray without ceasing," he may have in mind being regular (not occasional) in daily prayers—but I suspect there is more. *The Practice of the Presence of God* is a classic by Brother Lawrence, a seventeenth-century lay brother in the Parisian Carmelite Order, who worked as a cook in a kitchen.[6] Brother Lawrence went through each day consciously praising God, asking for his help, loving God, and being aware of his presence. It is like having a colleague alongside you and chatting with him or her through the day's work. I am not recommending that we disrupt (and maybe

---

6. Brother Lawrence, *The Practice of the Presence of God*, Hendrickson Christian Classics (Peabody, MA: Hendrickson, 2004).

worry!) our colleagues by a lot of *audible* chats with God in our workplace! But I am recommending that—not just for crises and emergencies—we cultivate more of a sense of God's presence and get comfortable "chatting" our praises and requests to God throughout the day.

Think about this as the polar opposite of profanity. Our vulgar, disrespectful culture is full of outbursts of profanity that use the Lord's name in vain. But people who do this have zero interest in actually getting God's attention and speaking to him. Here is a little thought experiment: How would you feel if people called out your name all the time, especially when angry or whenever something bad happened? You would perk up at attention, only to find they have no interest in actually communicating with you. *Think of what God has to put up with every day as casual and constant cursing rises from our planet toward our loving God.* Our intermittent "chat" prayers through our days are just the opposite. "Oh Lord, thank you for helping me figure out this math problem." "Lord, what a wonderful group of customers you just brought in here." "Lord, please help me get my computer to function again." And so on. Amid the vulgar, profane din of a world full of casual cursing and taking God's name in vain, imagine how God might be pleased to hear a bunch of us "chatting" (and maybe even singing!) our praise and thanksgiving to him throughout our workday.

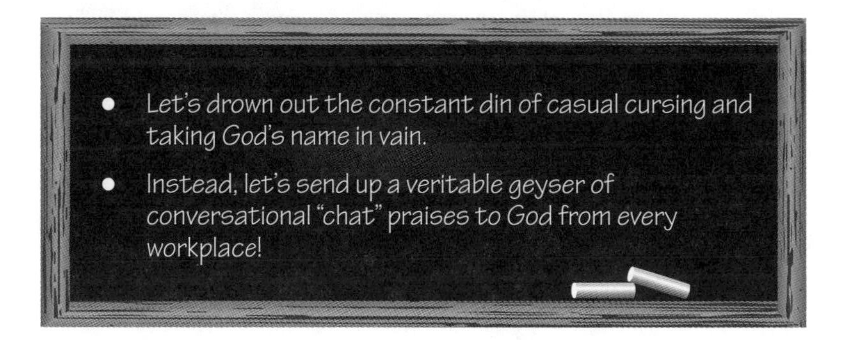

In our thinking about prayer, just like every other aspect of discipleship, we must not get too down on ourselves or forget that we are not alone in the struggle. I love Paul's reminder that "the Spirit helps us in our weakness; for we do not know how to pray as we ought, but that very Spirit intercedes with sighs too deep for words" (Rom. 8:26). Isn't that amazing? We do our best to have a good prayer life but—no matter what—God's very own Spirit is praying and interceding for us. Rest on that promise.

Let's make the commitment to a life of prayer as workplace disciples with (1) our emergency, crisis calls for help in the day of trouble; (2) our regular, intentional, proactive prayers about our work; and (3) our casual "chat" prayers throughout the day. Now we're talking!

Of course, "conversation" is a two-way street, and we should not do all the talking. Our next move, therefore, is to explore what it means to listen to God speak to us by his Spirit through his word in Scripture.

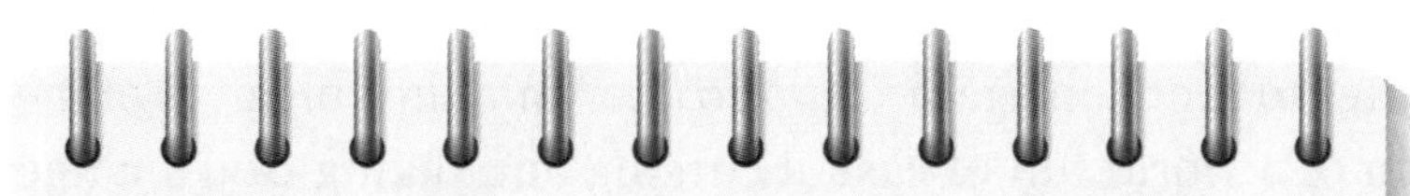

To Do

- ✓ Summarize the reasons why prayer is an essential component in workplace discipleship.
- ✓ Make a specific plan for (at least) weekly workplace-related prayer that is proactive and holistic, not just reactive and emergency oriented.

For Reflection & Discussion

1. What have been your experiences of trying to have a regular, personal, or small group prayer life?

2. Have you ever tried to focus your prayers on your education, work, or career in a proactive (not just emergency) way?

3. Have you ever found a daily devotional guide or prayer book to be helpful in your prayer life?

3

Listen

Ask God to Speak to You about Work through Jesus and Scripture

I heard a funny story once about a business owner whose company was in serious trouble. When it finally got so bad, the owner, Bob, went to his pastor in desperation.

> "Pastor," Bob said, "my business is about to go under. I need help from God. What should I do?"
>
> The pastor replied, "Well, Bob, when I need a clear message from God, I close my eyes, let my big Bible fall open as I hold it in my left hand, and—without peeking—put my right index finger on whatever verse on the page where it falls open. When I open my eyes and look where my finger is pointed, I take that particular verse as God's special message to me."
>
> Months later, the business owner showed up again at church driving an expensive new BMW. The pastor said, "Bob, we haven't seen you around here for months. What happened to you, and where have you been?"
>
> "Oh pastor," replied Bob, "your advice on faith at work was really helpful. Thank you so much."
>
> "Tell me—just out of curiosity, Bob—what was the message from the Holy Bible that helped you in that crisis?"

> Bob answered, "I did as you said and closed my eyes, let the Bible fall open, and put my finger down. When I opened my eyes, I saw my finger pointing directly at the message: 'Chapter Eleven.' "[1]

Needless to say, *that* will not be the recommended strategy for acquiring God's guidance for our workplace discipleship.

In the previous chapter, we explored the importance of talking to God in our prayers. Now we want to explore how to listen to God. God can, of course, speak to us in all kinds of ways. Remember the story of the prophet Balaam, who heard God speak to him through the donkey he was riding (Num. 22:21–35)? Remember all the dreams through which God spoke to Joseph, Daniel, Peter, and many others? Remember how the three "wise men" followed a star? Remember how Paul wrote to the Roman Christians that we can learn some things about God from the world he has created and from our conscience and from the law written on our hearts (Rom. 1:19–20; 2:14–15)? Remember how Paul made an argument about God to the people of Athens, based partly on their old classic pagan poets (Acts 17:28)? God can speak to us through nature, through music and art, through history and literature, and through the circumstances of our life. In the next chapter, we will highlight how God helps guide us and speaks to us through our brothers, sisters, and friends.

So, there are multiple channels and locations to hear God speak to us, and as Jesus often said, "Let those who have ears to hear, hear!" But I'm going to argue that in the end the central, clearest, and most authoritative way God speaks to us is through the *written word* of Scripture (the Bible), centered on the *incarnate Word*, Jesus Christ. In Jesus Christ, God's Word "became flesh" so we could see what it looks like (John 1). With all the communication channels

1. In other words, "declare bankruptcy."

of God's messages mentioned above, the Bible—with Jesus at the center—remains the most important primary source and channel. But biblical illiteracy is a terrible handicap in today's workplace discipleship. How and where can we listen to God speak through the Bible? I want to urge all of us to think about that and do something about it.

Listening to God in Church, Parachurch, and Educational Settings

To begin with, God can speak to us about our work when we are at church. I hope we attend church regularly and expectantly. I pray that our church worship will bring us into the presence of God and that we hear his voice in the reading and preaching of Scripture, in song, and even in moments of quiet. But I think we should not count on church attendance *alone* (or maybe even *primarily*) to listen to God's word about our work. For one thing, the gathered church is (and ought to be) about a lot more than lessons on work. And let's be realistic: few pastors have much experience working outside the church context, and fewer still have been helped in their seminary or Bible school courses to recognize the workplace discipleship lessons of Scripture. The late Gillette CEO Colman Mockler is reported to have said, "I have been attending church faithfully for fifty years, and I have never heard even one word from the pulpit that recognized or encouraged my work as a service to God that mattered and had value."[2] Beyond the worship context, few churches have

2. To improve the workplace discipleship education of future pastors, Colman's widow, Joanna, honored her late husband by endowing the Mockler Center for Faith & Ethics in the Workplace and the Mockler-Phillips Chair in Workplace Theology and Business Ethics at Gordon-Conwell Theological Seminary. I was privileged to be the first occupant of that professorship (2010–16).

Christian education classes or small group studies focused on God's will for our work. I am not really interested in criticizing our churches here—I am only saying that we need something more to help us hear God teach about work.

Still, hearing God's word in the context of church is important for at least two reasons. First, church is a *community* of learners, where we can build relationships, learn from one another, and correct, augment, and encourage one another. Individualism is not biblical, and we can go astray when we become isolated from others. Second, church is a *worshipping* community where biblical insights are not just good ideas but reasons to celebrate together and praise the living God. We never want to reduce Christianity to a set of abstract doctrines and good ideas separate from life and relationships to God and others.

The situation is almost the same when it comes to parachurch ministries (mission groups, campus fellowships, etc.). Parachurch leaders are not often trained to see and share workplace insights from Scripture. Their emphases are more likely to concern good doctrine and theology, evangelism, prayer, spiritual formation, sex and relationships, missions, church planting, or God's concern for the poor and others who need help. Of course, any way of getting people focused on line-by-line, paragraph-by-paragraph, book-by-book study of the text—or even memorization of biblical texts—is wonderful. But it is sad that even the simplest workplace lessons are so often overlooked by leaders of parachurch ministries.

The exciting exception to this picture is the incredible growth of faith at work and marketplace ministry organizations. Over the past forty years, there has been a boom, a revival, in this arena. There are Bible studies in many businesses and organizations, in many industries, many cities, on many campuses. The opportunities to study the workplace lessons of Scripture with other kindred spirits are a huge gift these days. Look around, ask around, and you will almost surely find something.

There are also many study centers, online study opportunities, and helpful books focused on workplace discipleship and its biblical foundations. In *Work Matters: Lessons from Scripture* (Eerdmans, 2012), Paul Stevens gives samples from Genesis to Revelation of what the Bible teaches about work. The *Theology of Work Bible Commentary* (Hendrickson, 2016) provides real-life lessons on what the Bible says about work. There is also the Theology of Work's "The Bible and Your Work Study Series" to go along with the commentary. Each helpful Bible study (based on either a biblical book or topic) is created for either group or personal study during a thirty-minute lunch break. Other excellent examples of reading the Bible and inviting God to teach us about our work are *The Accidental Executive: Lessons on Business, Faith, and Calling from the Life of Joseph* (Hendrickson, 2015) and *The ServiceMaster Story: Navigating Tension between People and Profit* (Hendrickson, 2020) by Albert M. Erisman.

Listening to God on Our Own

At several points in this book, I criticize "individualism"—that is, when people try to go it alone in the Christian life, including workplace discipleship. But there is, of course, an individual side to our discipleship; we can't just depend on some group to make our learning and discipleship happen. It is necessary for us to try to listen to God speak to us as individuals about work.

When I was about ten or twelve years old, I decided to read at least something in the Bible every day (I think either my dad or my Sunday school teacher must have leaned on me to start doing this). I failed to do it every day, but I am sure that *most* days of my sixty years since then I have read the Bible, often a chapter a day. Some time back then, I was also encouraged to keep a pen in my hand when I read, so I could underline, circle, outline, and write down comments or questions as I read.

No matter how great my church's teaching and preaching, I came to believe that there is no substitute for personal Bible study. The Bible—from Genesis to Revelation, cover-to-cover—is a gold mine of inspired insight and guidance for our work lives. Most of us can easily afford to buy a personal copy of the Bible, and most of us have the freedom and capacity to read it every day, maybe one chapter, maybe thirty minutes a day, maybe more.[3]

Let's read with a pen in hand, underlining and marking ideas and passages that come across to us as especially important and relevant. Notice patterns and lists and repetitions—and mark them in your Bible (or keep a journal if you hate the idea of marking it up!). Reading becomes *active* listening when we write in our Bible or journal. Then, when your Bible is all marked up, you can go buy another copy and start over. Whenever I finish reading any one of the sixty-six individual books of the Bible, I write the month and year in the table of contents. I am compulsive about wanting to put a date by every one of these books in the table of contents. This way, I make sure that I read the whole Bible, not just a few favorite parts.

There are also Bible reading plans and Bible apps for smartphones and computers that could help. My only caution is that while the apps can, for example, find a familiar phrase or text in seconds, such technology short-cuts unfortunately can also undermine our understanding and memory of Scripture (just as GPS programs often undermine our sense of place and direction and our capacity to read maps, or take us

---

3. For Bibles of all translations and types—affordable paperback or expensive leather—visit www.christianbook.com.

on a wild goose chase!). There is no substitute for "old school" reading, study, and memorization of the text. Nevertheless, as tools to assist our Bible study, there are wonderful online resources available.

The Listening Attitude: Our Agenda & Questions . . . *God's* Agenda & Questions

Our attitude when reading the Bible is critical. We want to listen to God speak to us. Of course, we would like answers to all our questions, but above all we want to hear his message to us—not just about our questions, but whatever God has to say to us. Jacques Ellul observed that people are quite bold and free in bringing their own questions to the Bible. Critical professional scholars are known to question who wrote one text or another, when and in what circumstances it was originally composed, and whether it represents a primitive worldview we must question today. They often do not, however, get around to asking, "What might God be trying to say to us through this passage?" Even sympathetic ordinary readers can let personal questions dominate their study: What is this prophecy teaching? What is this doctrine? What is the theological message here? How do we reconcile this apparent contradiction? Is this behavior of mine okay?

In the Bible, the disciples questioned Jesus: "When will your kingdom come?" "How many times should I forgive my brother?" But, Ellul argued, the most important questions were the ones *God* addressed to the people, such as: "Who do you say that I am?" "When the Son of Man returns will he find faith on earth?" "Adam, where are you? What have you done?" "Cain, where is your brother?" Ellul argued that humanity's fall from grace was occasioned by Satan's question in the garden, "Yeah, hath God said?" As we approach any part of Scripture, our questions do matter, but even more important might be the questions God is addressing to us.

As we read the Bible, let's constantly be inviting God to teach and challenge us. What does this or that text imply for our work? It is not just the passages that speak directly and explicitly about work that matter. A passage warning about idolatry or misplaced love has major relevance to our work lives. A passage calling us to patience or to nonconformity has huge workplace relevance. It is all about our attitude and stance as we read and study Scripture. We want to know God's agenda, not just our own; God's questions for us, not just our questions for God; God's will, purpose, and values, not just our own.

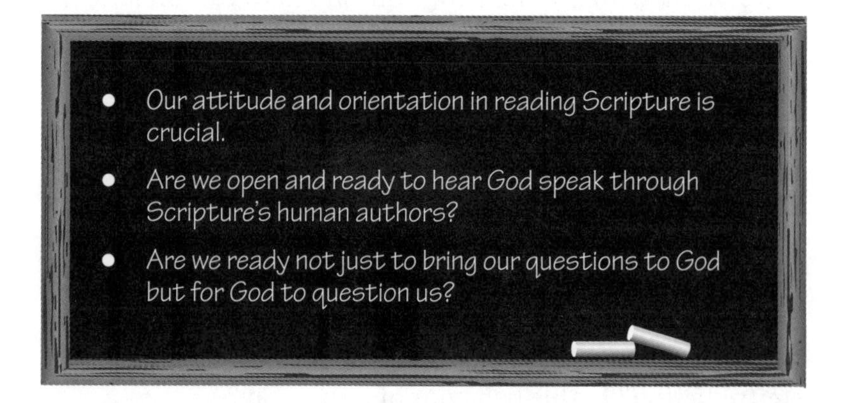

Focus 1: The Center and Everything Else

What are we listening for as we read and study God's word in Scripture? As part of the historic community of Christian faith, we affirm with Paul that "all Scripture is inspired by God and is useful for teaching, for reproof, for correction, and for training in righteousness, so that everyone who belongs to God may be proficient, equipped for every good work" (2 Tim. 3:16–17). The Bible is composed of sixty-six individual books, written in many different times, places, and circumstances by different human authors. This is an incredible virtue, because it shows how God can and will enter our human situation in all manner of circumstances. But there are difficult passages that are sometimes hard to understand, often mysterious, and occasionally appear contradictory.

All of it is God's word to us—sometimes by way of poetry, sometimes in history or chronology, sometimes in dramatically symbolic apocalyptic visions, sometimes in strong prophetic denunciation and exhortation, sometimes in laws and precepts, sometimes in parables, sometimes in sermons, speeches, wise sayings, letters of counsel or other literary forms, and sometimes by negative example as well as positive. The hand of oral tradition, original authors, editorial assistants, and others are part of this amazing collection. It is all "profitable"—worthwhile and deserving of our reading and reflection. Even long lists of building dimensions or genealogical lists can teach us that this kind of detail matters to God. Ancestors matter. Architectural detail. Legal detail. They all matter to God and teach us to care about such things. It is therefore good to read it all and try to figure out the "profit"—that is, the teaching message.

My former colleague Nate Smith used to say that the things the Bible teaches *clearly* and *frequently* are *nonnegotiable* parts of the Christian life; the things that are *infrequent* and *unclear* in the Bible need to be *negotiable*, and so we need to allow more freedom and diversity of interpretation in these latter cases. This is a good guideline. We always want to understand the vocabulary and original context as much as we can, but we are looking for the ongoing, living message that applies to ourselves and our era. What is the *substance*, the *essence* of the biblical teaching that has transcultural meaning and relevance? While we don't want to overlook the rare, occasional, eccentric, exceptional bits of the Bible, let's focus on the repeated, clear messages.

Another image that may help comes from the ocean. On the surface are the waves, but underneath are the powerful main currents (like the Arctic Current). If we restrict our focus to the waves, we may fail to see the main currents under the surface that are the decisive forces giving rise to those surface waves. So too, in reading the Bible we don't want to restrict our attention to discrete individual verses and miss the broader themes running sometimes just below the surface, which provide the context for understanding those verses. What are those main currents? Loving God and loving our neighbor, sin and evil, justice and mercy, violence and peace, land and creation, community and individual, flesh and spirit, kingdom of God present and future, and so on. Scripture itself also highlights such summary texts as the Ten Commandments and the Sermon on the Mount.

But there is one center and anchor to our reading of Scripture. This point is made explicit by the New Testament Letter to the Hebrews:

> Long ago God spoke to our ancestors in many and various ways by the prophets, but in these last days he has spoken to us by a Son, whom he appointed heir of all things, through whom he also created the worlds. He is the reflection of God's glory and

> the exact imprint of God's very being, and he sustains all things by his powerful word. (Heb. 1:1–3)

Jesus Christ is the full and *exact* representation of God. Jesus Christ is the Son of God, the creator, sustainer, and redeemer. Jesus of Nazareth is the Word made flesh, visible in human history (John 1). Paul wrote to the Colossians that in Jesus Christ "the whole fullness of deity dwells bodily" (Col. 2:9). So, as we read the Bible, our interpretive anchor and center is always Jesus. Jesus is the full and precise revelation of God in our world. All other revelation is partial and imprecise. Do we want to know how God would treat children? Jesus shows us most clearly (not the Proverbs, not the Law of Moses). What to think about money? The poor? The wealthy? Work and rest? Jesus is the center.

Focus 2: *God's Character and Mission*

The most important objective in our Bible reading, and our focus on Jesus, is to understand the character and mission of God. The first reason for this is that "discipleship" is about *following* God. We need to know who we are following. But the second reason is that every man and woman is made in the image and likeness of this God. God's character is, in a vital way, embedded in our DNA, no matter how broken or failing we may be. Of course, human beings are fallen and imperfect, and God's image in us is radically scarred by human sin, but it is not totally eliminated. We discover our own humanity, purpose, and identity not just in *pursuing* but also in *expressing* the reality of God. This means understanding God the Creator. God designs and builds things that are "very good," "useful," and "pleasing to the eye." This same divine creativity is in the DNA of human beings made in God's image and likeness. If men, women, and children are prevented from expressing this creativity, then they are radically dehumanized. Studying the characteristics of God's creation will teach us a major component in our understanding of what makes for good work.

Exactly the same thing can be said about God as sustainer and upholder of the world he has created. He doesn't just walk away and abandon what he creates! Studying the biblical drama of God's sustaining work is a key to our philosophy of good work. God is also the redeemer who saves the lost, fixes what is broken, heals the injured and hurting, reconciles the alienated, and liberates those in bondage. So too our human nature (in God's image and likeness) finds essential expression and meaning in such redemptive work. And, finally, as God chose to rest on the seventh day after six days of Creation, so we find rest essential in the framing of healthy and meaningful work.

This whole grand story from Creation to final new creation becomes our "metanarrative," our philosophy of life, the framework within which we understand particular texts and stories in the Bible. This is broadly taught throughout the canon of Scripture, and each of these themes is illustrated by Jesus who, as indicated in the Hebrews text above, is the creator, sustainer, and redeemer.

The ugly counterpart to the inspiring story of God, and of a humanity made in his image and likeness, is the story of the "fall" and sin. From the Genesis 3 serpent in the Garden of Eden to Revelation 20 and the final judgment of Babylon, the Bible describes in detail how "good work goes bad." Seeing the main themes in this fall (deception, lies, violence, greed, shame, hiding, arrogance, etc.) over and over truly helps us understand the challenges we face in the workplace.

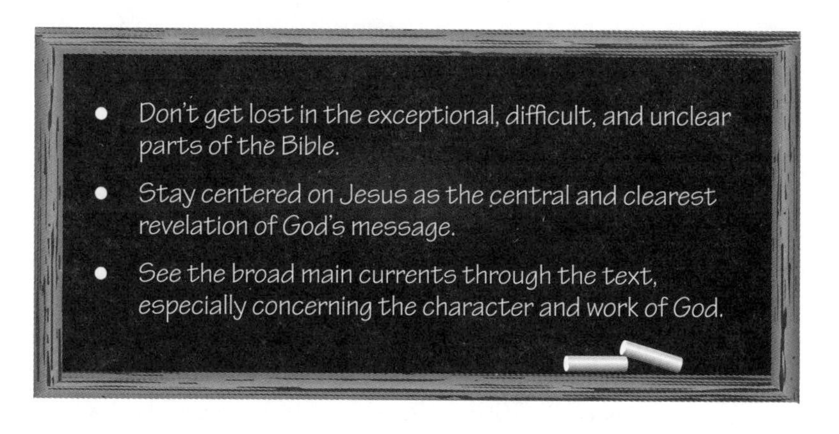

Focus 3: Specialized Topical Studies of Work in Scripture

Beyond this grand story of God's character and action, our attention as workplace disciples finds focus on themes and topics especially related to our work. Sometimes an index or concordance will help us find the verses and passages to do a study of what the Bible says about truth and lies, about debt and interest, about money, property, poverty, and wealth, about diligence and laziness, about greed and contentment, about pride and humility, and about other work-related topics. We may do a focused study on law, justice, and advocacy, on health, disease, and healing, on beauty, or on farming and animal husbandry. We may do a study of leadership and servanthood or on management.

As mentioned earlier, there are some great secondary sources to help our workplace biblical studies, such as the *Theology of Work* commentary and Bible study series. There are books seeking biblical perspectives on the arts, law, business, technology, science, and many other fields. But there is no substitute for each of us to engage directly in our own reading and study of Scripture, asking God to speak to us about our workplace discipleship.

Strategy: Read, Memorize, Practice, and Share

As we have discussed, active *reading* of Scripture (pen in hand, maybe writing in a journal as well as in our personal copy of the Bible) is a core, basic habit and practice in workplace discipleship. A next step to take is to *memorize* some of the passages of Scripture. Prodded on by my parents and Sunday school teachers, I memorized the Ten Commandments, the Beatitudes, Psalm 23, Romans 12, and many individual verses when I was younger—and I am grateful every day for imprinting those texts on my mind. Being able to call up those passages in an instant on our hand-held phones and other devices is great thing, but there is no substitute for having the text already in our own memory. The Navigators group and many other Christians make a habit of memorizing Scripture throughout their adult lives. It isn't just for kids in Sunday school.

It is also important to understand that we don't really know something (in the biblical sense) unless we live it, *practice* it. The Hebrew word *yada* was used in the Old Testament both for knowing a truth *and* for "knowing" your spouse in the sense of sexual intercourse ("Adam knew his wife and she conceived and bore a son . . ."). Knowledge is therefore participation, not just abstract cognition. You don't really know how to ride a bike until you ride a bike, or how to cook something until you cook it. In a wonderful statement, Paul prays that the Colossians will be "filled with the knowledge of God's will in all spiritual wisdom and understanding, so that you may lead lives worthy of the Lord, fully pleasing to him . . . as you grow in the knowledge of God" (Col. 1:9–10;

emphasis added). Notice the circle: increase in knowledge (not as an end in itself) so you can walk it, and then increase further in the knowledge. Think, act, think. We need to walk our talk, live out our faith in our works (James 2:14–26).

One final thought on strategy: If I really know and understand something, I should be able to distill it down and share it in an understandable way with others. If one pathway to understanding something is to put it in practice and "live" it, then another is to vocalize it and share it with others. We have all heard the saying, "Practice what you preach." A corollary is to "preach what you practice"—that is, share what you have learned and are trying to live.

Once again, after this robust challenge to listen and learn from God through Scripture and other channels, we must remember the caution that "those who are unspiritual do not receive the gifts of God's Spirit, for they are foolishness to them, and they are unable to understand them because they are spiritually discerned" (1 Cor. 2:14). Jesus promised his disciples that "the Advocate, the Holy Spirit . . . will teach you everything, and remind you of all that I have said to you" (John 14:26). Just as it is ultimately God's Spirit who empowers our prayers to God, it is ultimately God's Spirit who empowers and enables our hearing and understanding of God's voice. Work hard at it, but don't stress. We are not alone.

So now, we workplace disciples are in a real conversation with God. We pray, talking to God in all the ways described in the previous chapter. But we don't do all the talking. We listen to God in the ways described in this chapter: read Scripture, centering on Jesus and focusing on the great themes, especially the character and mission of God as described repeatedly throughout the text. Our eyes and ears are open, both during Bible study and at all other times, hoping and expecting our Lord will speak to us.

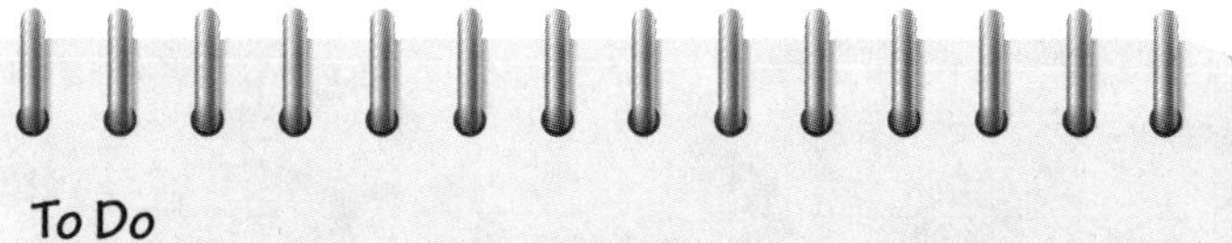

To Do

- ✓ Get a Bible you can feel free to write in, and keep it in a prominent place close to where you can read it for thirty minutes each day.
- ✓ Start reading one chapter per day, book after book, until all sixty-six books have your markings and comments on what you hear God saying to you in the text.

For Reflection & Discussion

1. Have you ever done any systematic or regular Bible reading and study? If so, what were the most satisfying and successful times when you did this?

2. Have you read the whole Bible? What were the most and least helpful parts for you?

3. Have you ever listened (e.g., while driving or exercising) to a recording of someone reading the Bible? Was that a helpful way to try to hear God speak through Scripture?

4. Have you ever felt like you heard God speaking or guiding you through nature or nonbiblical literature and art?

4

Partner

Form a Supportive Christian "Posse"— Don't Do It All on Your Own

Let's review where we are at this point in our course. First, we need to bring God into our workplace discipleship adventure through *prayer*. This means making a habit of not just crying out for God's help in emergencies and crises, but creating regular, daily planned communications to God as well as more casual "chat" prayers through the day. The next critical step is the counterpart to talking to God: listening to God's word back to us. Let's make a habit of listening to God speak to us, especially as we read his word in Scripture every day.

In this chapter, we'll see that the next big move is to carry out our discipleship in partnership with others. We shouldn't try to do this on our own as isolated individuals, if we can possibly find a comrade to journey alongside. These days, individualism has become a problem in our society and that includes our churches and workplaces. What we need to remember, however, is that Christian discipleship is a *team* sport—not a solo or an individual sport. Discipleship is like basketball or soccer—not sprinting or bowling.

This call to partnership and team is really common sense. Building teams and a collaborative work environment is widely praised and promoted in literature on work and business. As a modern classic on the topic argues,

> We believe that teams—real teams, not just groups that management calls "teams"—should be the basic unit of performance for most organizations, regardless of size. In any situation requiring the real-time combination of multiple skills, experiences, and judgments, a team inevitably gets better results than a collection of individuals. . . .
>
> Several well-known phenomena explain why teams perform well. First, they bring together complementary skills and experiences that, by definition, exceed those of any individual. . . . Second, . . . teams establish communications that support real-time problem solving and initiative. . . . Third, teams . . . build trust and confidence in each other. . . . [T]hey also reinforce each other's intentions to pursue their team purpose. . . . Finally, teams have more fun. This is not a trivial point. . . . For example, a more highly developed sense of humor . . . helps them deal with the pressure and intensity of high performance.[1]

Patrick Lencioni, one of today's most insightful and influential organizational consultants, writes, "If someone were to ask me to make a list of the most valuable qualities a person should develop in order to thrive in the world of work—and for that matter, life—I would put being a team player at the top. . . . Few people succeed at work, in the family, or in any social context without it."[2]

In the worlds of business and politics, there are still plenty of vicious, take-no-prisoners, looking-out-for-#1 individualists. The novelist Ayn Rand is their guru with her books *The Fountainhead* and *Atlas Shrugged.* We see this same attitude

---

1. Jon R. Katzenbach and Douglas K. Smith, *The Wisdom of Teams: Creating the High-Performance Organization* (Boston: Harvard Business Review Press, 2015), 15, 18.

2. Patrick Lencioni, *The Ideal Team Player: How to Recognize and Cultivate the Three Essential Virtues* (Hoboken, NJ: Jossey-Bass, 2016), ix.

sometimes in the entertainment world, in sports, and even in the church and the nonprofit world. It is our fallen humanity that leads us in this toxic direction. It wasn't meant to be this way, and it doesn't have to stay this way. There are plenty of inspiring examples of people in business, politics, and other fields choosing to work together as teams.

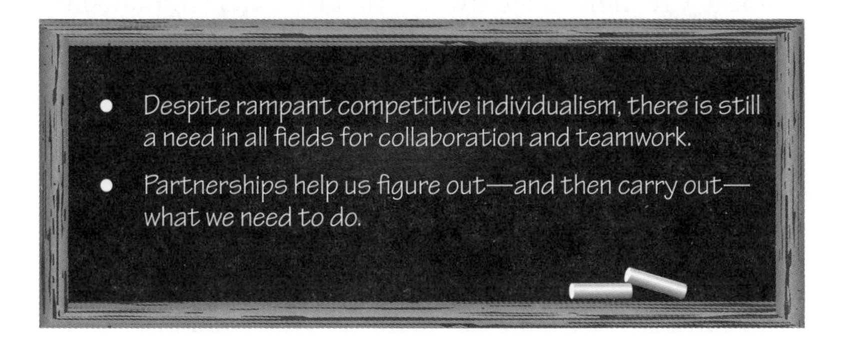

The Biblical Case for Partnership and Teams

The secular case for teams tends to be pragmatic: teams are embraced because they work and they improve the organization. The biblical case grounds the argument even deeper in our created human nature. In the beginning, God said,

> "Let us make humankind in our image, according to our likeness." . . . [S]o God created humankind in his image, in the image of God he created them; male and female he created them. God blessed them, and God said to them, "Be fruitful and multiply and fill the earth and subdue it; and have dominion." (Gen. 1:26–28)

When God created the world, everything was "good" or "very good"—except for one thing. As the second Creation story has it: "Then the LORD God said, 'It is not good that the man should be alone; I will make him a helper as his partner'" (Gen. 2:18).

Here is the core message: God is an "us" not just an "I/me." Christians understand this as the mystery of the Trinity. God is simultaneously One and Three. Three persons in perfect unity of being and action. The first, fundamental account of Creation explicitly says that God created humanity as a twosome, male and female. The second account presents one undifferentiated Adam, not the twosome of the first account. But in carrying out his mission and work, Adam's individuality is "not good" according to God. So, God separates Adam into a twosome-in-partnership, a man and a woman. It is important to note carefully that in both accounts of Creation, *both* male and female—in partnership—will have and raise children, and *both* will tend, cultivate, and protect the garden. It is only when sin and the fall occur (Gen. 3) that the man and woman suffer the curse of being alone (and being stereotyped) in either field labor or childbearing labor.

The point is that all human beings everywhere are created in the image of God; and because of this, it is deeply and essentially in our nature to live and work in partnership. It is not good to dwell or work alone. It is dehumanizing not to work and live in partnership. The Creation story, which presents the first partnership as a male/female one, certainly teaches us that we need the voices, gifts, and presence of *both* women and men on our work teams (and child-rearing teams) of all kinds.

Our sin and rebellion against God led to alienation and accusation, blaming and hiding, and then jealousy and murder. It then became necessary for Jesus Christ to reconcile us to God and to also overcome sin and its barriers between people. As we see in the Gospel accounts, Jesus built partnerships, and he sent his disciples out two-by-two, not one-by-one (Luke 10:1). His major teaching was to a band of disciples, not to individuals. People sometimes listen to the Sermon on the Mount and say that it's impossible to live out the Beatitudes. Well, it is a high standard but it was given to a community, not an isolated individual—you can be recklessly generous if you have a brother or sister who will give you a replacement coat after you give yours away. Jesus also gave considerable decision-making authority to partnerships, not to individuals: "Truly I tell you, if two of you agree on earth about anything you ask, it will be done for you by my Father in heaven. For where two or three are gathered in my name, I am there among them" (Matt. 18:19–20).

Remember how Paul had Barnabas as his sidekick. Two is good—the minimum—but three may be even better, as when Paul teamed up with Aquila and Priscilla, for example. A word used often in the early church was *koinonia* (Greek for "community"). The root word *koinos* means "common, shared." In the early Spirit-filled church of the book of Acts, the believers were no longer *idios* but *koinos*—it was no longer just about "me and mine" but about "us and ours." I love how *idios* is also a root of our word *idiotic*. It is idiotic to be an autonomous individual focused just on what is yours. Right after Paul's famous call to "not be conformed to this world, but be transformed" (Rom. 12:1–2), he urges us to not "think of yourself more highly than you ought to think" (Rom. 12:3–8). Paul stresses the importance of the various gifts of the members of the body of Christ (the church). Each of us has something to contribute; no one stands sufficient alone.

All of this in the New Testament was building on the Old Testament. Moses needed Aaron to get the job done, and Ruth made a covenant to be with Naomi, saying, "Where you go, I will go; where you lodge, I will lodge" (Ruth 1:16). David and Jonathan swore loyalty to a covenant with each other three times to watch out not just for the other but for their households as well (1 Sam. 18:3; 20:16; 23:18). The entire

Bible argues the practical benefits of working in partnership, but it goes much deeper by showing that this is embedded in our nature. We are made to live and work in relationships. It is dehumanizing not to seek and build such partnerships, but it is lifegiving to live and work in partnerships. Workplace discipleship needs to be pursued in partnership.

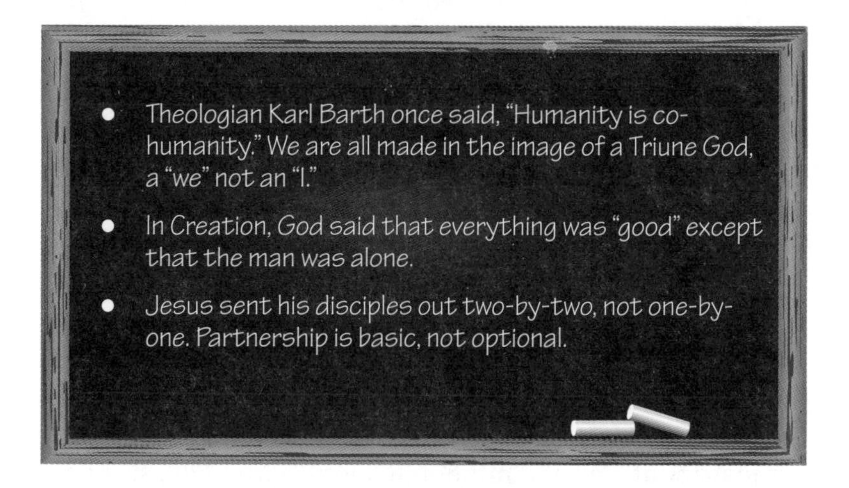

Three Partnerships That Get Us Partway

Let us look now at three forms of "partnership" and "team" that are helpful—if not quite sufficient—for optimal, high-performance workplace discipleship. First of all, let's think about friendships, partnerships, and teams in the places we work. In addition to the kind of work teams praised by Lencioni, Katzenbach, and Smith, we need to add the importance of *trusted friendships at work.* Such friends may not share our faith, but I would still urge the importance of finding and cultivating trusting and trustworthy friendships with a colleague or two where we work. Who in our department or company is wise, ethical, and reliable? Who could we go to for counsel, support, and encouragement?

This is not about a superficial willingness to gossip or gripe with someone in sympathy with us. We want approachability, wisdom, and loyal friendship—coworkers we can approach in confidence, at any time, to share concerns and questions and get some feedback and advice. *How* should I do this? *What* should I say? *Should* I speak up? Protest? Volunteer? It's also great to have some committed friends with whom we can celebrate successes and victories without fear that they will be jealous, and share humorous things without fear they will take offense. This is a kind of support group or partnership based in the workplace (or maybe just a little more broadly, in the industry). In my work history, this has meant special relationships with a couple of faculty and staff members where I have taught.

Second, in most *churches* these days, people are encouraged to become part of small groups (cell groups, fellowship groups, home groups, connection groups, etc.). Often, they are given common, churchwide curriculum to study with a meeting format to follow. Membership may be assigned by the pastoral staff or chosen by small group members themselves. All of this can be a valuable experience, and we may be able to share our workplace challenges with them and receive some objective counsel and support. I am all for this kind of small group fellowship in our churches.[3] But the kind of deeper, steadier counsel and support we need for our workplace discipleship may not be possible in this kind of church small group. This is partly because the small group membership may be fluid, with people joining and leaving, which is not a good context for trust and deep sharing. It may also be true that the needs and goals of most church small groups are broader than workplace

3. For more on starting small groups in your church, see Allen White, *Exponential Groups: Unleashing Your Church's Potential* (Peabody, MA: Hendrickson, 2017), and *Exponential Groups Workbook* (Peabody, MA: Hendrickson, 2020).

discipleship, or our small group colleagues may have little capacity to understand our particular workplace challenges.

Third, our *family, housemates, and close friends* are obviously valued partners. My wife of five decades is and always has been my primary confidant, advisor, and prayer partner. I have often gone to her for counsel and support, and she has often given me wise responses. But she can't—and shouldn't have to—carry alone the burdens of her husband's stressful work life. Nor is she an academic or a pastor as I have been. While I share the most critical matters of my work with her, we tend to be more focused on family, neighborhood, and church matters we share in common every day. Sharing about my work, yes. But "bringing my work home" to load my stress on her or my kids when they were growing up? No! I probably need another set of partners for that. My workplace discipleship "posse" (outside my marriage) has actually strengthened my marriage over the years. It is not a competitor.

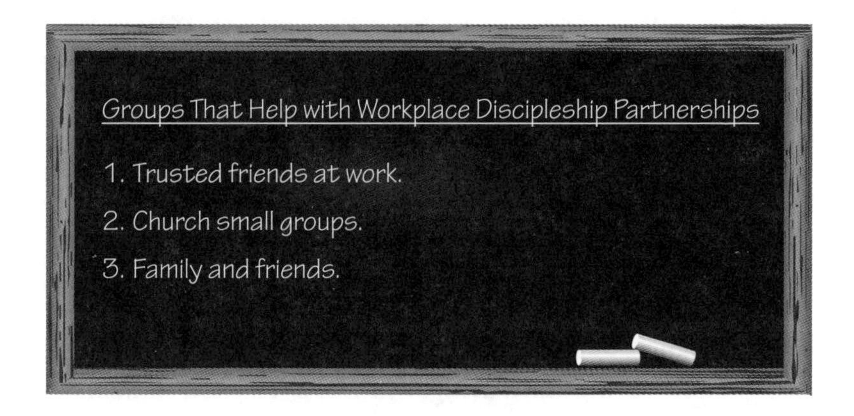

The Workplace Discipleship Posse: What It Is and Does

I often refer to the kind of optimum workplace discipleship partnership we are looking for as a "posse." The dictionaries define "posse" as a group called together to assist a sheriff in apprehending a criminal, keeping the peace, or searching for a missing person. There is a kind of "old West" feel to the word. More recently, in urban street culture usage, your "posse" can mean your "crew," your "homies," your close associates who "have your back." Another label for what I am talking about is "kitchen cabinet." This term was created to describe President Andrew Jackson's informal group of friends and advisors, but many political leaders since then have had such a group around them. They are not being paid, and they were not elected. They are close by, because you trust them to give you good advice.

A workplace discipleship posse has two main functions: first, it is to help us *figure out*—that is, discern the right thing to do, the will of God, that which God will call "good." Second, this posse will help us *carry out*, execute, what we together have decided is the best way to go. It's about discernment, support, encouragement, and accountability. Yes, we still bear the primary responsibility for our choices and actions, but we are no longer on our own. If our choices lead to difficulty or even to ruin, the posse that helped us choose that route will stick with us and help us as long as we need it. See what I'm talking about? What this requires is a *covenanted* partnership, not just another *casual* one. Our workplace posse cannot be a come-and-go, maybe-yes-maybe-no, here-today-gone-tomorrow matter. We can't have trust, we can't risk being vulnerable, without that intentional, conscious covenant. The "covenant" commitment may not be for life (like marriage), but it should be clear and conscious.

David and Jonathan's covenanted friendship is a great model.[4] It was based on an *affinity* they instantly had for each other—they liked and enjoyed each other. We probably need

4. The main story is in 1 Samuel. 18:1–4; 19:1–7; 20:1–42; 23:13–18; 2 Samuel. 1:17–27; 9:1–13.

some of that for our own workplace posse membership. The chemistry has to be right. A second basis for their relationship was their *common vocation*: they were both young warriors in Israel's army. They could talk about the military and political issues and threats they shared and faced. As already mentioned, three different times, David and Jonathan swore loyalty to each other in life and death. When they first committed to their friendship, they shared uniforms and weapons. As time went on, they warned and protected each other from danger and trouble. They represented and advocated for each other to those who misunderstood or threatened them. They made time for and listened to each other, even in moments of deep questioning and anguish. They encouraged each other and kept the dream alive. They strengthened each other in the Lord—the faith dimension. And finally, they cared not just for each other but also for their family and people. After Jonathan died in battle, David found Jonathan's disabled son, Mephibosheth, and brought him to live just like one of his own sons in the palace. This is the kind of workplace discipleship partnership we need and want.

I have given a talk titled "Every David Needs a Jonathan." This is a true brother or sister we can call on in the day of trouble as well as in the day of celebration. A few years later when David failed catastrophically in his relationship with Uriah and Bathsheba, think of how things might have been different if, when he saw her and was overcome with desire and temptation, he had been able to call Jonathan and say, "Brother, I am about to do something horrible. Get over here and kick my butt!" But he called Bathsheba instead of a discipleship covenant partner. If Jonathan had been around, he might have challenged David to be at work instead of hanging out on the palace roof (the text says this was "the time when kings went out to war"—but warrior king David stayed home). Bad move and big warning to us!

Like David and Jonathan, we need a partner or a posse with whom we can share what's going on—the highs and the lows, the good and the bad—and give each other counsel or encouragement, and pray together. Our posse will help us both pray and listen to God more faithfully, which we saw in the two steps described in earlier chapters. Our partners will pray for us, whether we are together or apart. They will pass on to us an encouraging word from God's word. We can ask them about an issue and know they will pray right away, during our hour of challenge. Whether we are together or apart, we can share our updates and news, our praises and requests. We can receive back encouragement, advice, clarifying questions, even warnings. This posse is capable of spiritual discernment and spiritual warfare, not just analysis on the secular, managerial, commonsense level (valuable as that is!).

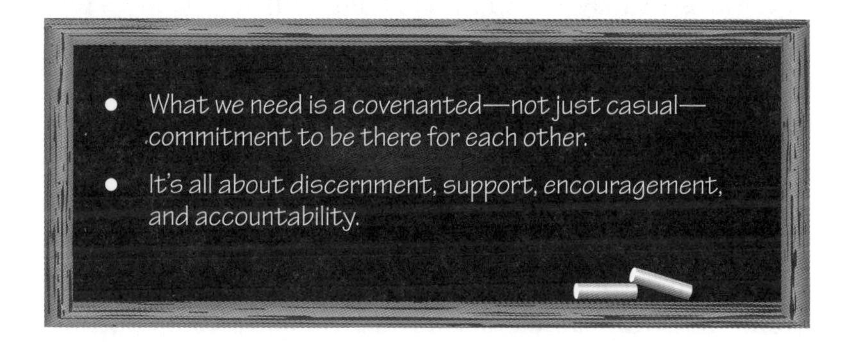

Finding or Creating a Workplace Discipleship Posse

While the argument is pretty convincing, some of us will have problems (1) finding the appropriate partner(s) and (2) making this a priority and regular part of a busy weekly schedule. The first challenge is to find fellow Christians who are either in our profession or close enough to relate to our work experiences. That is, techies need to find techie Christians, stay-at-home parents should find stay-at-home parents, artists find Christians in the arts community, and so on. This is not a hard-and-fast requirement of course. A good posse might be composed of three people in different jobs or professions (and even different generations), provided they share the covenant commitment and can come to understand and support one another's workplace discipleship.

How to begin? First, we need to find *one* potential posse member, starting with our church and personal network. Who in our church might be in our field of work and willing to get together? If need be, we can extend the search to other churches and Christian groups. For example, we might find a parenting group, an arts group, or business group where we can connect at our own church or one nearby. There may already be a Bible study or Christian fellowship group at our workplace, either publicly visible or flying under the radar. There already may be a Christian fellowship for business folk or artists or police or other work specialties in our city or region. Ask around. Go online and search for Christians in your vocation. If we are artists, we could join CIVA (Christians in the Visual Arts) and find other CIVA members in our area. If we are attorneys, we could join the Christian Legal Society, and so on. Whatever our work specialty, there may already be a Christian professional association or work group that will lead us to a workplace discipleship partner or two.

One possible strategy is for us to try to start a new Bible study or Christian fellowship group in our workplace (factory, school, art studio, business, police department, etc.). We may need to get permission to publicize it through company channels, but (even if denied) word of mouth and personal networking may be a better recruiting tool anyway. We can decide whether to have a study focus or a sharing and prayer focus—or some combination. Many organizations have (or allow) employee-initiated groups like this.

Vocation-specific fellowships—whether in our churches, cities, or organizations—are something extremely valuable in themselves, not just as recruiting grounds for a smaller posse. I have been part of various groups of historians, pastors, business ethics professors and consultants, technology critics, and business leaders at various times in my work career. I have visited and participated in some amazing company-based and community-based Christian fellowships. While many of the posse functions can happen in these groups, there are also some limitations on how deeply or frankly we can share our workplace challenges, especially when the membership is large and fluid. It may be best not to open ourselves up to newcomers we don't know well enough. I would encourage workplace disciples to be active members of these fellowships. Some of them actually encourage and assist their members/participants to form smaller posses of the type discussed in this chapter.

The posse/partnership goal is for all of us to find at least one other Christian (and eventually three or four) with whom to commit to an ongoing relationship in which we share our workplace struggles, opportunities, and questions; and then help each other with discernment, encouragement, support, and accountability. Once we have a prospect or two in sight, we can contact them and invite them to lunch or coffee. We can share our work stories and current situations with one another. If we feel like we have enough of a shared faith and calling, and can imagine hanging out together, then we can ask if they might be interested in a prayer and sharing support group of maybe three or four people. We can ask if they would be willing to commit to, say, a meeting every two weeks over the next three or four months to see how it goes. We have to really want it. We have to be intentional and persistent, even a little bold in finding the right workplace discipleship partners. Keep it casual and for a limited trial run in the beginning, as you don't want to prematurely commit and then find it doesn't work and be stuck in an unhelpful relationship.

What kind of people are we looking for? We want people we can respect and learn from. We want to be able to share (eventually) difficult and maybe extremely confidential stuff without fear of disclosure. It can be good if one or two of the members are older mentors, but not if they dominate and dictate rather than take a humble place alongside others. It can work if a couple members are younger, provided they can be committed and trustworthy. They may not have much advice for our situations if they haven't been around for long. Another thing: I tend to think it is best if our posse is the same sex as us, though I don't think this is a hard and fast rule. We don't want to have any kind of tempting male/female dynamic enter the picture as we get more emotionally vulnerable. It's better to go home to our spouse for emotional comfort. Someone in our posse might want to share about their relational temptation at work and ask for accountability and support. Open and frank sharing may be inhibited by having the opposite sex present. This is not a rule, just a caution.

How many partners? Finding just one Jonathan-type partner can be enough. But I think three or four or five is even better. Why? Because in today's mobile era, we are often out of town or temporarily unavailable. It's great if we have critical mass for, say, a weekly meeting even if one person is on the road or taken ill. Also, having three or four (not just one) trusted posse members with their different gifts, experiences, and perspectives can lift the wise advice potential. Is there a maximum size limit? Maybe twelve, since Jesus worked with that number, but remember that even Jesus often hung out just with Peter, James, and John.

How often to connect? I tend to think that a *weekly hour* together is the best target. Every two weeks may be all that is possible. Once a month is not good for staying current with one another unless we have a weekly email exchange or some significant midmonth communication. One of my longest-term posses, for about ten years through the 1980s, was composed of a pastor, a university campus fellowship leader, an urban mission leader, a retired (but itinerate) missionary legend, and me (a professor and dean of a theological school). We five met every Thursday morning from 7:00 to 8:00. Even with our busy travel schedules, we always had "critical mass."

A Posse Start-Up Plan

- Find one or two or three people who seem like they would be congenial, thoughtful, caring, understanding, trustworthy discipleship partners.
- Meet and talk about whether they would be interested in forming a small workplace discipleship support group/partnership.
- Commit to meet weekly or biweekly for a three- or four-month trial period.
- Share and discuss the issues, struggles, questions, successes, and failures each of you experiences in your work. It's about discernment and support.
- Pray together and keep in touch in between meetings as appropriate.

I remember when the wife of one of our guys was diagnosed with cancer and slowly died over the year. This became Topic A for us during that difficult time, and I am sure this brother would tell you he couldn't have made it without the posse's support. Another year, I think Topic A was my extremely stressful final year as president of a school I had founded and given my life to. Bleeding from friendly fire almost every week, I survived because of these guys. They helped me work through an agonizing decision of whether and when to resign—and then my next vocational step. They walked with me as I had to decide whether to fire a highly skilled but dishonest associate during my final "lame duck" year. I remember another time when one of our guys was going off to his high school reunion in another city where he would likely see his high school girlfriend (twenty years later!). There had been no contact of any kind since high school, and our brother's marriage was solid. But just to be safe, he told us about this possible encounter and said, "When I get back next week, I want you guys to ask me how it went and keep me accountable." We did. Not all of our posse sharing was strictly limited to workplace issues in any narrow sense, but what brought us together and remained our central focus was our commonality of calling and work.

My posse didn't study the Bible together every week—we each had lots of such study in our lives already. What we did was share our lives and concerns and pray for one another. We raised issues and questions coming up in our workplaces and received suggestions and counsel. We helped one another calm down and trust God. We helped one another get fired up and motivated when they needed it. Once a year, we went about an hour's drive away for an overnight mini-retreat, where we cooked and laughed, ate and drank, and did a couple Bible studies together. We also carved out one hour per person, during which they shared at length their sense of "where they were" and "where they were going" vocationally. After some discussion, we had him kneel down while we laid hands on him and prayed for him. This was a powerful experience for all of us. This lasted for ten years, until our different callings broke up our group and took us to different places literally all over the world.

This matter of partnership is critical. Having a workout partner massively improves the regularity and quality of our fitness workouts. Kicking an addiction is much more likely with a committed partner accompanying us over time in the struggle. Caring for children and family is never easy, but going it alone as a single parent is much harder than doing it with a committed partner (although, obviously, a toxic partner is worse than being alone, so choose wisely!).

Of course, we are actually *never* alone in our workplace discipleship. In the ultimate sense, God is always our partner—even when we ignore him and act as though we are alone, even if our posse were to abandon us. "Be strong and bold; have no fear or dread of them, because it is the LORD your God who goes with you; he will not fail you or forsake you" (Deut. 31:6; see also Heb. 13:5). As Jesus promised his disciples, "Remember, I am with you always, to the end of the age" (Matt. 28:20).

But as wonderful as God's presence is, it is still "not good" for someone to dwell (or work) alone without one or more partners! Let's be sure to find at least one committed, covenanted partner to accompany us on the journey of workplace discipleship.

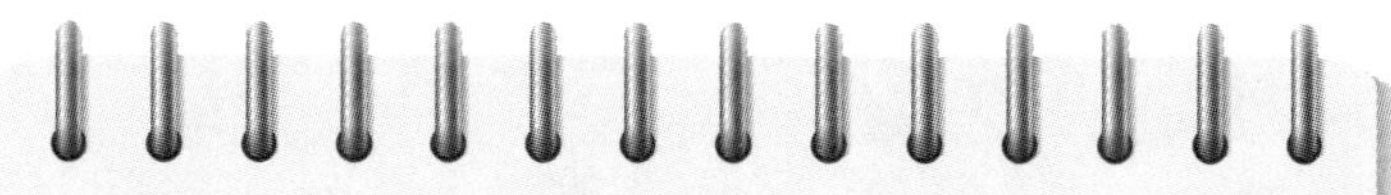

To Do

✓ Survey your network (and expand it), looking for potential posse members— workplace discipleship partners who seem like prospects for a discernment and support group.

✓ Invite one or two potential partners to join you in a three- or four-month experiment of meeting for an hour of sharing and prayer weekly or biweekly.

For Reflection & Discussion

1. What, if any, have been your experiences as a member of small groups in a church or parachurch ministry? Were they positive? Negative? Did you receive any kind of support or understanding for your workplace discipleship?

2. Have you been part of any Christian vocational group fellowship (for example, in health care, the arts, parenting, education, technology)? How and where did that happen? Was it helpful?

3. Have you ever had the experience of good, trustworthy, supportive friendships in the workplace—even if you didn't share the same faith?

4. What might be the major obstacles and challenges you face in trying to create a covenanted Christian posse (a fellowship and support group) as a regular factor in your workplace discipleship? What could help you overcome those obstacles and impediments?

5

Learn

Get Better at Your Job—and Get Broader, Deeper, and Wiser

In chapter 3, we encouraged *listening* to what God might have to say about our work. Mostly, this drove us to the life and teaching of Jesus and the daily study of Scripture. While that is going to remain the center of our educational agenda, there is more to learn. Faithful and wise workplace disciples must be *lifelong learners*. What—and how—can we learn, in order to serve well in the work God has given us?

I see four basic subjects in our workplace discipleship continuing education course—that is, our lifelong learning curriculum. The first and third of these four subjects are highly personalized, depending on our field of work, so I will frequently depend on examples from my own field of work—but you can easily imagine the parallels for your work. The second and fourth subjects are more general and not field specific. Much of this chapter is a kind of sample bibliography and study list, and it will really be up to each reader to look beyond my suggestions and do some searching to find the best resources appropriate to their workplace learning objectives.

Job Skills and Expertise

First of all, we workplace disciples want to be really good at our jobs! No matter what our work may be, let's be constantly learning and improving our job skills and expertise. Isn't this implied pretty directly by the Colossians text? "Whatever you do, in word or deed, do everything in the name of the Lord Jesus . . . wholeheartedly, fearing the Lord. Whatever your task, put yourselves into it, as done for the Lord and not for your masters" (Col. 3:17, 22–23). Isn't it important that we don't just go through the motions, put in our hours and go home, satisfied with mediocrity? Whether our work is painting buildings, raising kids, being a sous-chef, creating illustrations for an advertising campaign, or writing software programs, wouldn't God want us to get better and better at our work? Whenever we have an opportunity for a good continuing education course or session, let's be first in line. When there are training materials available, let's read or watch them. We don't want to go through life doing the minimum. We don't want to be average or just acceptable. We want people to see that we are trying to do a great job—and then give glory to our Father in heaven who (we hope they know) inspires us.

Here is my story (and I'm sticking to it!), but remember that my experience as a teacher and writer has meant a lot more "book learning" than most other vocations. Lifelong learning for your particular kind of work will have its own distinctive characteristics. For what it's worth though: I attended years of formal education from high school to college through graduate school, but that was just to learn some basics and to learn how to learn. My various employers have hosted required or optional in-service training programs (lots of work specialties, not just schools, offer opportunities like this). My wife also used to sign up for optional computer courses at a big bank she worked for; before she knew it, there was a steady stream of both managers and administrative support personnel coming by her desk to beg for her help (this included me!).

These formal and official learning requirements and opportunities, however, were only the beginning. Almost everything of truly great value I learned *outside* the classroom. I joined professional associations and learned from their annual meetings and journal articles and reviews.[1] I bookmarked a few web sites and subscribed to a few online newsletters or blogs that I found helpful. I attend conferences and lectures where I see opportunities to learn. I hear about these learning opportunities from my employers and colleagues, or see them mentioned in journals or newsletters. My workplace discipleship posse (which we discussed in chapter 4) is always on the lookout for resources and events that might be of interest to me.

Most of all I read a lot of *books* related to my workplace interests. I hear recommendations from my friends and colleagues. I see book reviews and recommendations in the publications I read, from newspapers to journals. I love to walk through bookstores and browse the new releases as well as the business, technology, and ethics-related shelves (which are my specialties). The footnotes and references in one book often lead me to another great discovery. I am always in the midst of reading a book. I have a "next up to read" pile on my desk. I don't read very fast, but I am "bulldog" persistent. I always read with a pen in my hand, so I can scribble notes in the margins. Although I am sometimes frustrated by not having enough reading time, I never give up.

So here is my counsel: look around online and in bookstores, pay attention to your particular professional

---

1. For me, this has been above all the International Jacques Ellul Society, Society of Christian Ethics, and Society of Business Ethics; but also, at times, the Association for Practical and Professional Ethics, the National Association for Science, Technology, and Society, and (as a sometime pastor) the Midwinter Conference of the Evangelical Covenant Church. Most of these organizations have a journal and a website with great resources.

publications and to their reviews and recommendations. What looks interesting and helpful to read? How, for example, are technology and globalization changing your field of work? What is the history of your field, your company, your competitors, and your industry leaders? Are there exposés of how leaders or companies went wrong that could be relevant to what's happening in your context? Ask your work colleagues and supervisors. Ask your friends. Ask Google (that is, do an Internet search).

This first objective in the curriculum is the same for everyone. Get better at our work. Strengthen our job skills and performance. Be the best we can be. Learn all we can. Let's make ourselves valuable, even essential, in our place of work because of our growing job expertise. And remember: we don't do this just for personal gain and promotion, but also to honor, obey, and glorify the Lord of our work life.

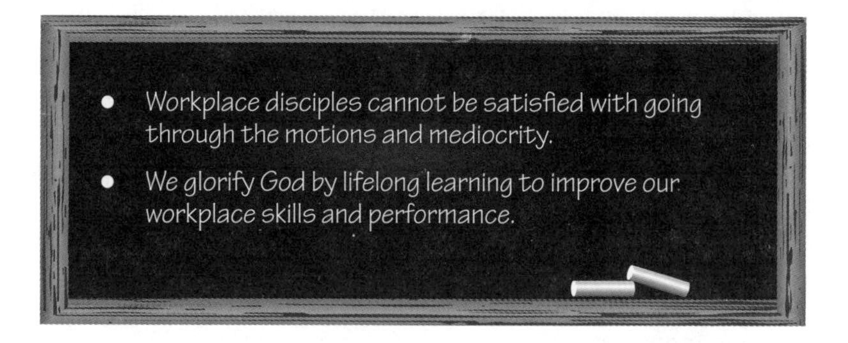

The Theology of Work in General

The second subject in our curriculum is "Christian Perspectives" on work in the broad sense, including all work fields and specializations. We could call this the "theology of work"—that is, what does God say about the truth and reality, the core mission and values, of human work? Of course, our basic studies in Scripture will move us a long way toward this goal, but we can find a lot of additional help by reading and listening to some veterans and experts on the topic. This deeper, biblical understanding of work will really help us bring a "salt" and "light" difference to our work, whatever it is.

There are some excellent one-volume introductions to a Christian theology of work.[2] Some of my recommendations go back to books written thirty years ago, while others are more recent.[3] Doug Sherman and William Hendricks's classic *Your Work Matters to God* (NavPress, 1987) was among the first comprehensive introductions. Lee Hardy's *The Fabric of This World: Inquiries into Calling, Career Choice, and the Dignity of Human Work* (Eerdmans, 1990) provides a great history of the way Christians have thought about work, a summary of some modern views, and some helpful applications. New Testament scholar Ben Witherington's *Work: A Kingdom Perspective on Labor* (Eerdmans, 2011) is a brief but thorough introduction. Tom Nelson's *Work Matters: Connecting Sunday Worship to Monday Work* (Crossway, 2011) is almost a modern classic. Nelson is a pastor who "woke up" to the critical value and importance of his parishioners' work. Amy Sherman's *Kingdom Calling: Vocational Stewardship for the Common Good* (InterVarsity, 2011) may be the single best introduction to a Christian view of work. Timothy Keller and Katherine Leary Alsdorf's *Every Good Endeavor: Connecting Your Work to God's Work* (Dutton, 2012) is deservedly among the best introductions to the general subject, and is the joint effort of an articulate, wise pastor

---

2. My own introduction, *The God of Good* Work, is in process.

3. Some of the best stuff was written decades, centuries, or even millennia ago. To understand the details of the latest technological gadgets, we need new materials of course. But to understand work or technology (for example) in a deeper, more profound sense, we must not ignore something just because it was not published in the past five years.

and an experienced business leader. Finally, Katelyn Beaty's *A Woman's Place: A Christian Vision for Your Calling in the Office, the Home, and the World* (Howard, 2016) is an outstanding theology of work and calling with special reference to women's challenges and opportunities. It is a scandal that Christians have sometimes uncritically or silently accepted the working world's habitual undervaluing (if not overt mistreatment) of women.

The one-volume book or one-time conference introduction is the minimalist approach. Several seminaries, colleges, and faith at work institutes have created one-day conferences or multisession study opportunities to help workers develop a better workplace theology, ethics, and practical presence in the workplace. My home church offers a six-hour seminar on "Workplace Discipleship 101" at least twice each year. The Center for Faith and Work at Redeemer Presbyterian Church in New York City created an intensive yearlong "Gotham Fellows" study program. We can also find online resources ready to help us develop this deeper, stronger theology/philosophy of work.

For what it's worth, let me describe an ambitious course I created and led with Al Erisman, former research mathematician at Boeing and currently co-chair of the Theology of Work Project. My hope is that readers will be excited and inspired, not intimidated or overwhelmed, by this description of an ambitious approach! On two different occasions (2011–13 and 2014–16) we recruited a cohort of fifteen men and women in various jobs and career stages for a study program meeting six different weeks, spread over two years. We actually lived, ate, fellowshipped, and studied together Monday noon to Friday noon. We stayed connected monthly on the Internet in between our periodic intensive sessions.

Each of our six intensive weeklong courses had a precise focus: Week One was about "Workplace Theology"—what is the truth and reality of work in a biblical Christian perspective? Week Two was about "Workplace Ethics"—in light of that theological truth and reality, what makes for *good* work and the *right* thing to do? Week Six (skipping to the end) was about "Workplace Leadership"—how can we influence individuals and organizations to embrace that reality and actually pursue those ethical standards? The primary foci of the other three weeks (three through five) were what we believed were the main drivers in today's workplace: we studied Christian perspectives on "Finance and Marketing," "Technology and Entrepreneurship," and "Globalization and Development." To get as real as possible, we spent those study weeks in New York City, Seattle, and Tegucigalpa, Honduras, respectively. The co-teachers gave their perspectives, often with a bit of critique of one another's presentations. Students shared their insights, often with some considerable work and study experience behind them. We discussed readings from both Christian and general market orientations. We interacted with guest speakers and visited work sites of all kinds. We prayed. We talked over meals. Students wrote up reviews, interviews, and essays.

While this was an ambitious learning experience, *something* along these lines could be replicated in the context of a church (or a group of churches) or perhaps a marketplace organization, not just by a university or seminary. A two-year commitment to one another and to a holistic study experience as described above is possible. A two-, three-, or even four-member leadership team could create the interactivity and multi-voice perspective that is so valuable. Instead of an intensive forty-five-hour study week every few months, it could be just one eight-hour Saturday together every month for two years.

Whatever our availability for study, whatever our work specialty, acquiring a deeper Christian perspective on work in general provides an essential foundation for the more specialized studies to which we now turn.

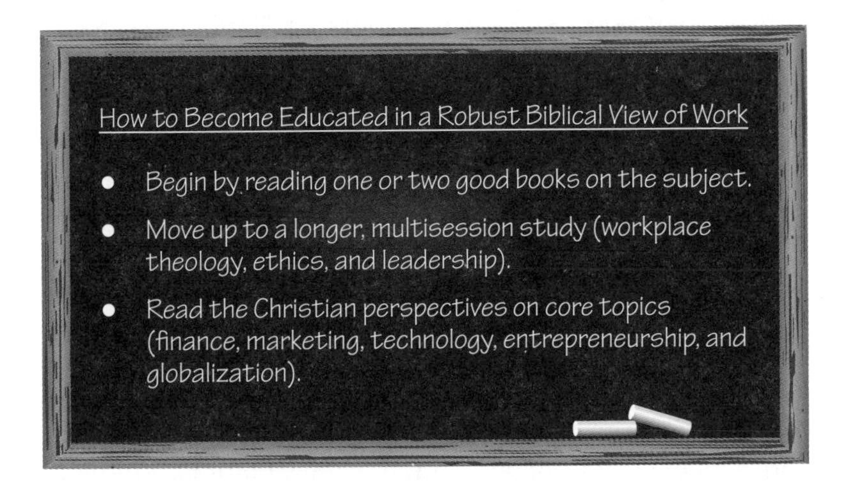

Christian Perspectives on Our Work in Particular

With the third subject in our curriculum, we seek to be more specific about our particular fields of work. Most of us have not had much help gaining Christian perspectives on our work specialty. If we went to a Christian college, we may have had some lectures or readings, but that would be an exception rather than the rule. Even if we did receive some help on the topic back in college, we are never done. Throughout our careers and lives, we need to continually look for more help and insight on the difference our faith should make in our particular work area. This might take some effort and research. How can our faith relate to cooking or to running a restaurant or food service? How about farming? Lab research? Artificial intelligence? Investment banking? Automobile manufacturing? City administration? Work in the hospitality and tourism industry? Homeschooling kids? Plumbing or carpentry? The list goes on . . . and on. Our goal is not just to think about God's will for work in general, but also for our work specifically!

Maybe my own story can inspire your quest. After earning my degree in history at Berkeley, I taught history courses in a public junior high and high school for four years. My workplace discipleship questions were as follows: How should my faith affect my understanding of history? Where is God in human history? What factors and forces does a biblical view of history focus on? I was not about to adopt a Marxist materialist perspective or a "great man" perspective or any other narrow, reductionist explanation. No theological seminaries had courses on this subject (I looked at their catalogs), but I was initially inspired by the bold, creative, swashbuckling historical interpretation of Francis Schaeffer.[4] That provoked me to look further, and I found the Conference on Faith and History and its longtime leader, Richard Pierard, professor of history at Indiana State University. Pierard and his colleagues were all reputable scholars in the American Historical Association, as well as committed Christians in their thinking and approach to history. I began reading their journal *Fides et Historia*. I was no longer alone! Professor Pierard and other veterans in the field encouraged me. Although this is my particular story, don't miss the pattern: a couple of helpful books and the discovery of a veteran or two in my field of work brought a giant leap forward for me in my workplace theology and discipleship.

Then I tried to take it to the next level: during those four public school teaching years, I enrolled (summer sessions and evening courses) at San Francisco State University and

---

4. Francis A. Schaeffer, *Escape from Reason*, IVP Classics (Downers Grove, IL: InterVarsity Press, 2006); and *The God Who Is There: Speaking Historic Christianity into the Twentieth Century* (Downers Grove, IL: Inter-Varsity Press, 1968). I moved away from Schaeffer's views as time went on, but I remain deeply grateful for his impact on me.

earned an MA with a thesis on "Contemporary Christian Philosophies of History: The Problem of God's Role" (1971). I did a comparative study of six different historians who had written on God's role in human history: Herbert Butterfield, Eric Voegelin, Gordon Clark, John W. Montgomery, Reinhold Niebuhr, and Rudolph Bultmann. Each of them had written a major book on the topic since the Holocaust, and I wanted to understand how they saw God and history, in full awareness of that hell-on-earth event. There was no consensus or easy answers, but I was launched on my career adventure of integrating faith and learning. I'm certainly not saying that we all could or should do a graduate degree or write a book on our field like a professor might do! The message is don't stop—keep moving forward, keep going deeper in understanding how your faith might relate to your particular work, strengthening and enriching it to the glory of God. This is the adventure of making Jesus Lord of our work.

Our task is to find people and resources to help us integrate our faith with our particular line of work. My friends back in those days who were entering scientific fields received a lot of help from the American Scientific Affiliation, a huge organization of Christians in science led by Stanford professor Richard Bube among others. People in literary studies often turned to works by C. S. Lewis, Dorothy Sayers, Owen Barfield, and the other Oxford "Inklings." More recently, people in the arts have found help in CIVA (Christians in the Visual Arts) and in books such as W. David O. Taylor's *For the Beauty of the Church: Casting A Vision for the Arts* (Baker, 2010). Those in music could start with Jeremy S. Begbie's *Resounding Truth: Christian Wisdom in the World of Music* (Baker, 2007). Those in law can turn to Michael P. Schutt, *Redeeming Law: Christian Calling and the Legal Profession* (InterVarsity, 2007). Among other possibilities in medicine and health care, I love Raymond Downing's *Death and Life in America: Biblical Healing and Biomedicine* (Herald Press, 2008) and *Global Health Means Listening* (Manqa Books, 2018). Amid a rapidly growing literature on Christianity and technology, John Dyer's *From the Garden to the City: The Redeeming and Corrupting Power of Technology* (Kregel, 2011) remains a great first step.

For the field of business, which generally includes more jobs than any other vocational specialty, there is now a rich (and rapidly expanding) trove of helpful literature alongside a growing number of organizations and fellowships for business folk of all kinds. It is wonderful that many Christian business organizations today give serious attention to the integration of biblical faith and values with business practices—and are not just social, spiritual, and evangelistic in their aims (as great and important as those can be). Some of the best books I have read on Christianity and business include *The ServiceMaster Story: Navigating Tension between People and Profit* by Al Erisman (Hendrickson, 2020), ServiceMaster CEO Bill Pollard's *The Soul of the Firm* (HarperBusiness, 1996), John D. Beckett's *Loving Monday: Succeeding in Business Without Selling Your Soul* and *Mastering Monday: A Guide to Integrating Faith and Work* (InterVarsity, 2006), AES CEO Dennis W. Bakke's *Joy at Work: A Revolutionary Approach to Fun on the Job* (PVG, 2005), R. Paul Stevens's *Doing God's Business: Meaning and Motivation in the Marketplace* (Eerdmans, 2006), Jeff Van Duzer's *Why Business Matters to God (and What Still Needs to Be Fixed)* (InterVarsity, 2010), and Kenman L. Wong and Scott B. Rae's *Business for the Common Good: A Christian Vision for the Marketplace* (InterVarsity, 2011). There are dozens or even hundreds of books out there with titles like these. There are also histories of companies and biographies of Christians in business leadership that can be helpful.

Again, the purpose of this third part of the workplace discipleship lifelong learning curriculum is to find resources—individuals, professional groups and fellowships, conferences, podcasts, books, journals, articles, interviews—that help us to integrate our faith with our *particular* job specialty (going beyond just work in general).

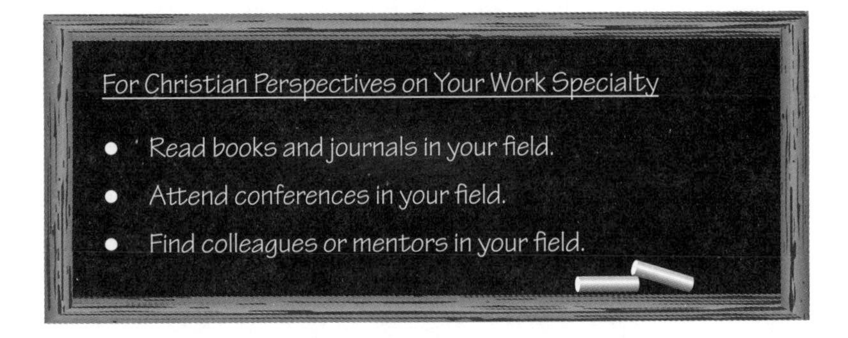

Wisdom, Depth, and Breadth

The fourth basic subject in our workplace discipleship curriculum we might summarize as "wisdom" and "good judgment." The ancient Greeks had several different words for knowledge. *Techne* (from which we get "technology") was skill-knowledge, know-how, knowledge of how to make and do things, practical tasks. But they also highlighted *sophia*, which means wisdom. The great philosophers, such as Plato and Aristotle, argued that *techne* without *sophia* was dangerous. Today, we live in a world overflowing with technical knowledge but desperately lacking wisdom and good judgment on how to use and direct that technical knowledge. *Techne* brings a kind of power. *Sophia* can guide that power in constructive directions. *Techne* is concerned with means and methods. *Sophia* is concerned with ends and purposes. Workplace disciples want to be experts, fully competent, even exemplary, on the technical aspects of our work. But God also wants us to bring wisdom to our work and our workplace.

Here is how King Solomon in Proverbs 4:5–11 puts it,

> Get wisdom; get insight: do not forget, nor turn away from the words of my mouth.
>
> Do not forsake her, and she will keep you; love her, and she will guard you.
>
> The beginning of wisdom is this: Get wisdom, and whatever else you get, get insight.
>
> Prize her highly, and she will exalt you; she will honor you if you embrace her.
>
> She will place on your head a fair garland; she will bestow on you a beautiful crown.
>
> Hear, my child, and accept my words, that the years of your life may be many.
>
> I have taught you the way of wisdom; I have led you in the paths of uprightness.

What can we do? For sure, "The fear of the LORD is the beginning of wisdom, and the knowledge of the Holy One is insight" (Prov. 9:10). My father was a midlevel executive in a corporation, and every morning throughout his life he read a chapter from the book of Proverbs (there are 31 chapters, so this means every month he read the whole book). There is no better foundation for becoming a faithful and wise workplace disciple than this habit of reading Scripture daily and praying about its message and applications. But beyond Scripture itself, workplace disciples need to work at acquiring and enhancing a broader, deeper education throughout our lives.

We live in a world of vast flows and deposits of *information*—but less real *knowledge* and *understanding*, and a veritable famine of *wisdom*. We have a serious learning deficit that has to do with (1) the way we have been schooled and educated, and (2) the craziness and chaos of today's society and culture. The schooling problem is that our educational curricula are more and more narrowly focused on a certain kind of job training and skills—for example, in business, communications, or computer science. Without any doubt, we need what is called STEM education in today's world—science, technology, engineering, and mathematics. We should encourage people to enter these fields and do well. This is hard stuff! People in these fields need our prayers and support.

What is weakening in today's education are the kinds of studies and experiences that deepen and broaden our thinking. To use the old metaphor, we become experts on the technical aspects of the "trees" but have little perspective or appreciation for the "forest" (or for different kinds of "plants" outside of our space). Learning foreign languages, living among people different from ourselves (racially, vocationally, politically, etc.), exploring and practicing music and other art forms, studying geography and history, religion and philosophy—it is these subject areas in the humanities that are often minimized or ignored, yet they bring us the kind of broader and deeper perspective that can yield wisdom and good judgment. An old way of putting it is that our education is about "making a life," not just "making a living" by way of our specialized expertise.

We also have to deal with the craziness and chaos of today's technological culture. We live in a culture of distraction, with constant noise and an assault of images and bits of information. Our world is in relentless accelerating motion. It is difficult if not impossible to disconnect from our phones (info hunting on the Internet, phone and text messages from friends, game playing, addictive viewing habits, etc.). Our screens bring innumerable bits of information and entertainment into our lives. There is no escape. Many are addicted, and the idea of unplugging or disconnecting is essentially unthinkable.

The quantity of our texts, tweets, and exposure to bits of info does not make up for the lack of in-depth quality, which would require longer, deeper, undistracted conversation and shared experience. And what is true for our interpersonal relationships is also true for our work, our political life, and even our faith. We have lots of bits of information but little depth, breadth, and integration. Seventy years ago, Jacques Ellul warned that in a world of swirling, disconnected bits of information, people can cope only by grabbing onto "explanatory myths" to make some sense of life.[5] These myths are simplistic overgeneralizations, maybe with some kernel of truth—but a poor replacement for more careful, truthful, comprehensive thought. In other places and times, other myths will replace these. We need to guard against simplistic, overgeneralized explanations, but people are vulnerable to these mental short-cuts when overwhelmed by the daily information overload.

How might we make up for the deficits in our education and the craziness and distraction of our culture? It is impossible to add another hour to each day or another year to each decade in order to participate in supplementary education. This may not be a welcome suggestion, but I think we need to do what we can (with the support of our posse!) to cut some things out of our schedule and make room for other priorities. It is interesting that the fourth commandment starts with "Remember the Sabbath day" and follows that with "Six days you shall work." We can't be legalistic or inflexible about these matters, but blocking out some time every week for reading and for activities that will broaden and deepen us

5. Ellul, *Presence in the Modern World*, 78–80.

is an important step. Make a priority list of material to read, podcasts to listen to, events and activities to attend or participate in, people to meet with—all to broaden and deepen our understanding and appreciation of the people and the planet.

We might read the Koran or the Analects of Confucius. It is never too late to try to learn another language or a musical instrument or a sport (perhaps no tackle football after age fifty though). Even taking up hobbies such as painting, cooking, astronomy, or bird-watching can broaden our take on life. If our work tends to be mostly about "thinking" (analysis, design, etc.), it could be refreshing to take a shop class or something else physical. We don't want to be dilettantes—people who dabble in everything without taking anything seriously. Nor do we want to become well-educated cultural snobs! But we workplace disciples do want to acquire a broad understanding and appreciation of life, history, the peoples around us, and their cultures.

Work on acquiring that deeper, wiser perspective we call "wisdom." Of course, this may mean a reduction in television, movie, or sports viewing, or something else dominating our schedule without much real benefit (less sleep is not an option!). No doubt each of us has to create a personal learning agenda in our own way. Talking this through with our workplace posse (chapter 4) is an important help in deciding how to proceed.

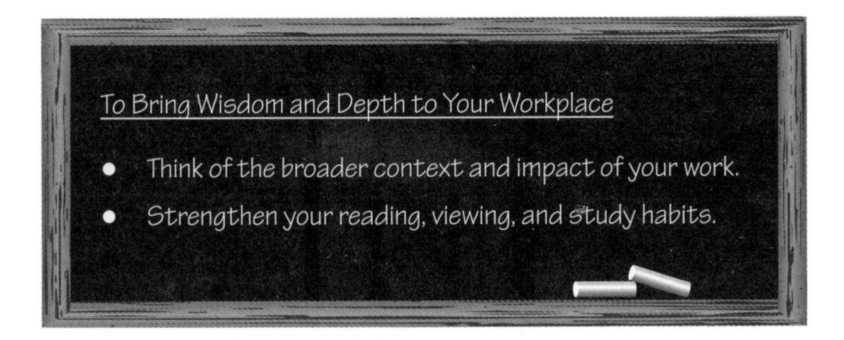

Awareness of the News

Much of the emphasis on wisdom here has leaned toward the past—understanding the roots and the background of today's work. But we can't leave the wisdom challenge without briefly thinking about our awareness of current events and challenges—that is, the news. The great Swiss-German theologian Karl Barth was famous for saying we should go through life with the Bible in one hand and a newspaper in the other in order to be well-informed. This does not mean wasting time on media newscasts and publications that jump from one gory accident to another, then some celebrity gossip, then a political scandal or public outrage, then some weather speculation, and so on. Nor is the all-politics-all-the-time jabbering of other news channels enough. And even if our news sources and channels are of quality, I don't think we want to become "news junkies" in the sense of 24/7 attention to the latest breaking news. But I think Barth had a point that we need to stay aware of what is going on around us.

How can we, then, acquire this basic awareness of the news of our place and time? Since I am a teacher, researcher, writer, and educator, people in other work arenas need to take my examples with a grain of salt. I share my own approach to news awareness (as other subjects in this book) not as the only or best way, but to illustrate the point. What I am proposing in this book is not a theory alone, but a practical plan that I myself have pursued (however imperfectly).

Some of my friends follow the news by scrolling through an online newsfeed and, occasionally, clicking to a longer story when something looks important. I have no criticism of anyone who follows this approach, but I prefer being a daily reader of my local newspaper wherever I happen to live as well as a daily national newspaper, such as the *New York*

Times or the *Wall Street Journal*. This usually takes me thirty to sixty minutes every day. Yeah, I like holding the paper in my hand rather than squinting at my screen (which may well demand my gaze for many hours the rest of the day). I look at every page, but I certainly don't read everything. I read some investigative articles and some opinion columns. I peruse things and stop for some reading about the arts and music scenes, fashion and sports, medical and religious news, and international news.

This way I am getting two things: first, I am exposed not just to politics but business; not just to local matters but also national and international ones; and not just to my narrower field of interest. There is a breadth and a serendipity in this approach that helps keep me from getting myopic (narrow vision) and stuck on some preselected favorite topics. The second benefit is that I am usually reading stories that are original, in-depth research. We live in a "McPaper"[6] world of brief, flashy, often secondhand news bits—when we need a deeper level of research and breadth of coverage. Another source of deeper, fuller presentation and analysis of today's world is in magazines such as *The Economist* or *The Atlantic*. Beyond the print media, I am a big fan of the *PBS News-Hour* (and PBS in-depth news research programs, such as *Frontline*). While nobody is perfect or above criticism, more than most of its alternatives, PBS attempts a dispassionate, multi-perspective, in-depth reporting and analysis of the day's news and trends.

The ideas and suggestions in this chapter are highly individual, and you are reading about what has helped me. You will need to find your own way, of course, and choose your

6. "McPaper" refers to a way of thinking about mass-marketed, lowest-common-denominator news, like comparing McDonald's to a fine restaurant.

own sources. The purpose of this fourth part of the workplace discipleship curriculum is to honor God by (1) getting really good at what we do, (2) developing a rich Christian view of work in general and (3) of our vocation in particular, and (4) acquiring a broader, deeper, godly wisdom. I hope that you at least found my suggestions helpful!

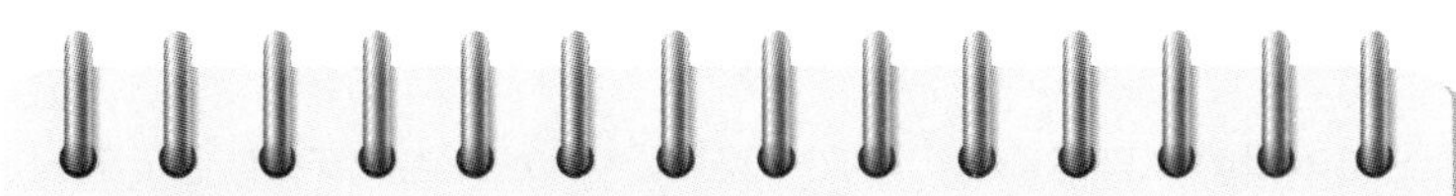

To Do

- ✓ Ask your work colleagues for recommendations of books or other materials on the best practices, current state, and likely future of your industry or field of work.
- ✓ Do an Internet search for books and other learning resources (articles, conferences, videos, podcasts, etc.) that provide some Christian fellowship and perspective on your field of work.

For Reflection & Discussion

1. How do you stay current (or even get ahead of the pack) in your field of work? What do you read, listen to, attend, participate in, and so on?

2. What have you read (or what conferences or programs have you attended) that deepened your historical or theological perspective on your work?

3. How might it be possible for you to create or participate in a serious workplace theology, ethics, and leadership study cohort like the one described in this chapter?

PART TWO

Impacting Our Workplace

All that preparation in Part One was about getting ready and able to implement Part Two. In Part Two, we now turn our attention to five concrete ways that workplace disciples are present in their place of work. First, if we can, we try to choose or, no matter what, do our work in harmony and alignment with God's mission in the world as creator, sustainer, and redeemer. Second, we try to set a great personal example, visibly modeling the values of the kingdom of God. Third, we try to share specific biblical insights and ideas about our work in our workplace. Fourth, we share our faith about Jesus—the foundation of our life, values, and philosophy of work. Finally, we try to be faithful and effective reconcilers and overcomers of any workplace evil with good.

6

Align

Work in Harmony with God's Work

Now, we go to work! What kind of presence and impact do workplace disciples have when they show up for work? We want to *work like God would work*. As much as possible, we want our work to be in *alignment* with God's work in the world. We want to hear God's "Well done, good and faithful servant" when our work is finished. There may come a time when we discern (with our posse) that we just can't continue in a certain workplace, because it totally prevents us from any alignment with God's work. If this happens, it can be difficult for us, especially if we can't see other, better work opportunities and we are dependent on income from that toxic workplace.

All of us would love to be able to choose or design our work and our place of work. The reality for many (perhaps most) people on the planet, however, is that their choice of work is near zero and *any* work, *any* job that can help them survive must be pursued. Long hours working in agricultural fields planting and harvesting, in mines or on construction projects, in manufacturing sweatshops, in minimum-wage fast-food establishments, in soul-numbing office complexes. People with these kinds of jobs are actually the lucky ones, because they have a chance to feed their families and put a roof over their heads. Of course, there are farms and kitchens and workshops where people's experiences are good ones.

That is, they have good colleagues, a safe and even beautiful workplace, a decent salary and benefits, job security, and they're creating products they can be proud of. Still, appalling work conditions, near slave-wages, and uncertainty characterize many workplaces around the world. In far too many cases, the poor and powerless are forced into degrading, unhealthy, and dangerous work.

Even in freer and more flourishing economies and cultures, we might be working on a project or for a company that is far from what we would prefer as servants of the Lord. But it may be that the job market is so tight we don't see any employment alternatives, and meanwhile our family is totally dependent on our maintaining our salary with its health-care coverage for our sick child. Trapped!

Another possibility is that God has actually placed us in a difficult working environment, or a less than ideal organization, that daily challenges our faith and values. Remember how Daniel was placed in the Babylonian administration of Nebuchadnezzar, Joseph served as number two to the Egyptian Pharaoh, Cornelius was in charge of an occupying Roman legion in Israel, and Esther was forced to marry the Persian king (she didn't really have much choice, given the power differential). Personally, I have serious objections to some of the big banks, fossil fuel companies, big tech companies, the casino industry, our regional gas and electric company, and the manufacturer of a diesel car I was once deceived into buying . . . I could go on. But I can't tell you how grateful I am that God has many of his workplace disciples working at all levels in these organizations! Thank God they didn't all leave in search of some more ideal workplace. Sometimes it is right to leave; but probably more often, we should stay where we are and serve as ambassadors of a better way, doing everything possible to work in alignment with God's work even in the belly of the beast (to put it vividly), even in Babylon.

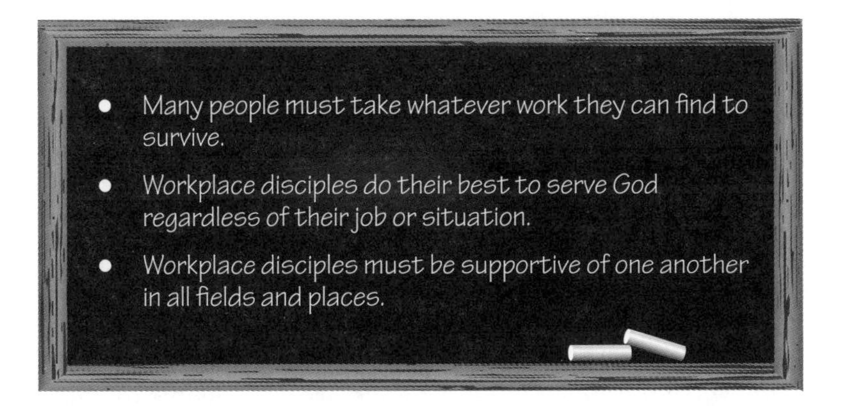

Let's remember again this advice from Paul (Col. 3:17, 22–4:1):

> Whatever you do, in word or deed, do everything in the name of the Lord Jesus, giving thanks to God the Father through him. . . .
>
> Slaves, obey your earthly masters in everything, not only while being watched and in order to please them, but wholeheartedly, fearing the Lord. Whatever your task, put yourselves into it, as done for the Lord and not for your masters, since you know that from the Lord you will receive the inheritance as your reward; you serve the Lord Christ. For the wrongdoer will be paid back for whatever wrong has been done, and there is no partiality.
>
> Masters, treat your slaves justly and fairly, for you know that you also have a Master in heaven.

We need to look past the ancient "slave and master" terminology to understand this as "employee and manager" (slavery was a common working relationship during the early Roman Empire in which the church began; while it was bad, it wasn't the same as America's abominable race-based slavery.

The point is: *whatever* work we do. We may have little or no choice as a "slave" (or an employee today). But *whatever* we do, *whatever* we say, let's do it "in the name of the Lord

Jesus." In Scripture, a person's name represented the character; for example, "Jesus" means "Savior" and "Peter" means "Rock," and so on. Let's do our work like Jesus would do it—that is, in his name. Let's do it *for* the Lord, wholeheartedly not halfheartedly, whether we're being watched or not. Let's count on God not only to reward us but also to deal with that nasty boss for his nastiness. And if we are a "master" (a boss or manager), we are called and commanded by God to treat our workers with justice and fairness—that is, what is *just and fair in the eyes of God*. Leaders are responsible to know and maintain God's ethical standards and values, and they need to remember that they are accountable to God himself.

Paul's advice to "obey your earthly masters in everything" is, of course, qualified by his other statement: "We must obey God rather than any human authority" (Acts 5:29). As long as our boss or company is not asking us to do something in clear violation of God's standards, we should normally be reliable, hardworking, honest, positive employees. We will come back to this—our workplace example—in a later chapter.

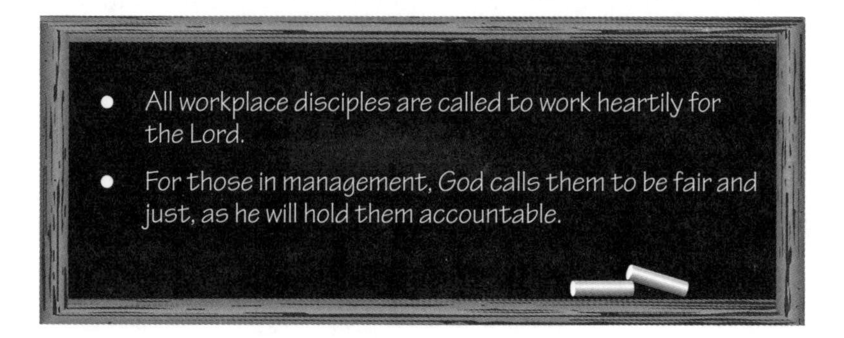

God's Work in the World

Now let's go back to the question of what God's work is in our world. The point and purpose of *our* work is to advance *God's* work in the world. We are here on earth not just to live and work for ourselves but also for God. How can I put my shoulder behind God's projects? A critical insight on this subject comes from the fact that every man, woman, and child around the planet and throughout history is made in the image and likeness of God. It is therefore not just the *command* of God to join in his work, but it is also his *example* that guides us. It is already part of our created DNA to do so—part of what it means to be human. Work that does not align with God's work in the world is *dehumanizing* (it violates what we were made to be and do in God's image) as well as *disobedient*. So, just what is God's work in the world? How can we describe it?[1] Let's summarize it under six headings. It is impossible to use just one term for each of the six.

1. Design, Create, Build, Produce

The first chapters of the Bible introduce God as the creator of all things. This is certainly about *innovation*—inventing something new. But we need to also use the term "productive." Not just the initial entrepreneurs but also the hardworking makers are following in our Creator's footsteps. Think about the characteristics of God's creative work: God creates things that are beautiful ("pleasant to the sight"), useful ("good for food"), lifegiving, complex, orderly, growing, dynamic, challenging, and flourishing. God creates as a team, an "us" ("let *us* make humankind in *our* image")—and he creates a team, a "them" (not just a "him" or "her"). God works brilliantly for six days and rests on the seventh (good work and good rest

1. My forthcoming book, *The God of Good Work*, describes in more detail a theology and philosophy of good work centered on the character of God in the Bible (and how the Bible says, "Good work goes bad"). As noted earlier, Michael Barram's *Missional Economics* gives a masterful description of God's mission, not just in the workplace but in all of life, from Genesis to Revelation.

are inextricably connected). It is no accident that in the grand vision of the afterlife, God is celebrated as creator: "You are worthy . . . for you created all things" (Rev. 4:11).

In the biblical story, designing and building things, innovating and creating goods and services, runs through the whole story as the work of God through the people. The first time anyone is said to be filled with God's Spirit, it is not a preacher or healer but a craftsman.

> The LORD spoke to Moses: See, I have called by name Bezalel . . . and I have filled him with divine spirit, with ability, intelligence, and knowledge in every kind of craft, to devise artistic designs, to work in gold, silver, and bronze, in cutting stones for setting, and in carving wood, in every kind of craft. (Exod. 31:1–5)

Think also about the design and implementation of Israel's amazing legal system, Israel's farming and ranching practices, and the construction of Jerusalem—its temple, palace, and walls. Think about the New Testament fishermen, Jesus' upbringing in a carpenter's home, his miraculous wine-making at a wedding and his bread-making for a hungry crowd. Think about the tent-making/leatherwork of Paul, Priscilla, and Aquila and the purple cloth business of Lydia. God will continue his creation in the end with a new heaven and a new earth. Creative designing and building are what God does. It's about ideas, designs, and plans but also about execution and production. This is phase one of the workplace mission of God.

So how can we express this godly creativeness wherever we work? This is an alignment question. Whatever our work may be, can we encourage and practice teamwork like our Trinitarian God does? Can our work be more productive . . . and our products not just "good for" but even "better for" their intended purposes and more "pleasant to the sight"—like God's work? Can we bring order and harmony where our workplace is experiencing some formlessness and chaos? Can we bring light into any darkness in our workplace? Can we practice and promote better stewardship of God's creation, better "dominion" before God? Can we better "cultivate" as well as "protect" people and the planet?

Sometimes our opportunities to express these creational characteristics will be confined to the small details of how we carry out our work. Other times we may be able to advocate and innovate in creative directions—new products or services or new and better ways of doing the existing things. Our creativeness/productivity could be in technology, building architecture and construction, child care, food production and preparation, transportation, hospitality, art and music . . . the list is long. No matter what or where our work, let's try to align our effort and approach with our creator. Let's pray that God can see what we have created, cultivated, and produced and call it "good."

2. Sustain, Uphold, Support

God is not just the creator of things; he is also the sustainer. Two powerful and explicit descriptions are given in Hebrews and Colossians: God "sustains all things by his powerful word" (Heb. 1:3); "All things have been created through him and for him . . . and in him *all things hold together*" (Col. 1:16–17; emphasis added). God doesn't just make something and walk away. This is a crucial point and not emphasized nearly enough. God stands by what he has created, tweaks it if necessary, supports it, and holds it together. Think about how God created Adam in Genesis 2. But, as we have already noted, God saw that "it is not good for man to dwell alone." So, God tweaks the creation and modifies it into male and female in partnership. God doesn't just plant a garden; he arranges for its caretakers (Adam and Eve). He waters it. But then, man and woman mess up and make themselves rudimentary clothing out of leaves, until God replaces their clothing with better, stronger, more durable, sustainable garments. They must be ejected from the garden after the rebellion, when it would be dangerous for them to have continuing access to the tree of life—they might eat it and get locked into their lost condition forever. So, God creates a barrier back into the garden to protect them from that danger. When Eve has a child, God is right there to help; he does not leave her to struggle by herself (Gen. 4:1). God is a sustainer.

How can we likewise express this godly "sustaining, upholding, and supporting" where we work? This is the alignment question again. Whatever our work may be, can we be upholders and sustainers like our God? As people made in God's image and under his command, this is an essential part of our work. We live in a throwaway, fall-apart, temporary world. Things are no longer built to last or to be repaired and sustained for long-term use. There is planned obsolescence all around us. Even people get worn out and sometimes discarded, so supporting our fellow workers could be a big part of this. Nature itself is severely stressed through being used up, wasted, and polluted; creation groans, eagerly waiting for our Lord's return. Wherever we work, whatever work we do, can we be sustainers and upholders of our products, customers and contracts, teams and relationships, and of our planet and environment? Maybe our workplace is irretrievably and unapologetically wasteful—but in our little functional arena we can do better: we can bear witness to our sustainer God.

3. Bring Wisdom and Realism

A third phase or characteristic of God's work and mission in the world is bringing truth and wisdom. Our world and its workplaces are often unrealistic, deceived, even foolish. But we know that God is the God of truth and wisdom and that

Jesus is the way, the truth, and the life (John 14:6). In Christ are "hidden all the treasures of wisdom and knowledge" (Col. 2:3). "The LORD by wisdom founded the earth; by understanding he established the heavens; by his knowledge the deeps broke open" (Prov. 3:19–20). Throughout the whole Bible, we see God giving us truth and practical wisdom. This wasn't just about some kind of philosophically true ideas hovering above us, but rather "the Word became flesh and lived among us" (John 1:14). Truth and wisdom were demonstrated in human life through Jesus Christ.

If this is such a part of God's mission, then it is part of our mission as well. How can we bring truth, wisdom, and realism to our workplaces? First of all, we can try to help our colleagues and companies not to worship false gods such as money, fame, power, technology, or work itself. That's about realism (think Ecclesiastes). We can encourage diligence, keeping agreements, generosity, and good communication (think Proverbs and Jesus' parables). This is a key part of our mission: aligning with the God of truth and wisdom. Let's bring it to our work.

4. Bring Goodness, Justice, and Righteousness

A fourth aspect of God's mission in the world is to exhibit and promote goodness, justice, and righteousness. "Ethics" is the best general description, but we need to think of ethics in a bigger sense than normal, as it is more than just compliance with rules. "The LORD is righteous; he loves righteous deeds" (Ps. 11:7). "I the LORD speak the truth, I declare what is right. . . . Only in the LORD . . . are righteousness and strength" (Isa. 45:19, 24). "We have an advocate . . . Jesus Christ the righteous" (1 John 2:1). What is true of God is to be true of his followers: "Let justice roll down like waters, and righteousness like an ever-flowing stream" (Amos 5:24). And to do justice, to love kindness, and to walk humbly with our

God (Mic. 6:8). "Hunger and thirst for righteousness" (Matt. 5:6). "Strive for the kingdom of God and his righteousness" (Matt. 6:33). "Present your members [of your body] to God as instruments of righteousness" (Rom. 6:13).

The alignment question is how can we demonstrate in our own lives and work the goodness and righteousness of God? What does that mean in our practical day-to-day work? And what does it mean to stand up for what is right when it comes to workplace behavior, customer service, environmental practices, and so on? This is a huge part of God's mission in the Bible from the ancient lawgivers and judges to the courageous, fiery prophets to the apostles of the kingdom of God and its righteousness.

5. Redeem, Repair, Heal, Reconcile, Liberate

God is not just the creator and sustainer, not just the bringer of wisdom and righteousness; he is also the redeemer—the fixer of broken things, the healer of the injured and brokenhearted, the liberator of those in bondage, the reconciler of the alienated, the savior of the lost. We don't live in Eden but in Babylon, a broken world full of hurting people. It is no accident at all that in Revelation 4 the first great song of eternity celebrates God as creator but in Revelation 5 the second great song celebrates the redeemer. This is the flip side of creational work: create good things; fix bad things. Throughout the Bible, God and his people do redemptive work. Noah builds an ark to save people and animals from the great flood. God uses Moses to set his enslaved people free. Jesus and his disciples not only preach the good news of the kingdom, but they also heal the sick, feed the hungry, and liberate people from the demons that haunt them. And, of course, Jesus endures crucifixion and is resurrected in order to save the human race: this is the redemptive work of the cross and our salvation. Our God is a redeemer, and we are all made in his image.

So how can we express this redeeming, fixing, healing, and liberating mission of God wherever we work? This is the alignment question yet again. Whatever our work may be, can we be redemptive like our Triune God? As people made in the redeemer's image and under his command, it is an essential part of our work. Maybe there are problems, even dangers, in our workplace that we can help fix—whether they primarily concern our fellow workers or our customers (patients, students, employees, and so on). Maybe there are broken relationships we can help heal. Of course, it would be great if in some more dramatic ways we could steer or influence our workplace or organization to become intentional about fixing some of society's problems, finding cures for diseases, and resolving educational or social issues. But even on a smaller, individual scale, workplace disciples can still make efforts to have a redemptive, healing impact in alignment with our Redeemer.

6. Finish, Flourish, Fly

The sixth characteristic of God's work is that he finishes what he starts—and sets it free to flourish. His work is able to "take off" and "fly" when he has finished. Think about how the Bible describes it: "And on the seventh day God finished the work he had done . . . all the work he had done in creation" (Gen. 2:2–3). And on the cross, "Jesus knew that all was now finished . . . he said, 'It is finished'" (John 19:28–30). Referring to the law and the prophets Jesus said, "I have come not to abolish but to fulfill" (Matt. 5:17). "Fulfill" (Greek *pleroma*) means literally to "fill full." There would be no unfinished loose ends in Jesus' teaching and action. It would all be "accomplished." I also love how at the close of his life, Jesus could pray to his Father, "I glorified you on earth by finishing the work that you gave me to do" (John 17:4). Paul writes to the Philippians, "I am confident of this, that the one who began a good work among you will bring it to completion" (Phil. 1:6).

The point is clear: God does not just start a work . . . and sustain it . . . and fix it when needed . . . he sticks with it to the very finish. And the finish is good. The product is very good.[2] How can we invite this theme to be an aspect of our work? Can we have a reputation (a testimony) we don't walk away from until our projects are finished well? Will we stick with our kids, even when they struggle as adults? Finishing well is our goal.

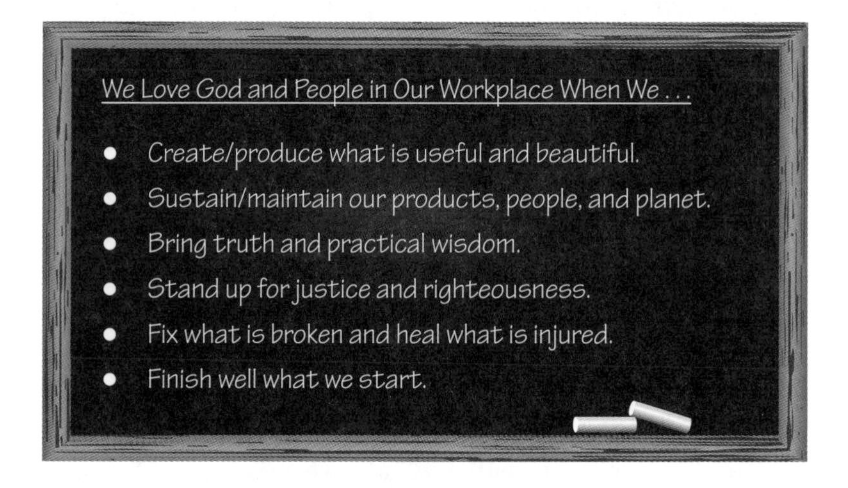

God's Worker Image and Likeness Are Embedded in Our Human Nature

This philosophy of good work is not just some abstract theory. It has a foundation in biblical revelation first of all, but there is also a basis in our anthropology (the study of our human nature). Think about the following three experiences (related to three of the six characteristics of God's work we just reviewed).

2. In my forthcoming *The God of Good Work*, we will explore the key characteristics of the end, the finish, of God's work in the world (including what he does through us). In theological terms, we will be thinking eschatologically—asking how our work today should be motivated and guided by the coming Day of the Lord.

First, how does it feel whenever we are given the opportunity in our work to be creative/productive? Maybe our boss or colleagues ask our opinion about some challenge? When we get to contribute our ideas and labor to produce something good or beautiful, we feel a sense of fulfilment. I know that when I have finished building a deck off my house, received the first copy of a new book back from my publisher, or succeeded in making a tasty dinner . . . it feels good! I'm probably sitting out on my new deck until way past dark (enjoying my new book?) and just feeling a deep sense of satisfaction. On the other hand, when our creative ideas are rejected, our labor is repetitive and boring, or we are assigned some little task but never get to see the fruits of our labor . . . then we do not get that same sense of fulfillment. This all shows that we are talking about something embedded in our human nature as created in God's image.

Second, when we step in and help sustain or uphold something or somebody, that can also bring deep satisfaction. For example, say someone's project or group is faltering, and they reach out to us for help. We stop everything, give them our best, and help them find stability so they can move forward. Or an elder is crossing the street in the rain and is obviously struggling. We jump out of our car and run to them, helping them across the busy street. We get back in the car and drive on . . . feeling good about the episode. It can't feel uplifting and good to close our eyes and let someone or something fall when we could have easily enough been sustainers. This is also about our human nature as created in God's image.

Third, when we can actually repair something broken, heal a relationship, or help free someone, we feel a deep satisfaction and pride that come from God and our innermost nature. This is more than just sustaining something and keeping it going. This time it is about actually fixing something broken, overcoming ignorance with knowledge and insight, healing a sickness or injury, restoring a fragmented relationship, or helping someone break free from an addiction or an abuser or tyrant. Human nature in God's image!

These three examples of a deeply human appetite or instinct and its satisfaction are not about getting paid for our good deeds. We feel a deep sense of satisfaction whether we are paid or not. We feel great about these three movements even if no photographer reports our activities on the evening news, even if the person we helped doesn't thank us. Of course, it is nice to be paid and thanked for what we do—but the argument here is that creating, sustaining, and redeeming work brings its own intrinsic rewards. Our explanation of this is that we are created in the image and likeness of a God who is the creator, sustainer, and redeemer of the universe. It is in our DNA, or created human nature, to act these ways, just like it is in our nature to eat and drink, communicate and love. This is certainly a generalization and there are people in our broken world who don't seem to want to be creative, productive, sustaining, or redemptive. We see too many people who are destructive and hurtful. My experience, though, is that such people are usually broken by horrible choices and life experiences, but these people can oftentimes be renewed if we can draw them toward life and work that aligns with God's mission and their God-created humanity.

The implications of this understanding of God's workplace mission are: (1) Let's try to exhibit these characteristics (all six) wherever and whenever we work each day; and (2) to the extent that we can, let's try to empower and encourage our coworkers toward the expression of the same God-aligned work. This will bring them more fulfilment in their own work. It is dehumanizing to do otherwise.

Yes, we need to work to make some money so we can survive and pay our bills—and also so we can be generous and help others. Making money is usually a good thing. But we must not put money up at the top of our philosophy and value system. Jesus said, "No one can serve two masters; for a slave will either hate the one and love the other, or be devoted to one and despise the other. You cannot serve God and wealth" (Matt. 6:24). We don't put technology, or our country, or our ambition, or anything else up at the top. Our life and work are about knowing and loving God and our neighbors, and about working in alignment with God.

If We Can Choose Our Work: Education and Career

Up to this point, our discussion has been about "whatever" work we have to do. No matter what work we have, we always want to be "on a mission from God," working in harmony and alignment with the way God works in the world. We can always find small ways to do this, even when big ways are out of reach. We need to trust God to bless our efforts and make them fruitful.

But what if we can actually choose what kind of work specialty to invest ourselves in over the long haul, through our "career" or "profession"? Can we ask the "alignment" question about our career choices? If we have any freedom of choice in this matter, then let's grab it and use it! Usually, this starts in our education: What subjects do we choose to study? What electives? What do we choose as an undergraduate major? What apprenticeship, what graduate, professional, or vocational study program do we choose, and with what career dreams and objectives? The top priority in these decisions for a faithful workplace disciple is how you can choose a career direction that will be in harmony with God's mission.

There are many, many career options and opportunities to contribute to God's creating, sustaining, and redeeming work in the world. We must say no to educational and career options that are likely (or maybe even certainly) to be in conflict with God's mission. Can we agree that robbing ethically admirable community banks, dumping toxic waste into the local water supply, and youth sex trafficking would be on all of our lists?[3] I leave it to you to add to this list of "careers-to-avoid-because-of-conflict-with-God's-mission."

The Typical Path

How do people usually choose or wind up in their work and job situations? For some, this choice is *decided by family tradition and pressure*. We are just expected to work in the family business, whether that is a farm, bakery, grocery store, manufacturing firm, law office, home-based parenting, or pastoring a church. Gender and birth order often have huge and decisive influence. We might be expected to attend a certain college and follow the career path of our father or mother. Sometimes, parents load up their kids with specific educational and career expectations based on what they personally dreamed but could *not* achieve for financial or other reasons. There are recent immigrants fighting their way up, who work day and night and expect their kids to receive sufficient education and become professionals of one type or another. This can be pretty complicated. We want to honor (and care for) our parents and family. We don't want to squander the blessings of a family business we are in line to inherit. But do we have any choice here?

We wind up in one kind of work and career under many informal influences and pressures of family and society as

---

3. Many of my faith-at-work leader friends reject any idea of a hierarchy of jobs. For example, the concept that a pastor or a nurse is on the top, and a card shark or a used-car dealer is at the bottom. While I basically agree, can't we say that some kinds of work are to be avoided or rejected at all costs? For example, an assassin or a sex trafficker.

we grow up. We find certain jobs more interesting and attractive than others. We are influenced by the positive and negative comments about different jobs that we hear from people around us. At school, we are steered by teachers and counselors toward subjects in which we seem to have ability, promise, and success. Our grades and maybe some "aptitude" and "vocational guidance" tests influence our directions.

We also receive forecasts about the coming job market. What kinds of work will be needed in our society and economy going forward? Where will the jobs be? Which jobs will pay the most? Who will be hiring? Technology-related jobs are all the rage in our era. Every corner of the world and every aspect of human life that can be invaded, assisted, mastered, or colonized by technological processes and devices will be submitted as quickly as possible to artificial intelligence and robotics, like it or not. Who knows how successful or socially acceptable the promised robotization of our working world will be? Of course, we need to choose our careers partly in light of where the jobs are and likely will be.

The Vocation and Calling Path

While the typical career guidance questions are important, we workplace disciples have some additional questions. What work does God want us to do? What work has God gifted us for? What market needs does God want us to address? The traditional term for this way of looking at work is referred to as a "calling." Our work isn't just a job. It isn't just about us. It's fundamentally about God. What is God's will for my work? The Latin term for "calling" is the root of our word *vocation*. "Vocational education" basically meant education to discern, prepare for, and execute God's calling for our work. (Obviously, the term has lost its original breadth and depth.) The core idea is that our work is a response to a call from God. We remember that the basic, core calling is to follow Jesus Christ with our whole life—and for our work to *align with God's work*. But is there a more specific calling to each of us as individuals?

In this career guidance process, workplace disciples pray, listen to God's word, and partner with others who care about God and us. We are not going to make important career decisions on our own. God will guide us individually through his Spirit and his word as we pray, but we will bounce this off of our prayer and support partners to make sure we are hearing God clearly. Never forget that while Christ is the head of the body, our brothers and sisters are the members of that body, including the fingers that may point us in the direction God intends.

So, if the first step in vocational guidance for workplace disciples is to understand and firmly embrace God's work in the world as our own, then the second step is to *figure out our own gifts and abilities*. What special capacities can we bring to God's work in the world? God may want some beautiful music—but if we can't sing or play an instrument on key, forget it. God may want helpful virus protection—but if we are technologically clueless. then that's not for us. What do we have to offer to the work of God? The earlier review of "typical" vocational guidance is a place to begin. Our schooling, our grades, the opinions of our counselors, and the suggestions of vocational aptitude tests can help. A lot of our educational and vocational directions are also a result of finding out through trial and error that we are better at some things than others.

The Bible teaches us that it's not just our genetics and education, but also that the Holy Spirit gives us various gifts (teaching, leadership, administration, helping, etc.). Of course, God is really the giver of *all* of our skills and abilities (mathematics, athletics, aesthetics, entrepreneurship, counseling, etc.). Discerning those gifts and abilities is an important exercise. In addition to the various tests and questionnaires we use to identify our personal gifts, let's ask our honest, true friends what they have seen in us. What do they think are our best gifts and abilities on which we should focus? Do they see any weaknesses or dead ends we should abandon or avoid? Any self-deception we need to acknowledge? Undeveloped potential? Let's share our thoughts, dreams, fears, and options, and ask these trusted confidants to discuss and pray with us.

The passions and concerns of our heart do matter a lot and are often placed there by God. But we need some humility and realism, along with our dreams and ambition. Our close friends and partners can help us by encouraging the gifts they see in us—and by telling us the truth even when it is painful to hear. The bottom line here is that, after embracing God's mission and values, we need to discern what our particular, best contribution to God's mission might be.

The next vocational guidance question is where is there a workplace need or "market" that you can serve with your gifts and skills? Where is there an opportunity for you to deploy your work skills? Using the term "market" means that you could be paid for your work—and that is almost always a necessity! The existing job market, however, may not offer the right opportunity to us right now when we need it. We may need a lot of patience, persistence, and flexibility to find the right job. To pay our bills, we may need to take a job that is nothing like what we really hoped or prepared for. Remember the Colossians text earlier in this chapter: "*Whatever* you do . . . do everything in the name of the Lord Jesus." I've had those jobs in factories and gas stations. But I tried to have a good attitude, work hard and well, and show some care to my fellow workers. I also expressed my gifts and passions as a volunteer teacher and writer until I finally found someone who would pay me (a little!) for it.[4]

---

4. Amy Sherman, *Kingdom Calling: Vocational Stewardship for the Common Good* (Downers Grove, IL: InterVarsity Press, 2011), describes

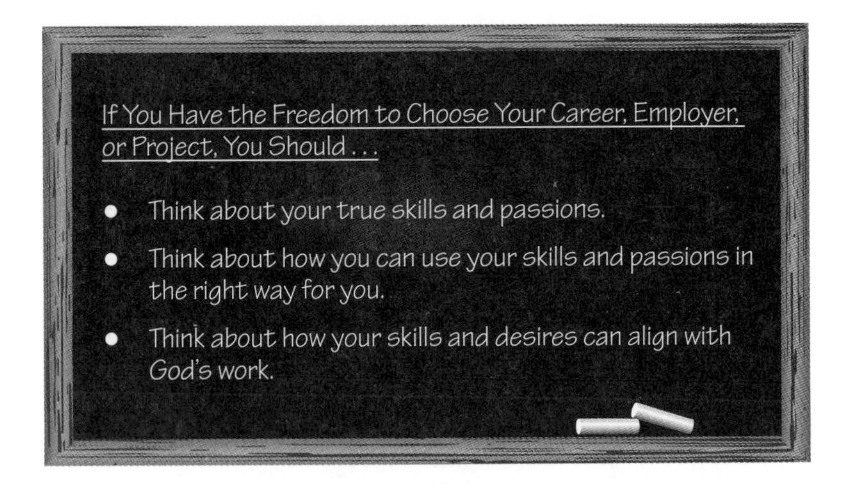

If We Can Choose Our Work: Workplaces and Projects

When we finish our education and start looking for an organization or company to work for (or are in a midcareer job change), the same basic philosophy of work applies: What is the mission and what are the core values of this organization? How do they align with—or contradict—what God is doing in the world? Let's try to find organizations that will enable and maybe even empower us to thrive on God's mission, even if we make less money. Then within our organization, let's try to choose or create work projects that let us be as creative, sustaining, and redemptive as possible. Let's try to influence our organization toward products and services that exhibit creation, sustaining, and redemption.

None of this alignment is particularly easy! It is a lifetime challenge. We need to regularly check our alignment and adjust it. Any work in which we can be creative, sustaining, and

---

four pathways in which to express our calling: (1) in our current job, (2) as a volunteer somewhere, (3) creating a new enterprise, and (4) in a church-based initiative.

redemptive is far better than work that is destructive, dishonest, and poisons people and the planet! But there are no perfect or permanently ideal workplaces. And remember that sometimes God places us within imperfect, even toxic, workplaces with a calling to stay there as God's representatives and agents, doing our very best to have a creative and redemptive impact. Alignment with God's mission is always the primary concern of our workplace presence, wherever that may be.

Whether we are still in school, at the launch of our career, in midcareer reevaluation and transition, or post-employment "retired," our task is to find the best alignment of our work with God's. Usually when we retire, we are in a position to use our skills to pursue God's mission without needing to be paid for it—and that is what we should do; not just sit back and avoid work. The double commandment to work six days and honor the seventh day as a Sabbath never ends throughout our life. We work for God's mission whether we are paid or not.[5]

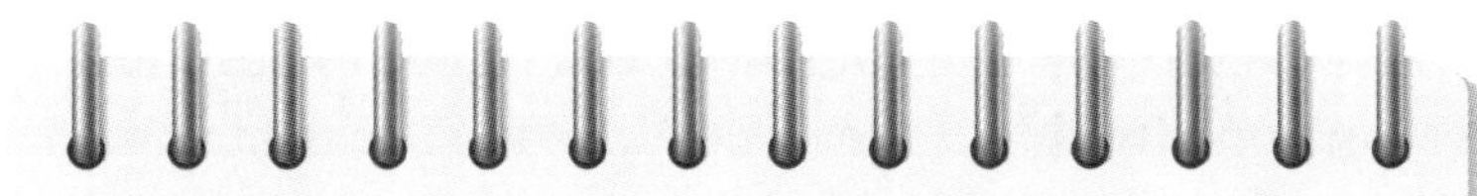

To Do

- ✓ Write up a couple pages of summary of your jobs and work experience up to the present, and your ambition and dreams for the future, and then summarize the lessons you learned about work.
- ✓ Talk to two people—a work colleague and a fellow church member (both of them peers or senior)—and ask them how and why they got into their current jobs and careers and whether they are happy with those directions.

5. For a helpful book on this subject, see Rodney Macready, *Retiring Retirement* (Peabody, MA: Hendrickson, 2016).

For Reflection & Discussion

1. Have you ever taken a vocational aptitude test or had formal vocational counseling? Did it help at all?

2. Have any of your jobs given you opportunities to create, sustain, bring wisdom, promote justice, and redeem in ways that could impact your colleagues and customers (students, patients, clients, etc.)? In other words, could you say that your work "aligned" at least to some extent with God's work?

3. How would you like your work colleagues to describe your contribution if they were asked to speak at your funeral some day?

7

Model

Set a Great Personal Example at Work

Workplace disciples don't just bring a different internal motivation and purpose to work. They don't just bring a different theory or set of ideas. They bring a different *character*, a different behavioral *model* to their workplaces. They try hard to be a *good example*. In the era of sexual harassment, hate speech, insults, cheating, arrogance, rudeness, bullying, and epic lying, what is the example Christians need to bring as a gospel alternative? Ralph Waldo Emerson said, "Your actions speak so loudly, I cannot hear what you are saying." Then there's the cryptic statement attributed to Saint Francis of Assisi: "Preach the gospel at all times. When necessary, use words." I read somewhere that what Francis said was, more precisely, "It is no use walking anywhere to preach unless our walking is our preaching." And according to the commonsense saying, "Actions speak louder than words."

The New Testament is full of exhortations to "walk" and live out our values, not just talk about them. Our life is a message, even before we open our mouth. What kind of message are our Christian examples sending in our workplaces? Jesus called us to be the "salt of the earth" (a metaphor we will come back to below), but we should remember that salt is not particularly visible when it is doing its work of preservation. There is nothing overly noticeable about our topic in this chapter (though your surroundings may be so bad that you do stand out!). It is about our day-to-day steady, reliable presence.

Paul's comment to the Philippian church is well known: "[Conduct yourselves] in a manner worthy of the gospel" (Phil. 1:27). Peter made a similar point to his audience: "Conduct yourselves honorably among the Gentiles, so that, though they malign you as evildoers, they may see your honorable deeds and glorify God" (1 Pet. 2:12). James exhorted his readers: "Be doers of the word, and not merely hearers who deceive themselves" (James 1:22). This is about our character, about the kind of person, or worker, we are. It's about our "walk"—not just our talk. It's about our character and example. In John 13:35, Jesus told his followers, "By this everyone will know that you are my disciples, if you have love for one another." It's about character, our habitual example and model.

Our character is who we are, and our characteristics are the usual, predictable traits that our lives exhibit: our virtues and our vices. We are not talking about our occasional slip-ups or acts of heroism, but about our habitual attitudes and behaviors. An interesting thought experiment is this: How would your bosses, coworkers, customers, and clients describe you, day in and day out? This isn't just about what they might say in public, but what they say among themselves out of your hearing. What people say is not always fair, right, or our ultimate standard, of course. But the question remains: What kind of example or model do we present in our workplace? Let's first review the typical characteristics of a bad workplace model. Then let's consider three biblical models of a good worker.

The Toxic Worker

How would we describe the characteristics of a bad or even toxic worker today? "Toxic" means poisonous—not just bad for us and our career, but also infecting and negatively impacting those around us. We don't need a detailed scientific study to get at the answer. A bad worker is one who does not show up on time (or maybe not at all), or disappears for overly long breaks, or leaves early. A bad worker is unprepared (wrong clothing, ignorance of task, failure to pay attention, etc.). A bad worker works half-heartedly and lazily. The bad worker is unreliable. The bad worker is dishonest, telling lies and half-truths on an application form, a quality report, or a sales pitch. The bad worker cheats the boss—or is a boss who cheats employees, customers, investors, or business partners. The bad worker steals—whether by accepting payment for hours not fully worked or taking materials, tools, or intellectual property from the workplace and coworkers. The bad worker is abusive and divisive, treating others disrespectfully or prejudicially or in a hostile fashion. Bad workers gossip and gripe. Bad workers engage in sexual harassment and racism The bad worker is selfish, caring for himself or herself alone.

We could all probably add to this list from our own experiences. And look at how Paul provides a famous "vice list" that he calls the "works of the flesh" in his letter to the Galatians (5:19–21): "fornication, impurity, licentiousness, idolatry, sorcery, enmities, strife, jealousy, anger, quarrels, dissensions, factions, envy, drunkenness, carousing." We could summarize Paul here as criticizing: (1) inappropriate sexual behavior and talk; (2) making an idol of money or personal or company success; (3) bad attitudes such as anger, jealousy, and envy; (4) creating conflict, strife, and dissension; and (5) showing up under the influence or carousing around. When Paul calls these "works of the flesh," he means they are sinful, negative, and against the will of God.

Immediately after the "works of the flesh," Paul writes, "By contrast, the fruit of the Spirit is love, joy, peace, patience, kindness, generosity, faithfulness, gentleness, and self-control"

(Gal. 5:22–23). God's Spirit will produce love in us as workers—meaning generosity, forgiveness, caring, and kindness. We will be team players, peacemakers, not divisive faction creators. There will be joy and a positive, cheerful attitude, not the grumpiness and bitterness we might otherwise fall into. Patience and gentleness (not impatience and aggressiveness) and faithfulness (not disloyalty and untrustworthiness) will be part of our behavioral witness. This is the spiritual antidote to a toxic "fleshly" workplace. In addition to this "fruit of the Spirit" account of good character, let's look at three other helpful, inspiring models in the Bible.

Kingdom Character: Three Basics

My favorite text in the Bible—what I often call my "philosophy of life"—is Romans 14:17–18: "The kingdom of God is not food and drink but righteousness and peace and joy in the Holy Spirit. The one who thus serves Christ is [well-pleasing] to God and has human approval." I call this text "the three most important things." Think about how this would play out in the workplace.

What if our habit, our day-to-day example, in the workplace was to stand up for *righteousness*—justice and fairness? Not to be self-righteous and judgmental, but nevertheless to advocate for fair wages and treatment of our colleagues at work? Equal pay for equal work, for example, fairness in the way we treat customers, and justice in our respect for laws and regulations. Opposing prejudice and discrimination.

And what if we were *peacemakers* at work—overcoming conflict and misunderstanding, encouraging teamwork and healthy collaboration instead of toxic competitiveness, divisive talk, and community-undermining behavior?

Finally, what if we were known as people who bring *joy* into our workplace—a good sense of humor, a ready smile, and an upbeat attitude? Life and work can be tough, so let's bring some joy.

Paul says that this kingdom example will not just be well-pleasing to God, but that it will also win the positive approval of the people around us. This is so simple. But when you think about it, you can easily see how a workplace disciple with these characteristics can have a wonderful impact. No wonder Paul says that people like this are not just pleasing to God but also "have human approval."

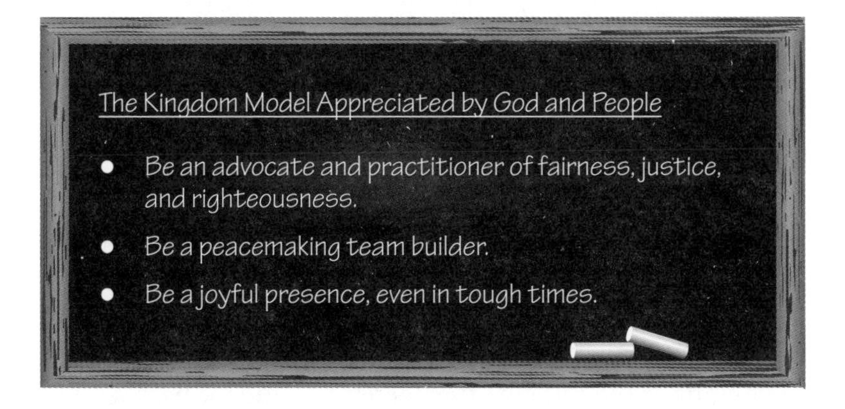

Wise, Commonsense Character: Five Themes

A second example of a solid workplace disciple's character comes from the Old Testament book of Proverbs. This represents a kind of commonsense wisdom that relates directly to our workplaces. In an earlier chapter, I mentioned that my own father committed to reading one chapter of Proverbs every day of his life. I am sure that this habit was part of what kept his workplace example strong at the corporate headquarters where he spent his career as an accountant. Proverbs is an incredible collection of advice and counsel.

Without trying to cover all the bases, we can summarize five important and recurring messages from Proverbs that can shape our workplace example and model. The first and central characteristic is *wisdom*—sometimes described as discernment, insight, prudence, or good judgment. In the previous chapter, we saw this as one of six characteristics of God's work mission. While all of Proverbs is about wisdom, the first nine chapters make it central and explicit. Wisdom is more than just knowledge, more even than understanding. It is knowing how to apply that knowledge, how to move from understanding to responding. Wisdom keeps us from evil and folly and guides us toward justice. "Wisdom is better than jewels, and all that you may desire cannot compare with her" (8:11). Wisdom partly comes from the pursuit of learning and knowledge and partly from the counsel of others: "In an abundance of counselors there is safety" (11:14).

Ultimately, "the fear of the LORD is the beginning of wisdom" (9:10). The foundation and anchor of our wisdom in the workplace and everywhere else is in our respectful, appreciative relationship to the God who created and loves everybody. The wise person sees fully and accurately not just the details of life but also the deeper and longer perspective. This is the key: We do not seek the perspective of some tribal or personal deity but the God of all creation, made known in Jesus and Scripture. The justice and wisdom that come from God are fair to everyone, insightful for every challenge. We don't just want to be smart and know a lot of stuff. We want to be *wise* on the job!

A second theme is *sexual purity*. Proverbs was compiled in a traditional, patriarchal culture, so its examples tend to be of some foolish guy giving in to temptation by a vampish woman whose husband is away on a business trip.[1] She

---

1. It is important, however, to note that while the sexual tempter of Proverbs 7 is a woman, wisdom is personified as a woman in chapter 8—and the whole collection ends with the exemplary businesswoman in chapter 31.

flirts and seduces; he can't resist and goes like an ox to the slaughter. Although it feels so good for the moment, it is a path to disaster. This message is repeated multiple times throughout Proverbs, though chapter seven is perhaps the most fully developed. The tempted young man is warned to think about the price he may have to pay, or resist and go home to enjoy his appropriate sexual relationship with his own wife (5:18–19 is the most explicit counsel on this). We should focus our passion on getting wisdom, not on getting temporary physical pleasure.

Proverbs is not anti-sex or anti-pleasure; it is anti-infidelity, anti-idiocy. This is an important workplace lesson for today. The multiple cases of workplace sexual harassment and abuse now publicized by the "Me Too" movement are a scandal. It is actually a disgrace that our churches do not more strongly and more frequently condemn this behavior from the pulpit to make sure our parishioners don't drift this way. The bottom line here is that workplace disciples must not initiate or respond to inappropriate sexual talk or behavior in the workplace. This is first of all about our own behavior and example—but it is also about speaking and acting to protect others who might be harassed, and calling out the perpetrators (even to the point of official whistle-blowing). Workplace disciples need to be exemplary on this topic.

A third theme in Proverbs is *diligence*, the opposite of laziness. "A slack hand causes poverty, but the hand of the diligent makes rich" (10:4). "Like vinegar to the teeth, and smoke to the eyes, so are the lazy to their employers" (10:26). "The appetite of the lazy craves, and gets nothing, while the appetite of the diligent is richly supplied" (13:4). "One who is slack in work is close kin to a vandal" (18:9). The lazy stay in bed too long, make excuses, and bring shame and poverty to themselves and others around them. How different from this are the diligent and industrious. Remember Paul's statement:

"Whatever your task, put yourselves into it, as done for the Lord" (Col. 3:23). Let's see some competence and responsibility, then, with a hearty effort.

A fourth theme is *honesty* in speech and action. "Put away from you crooked speech, and put devious talk far from you" (Prov. 4:24). We are to speak truth in love (no lying, no gossip). In an extraordinary statement, Proverbs says: "There are six things that the LORD hates, seven that are an abomination to him: haughty eyes, a lying tongue, and hands that shed innocent blood, a heart that devises wicked plans, feet that hurry to run to evil, a lying witness who testifies falsely, and one who sows discord in a family" (6:16). It is worth noting that *two* of the seven items are about lying. Jesus put it very directly: "You are from your father the devil; . . . he is a liar and the father of lies" (John 8:44). Revelation 12:7–9 gives a powerful and unmistakable description of Satan (the Hebrew name) and the devil (the Greek translation) who comes either as a roaring, bellowing dragon or a sneaky, slithering serpent—always to divide, to lie, to bring false accusations. Much of Christian tradition would seem to believe that the heart of darkness must be about sexual sin. Yes, sexual infidelity and decadence are nasty and destructive stuff (see the second characteristic above). But lying and false witness are the number one problem at the heart of the devil's work. It is appalling that Christians would ever approve of lying or deception by leaders or participate in it themselves in the workplace or anywhere else. Our example must be set by Jesus, who speaks—and is—truth.

Proverbs also condemns false weights and balances: "A false balance is an abomination to the LORD, but an accurate weight is his delight" (11:1). "Differing weights are an abomination to the LORD and false scales are not good" (20:23). What? An "abomination" that has the same condemnation as for, say, bestiality? Yes. This is not merely twice spoken;

it is a constant theme in Proverbs and throughout the Bible. Dishonest marketing and sales practices, failure to account accurately for time and actual services rendered—this is horrible. It not only offends God, but it also trashes the kind of trust that must be at the foundation of business and trade. Workplace disciples don't go there; we need to model integrity and honesty in all things, every day.

A fifth and final theme is *generosity*. We would call fairness (justice) the "moral minimum." Here is the continuum: ripping people off (one extreme) is terrible; fairness lifts us to the minimum; generosity (the other extreme) is the high goal. Over and over, Proverbs urge us to be generous to the poor. "The field of the poor may yield much food, but it is swept away through injustice" (13:23). The poor are rarely poor because of a lack of effort. Sometimes that may be true, and Proverbs warns against laziness. But most of the time, poverty is caused by a combination of factors such as bad weather, wars or violence, and injustice served up by the powerful (in government and in business). God has a persistent, deep concern for the poor—those with little voice, influence, opportunity, or means. "Those who oppress the poor insult their Maker, but those who are kind to the needy honor him" (14:31). "Whoever is kind to the poor lends to the LORD, and will be repaid in full" (19:17). "Those who are generous are blessed, for they share their bread with the poor" (22:9). Some businesses and some employees live out this kind of generosity toward others: fellow workers, employees, customers, and even neighbors and strangers. The dominant attitude in our culture, however, is one of entitlement ("I earned this, I own it, and I have every right to keep it to myself") and a judgmental attitude toward those who have less.

In summary, the workplace disciple who is shaped by the wisdom writings in the Bible will try to model from day to day a character that is wise, sexually appropriate, diligent, honest, and generous. As we will discuss in coming chapters, this not only has an immediate impact on the workplace, but it also earns us the right to be heard about our faith and opinions on other matters.

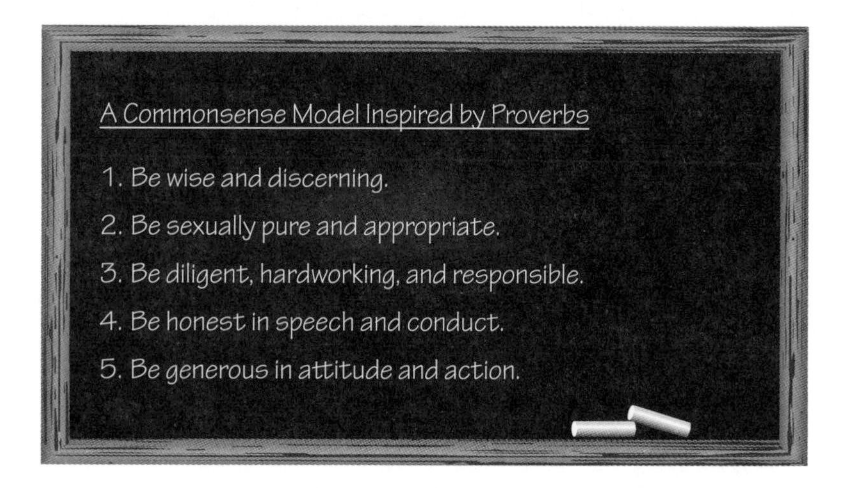

Salty, Luminous Character: Eight Beatitudes

The best account of character is provided by the Beatitudes, coming at the beginning of Jesus' Sermon on the Mount. It is these characteristics, Jesus said, that render us the "salt of the earth" (a metaphor for retarding its decay) and the "light of the world" (a metaphor for enabling it to see reality, enabling it to grow). Isn't that a big part of what we want to accomplish in our workplaces? Slowing down if not eliminating decay and disaster (by salting them)? Enabling and encouraging good vision, purpose, and growth (by lighting them)? Bringing glory and honor to God? For that matter, aren't we also looking for lives in which we, and those around us, are blessed (Greek, *makarios*)—objectively doing well, not just feeling happy?

> Blessed are the poor in spirit, for theirs is the kingdom of heaven.
>
> Blessed are those who mourn, for they will be comforted.
>
> Blessed are the meek, for they will inherit the earth.
>
> Blessed are those who hunger and thirst for righteousness' sake, for they will be filled.
>
> Blessed are the merciful, for they will receive mercy.
>
> Blessed are the pure in heart, for they will see God.
>
> Blessed are the peacemakers, for they will be called children of God.
>
> Blessed are those who are persecuted for righteousness, for theirs is the kingdom of heaven. . . .
>
> You are the salt of the earth. . . . You are the light of the world. . . . Let your light shine before others, so that they may see your good works and give glory to your Father in heaven.
>
> (Matt. 5:3–16)

Just imagine if these were the core values we demonstrated in our personal character and tried to build into our organizational culture.[2] Here is a rough "workplace translation":

---

2. For a fuller study of the Beatitudes and biblical teaching on character, see David W. Gill, *Becoming Good: Building Moral Character* (Downers Grove, IL: InterVarsity Press, 2000). For a fuller study of how the Beatitudes might be translated from "Bible-speak" to "business speak," see David W. Gill, "Eight Traits of an Ethically Healthy Culture: Insights from the Beatitudes," *Journal of Markets & Morality* 16, no. 2 (Fall 2013): 615–33. Also, see my general market business ethics book *It's About Excellence: Building Ethically Healthy Organizations* (repr., Eugene, OR: Wipf & Stock, 2011), esp. 119–39 and 183–94.

To be "poor in spirit" means not to be full of ourselves but rather to be humble, open, and teachable in recognition that we don't know everything or act perfectly.

To "mourn" means to actually lament our weaknesses and mistakes rather than blaming others for them, embracing them with responsibility.

To be "meek" means to be gentle, to give up the need to control everything. We stay strong but we are "leadable."

To "hunger and thirst for righteousness" means to be on a passionate quest to do the right thing as well as to do things right. It's about excellence as well as ethics.

To be "merciful" means to temper and apply the high standards and principles of ethics and justice with some forgiveness. Nobody's perfect.

To be "pure in heart" means to have integrity, a consistency in our attitude, our speech, and action. Our justice and mercy must not be a surface fake.

To be a "peacemaker" is the crown of good character. In a workplace context, it means good team-building and collaboration as we pursue our mission.

To be "persecuted for righteousness" is really about courage and persistence in the face of resistance and misunderstanding. We don't quit when our best intentions and efforts are attacked, misunderstood, or thwarted. We keep going.

Think about what all this implies: we want to be the kind of workers and managers whose habitual orientation is to bring together teams (high-performance teams!), whose work improves the bad stuff in our world (salt) and builds the good stuff (light). To build those teams, we need to start out by being humble, responsible, and noncontrolling. Out of that stance, we hope to see clearly and then pursue what is right. Our high ideals will be accompanied by realism, patience, forgiveness, and integrity. At that point, we will have optimized our chances for great teams to emerge!

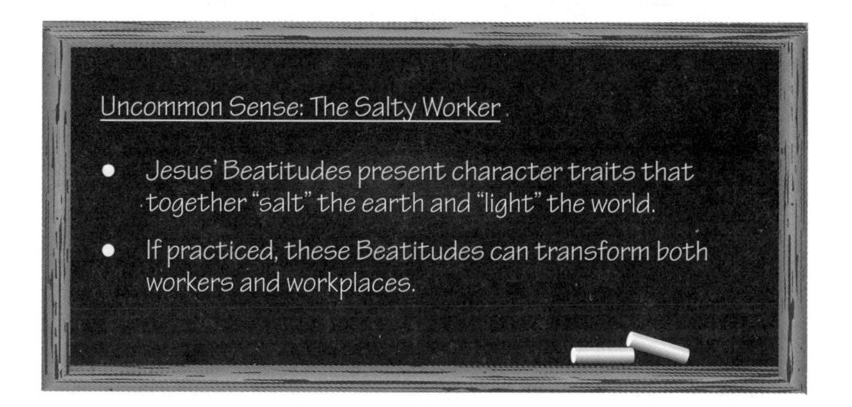

Our Day-In/Day-Out Model

When in trouble, today's workplaces typically focus on specific problem situations ("dilemmas") that arise and then ask the question, "What do we do now?" The first weakness of this approach is that it is *negative* and *narrow*. It lets problems and dilemmas—rather than positive opportunities—get our attention and drive our agenda. It is reactive rather than proactive. Second, this approach focuses on finding an immediate response without reflecting on either (1) the system, structure, and culture within which the problem has arisen, or (2) the character and capabilities of the human agents involved. Think about a sports analogy: We can't have a great basketball team if our players are not in good condition and well trained. Character and our example or model are like fitness and training in this analogy. A worker with a character habit of being honest, for example, is less likely to wind up as part of an employee theft problem.

A steady, day-in/day-out example of a solid set of habits and characteristics, like the three models we reviewed here, exercises a salting and lighting impact on a workplace and its people. Without this kind of personal example in the workplace, chances are that a bad situation is unlikely to improve—and that people are much less likely to listen to our opinions about our operations or products, to say nothing of our faith and values.

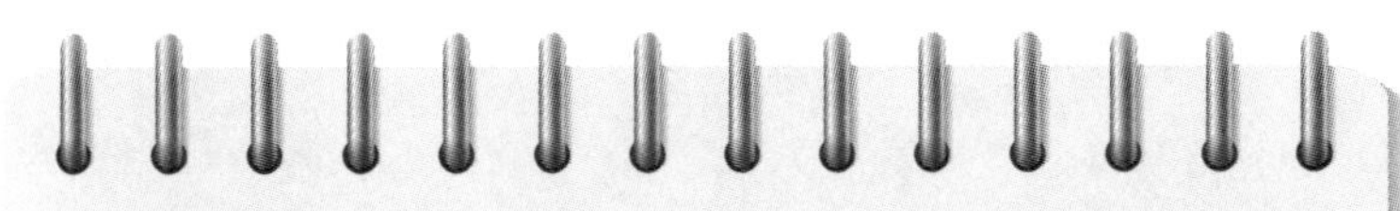

To Do

- ✓ Read through the book of Proverbs and underline and circle all the workplace-appropriate lessons and advice you see; then do the same thing with the Sermon on the Mount (Matt. 5–7).
- ✓ Discuss with a workplace colleague (Christian or otherwise) the most important behaviors you see in your workplace that could be improved. Then discuss what you can do about them.

For Reflection & Discussion

1. In your experience and opinion, what are some of the worst attitudes and behaviors you have seen in the places where you have worked? Were some of those commonsense Proverbs issues part of it (e.g., dishonesty, lack of effort, sexual harassment or inappropriateness, stupidity)?

2. Can you describe some colleagues or managers you have worked with whose character, attitude, and example were really outstanding? What made them so admirable? What was their impact on you and the organization?

3. As you think about it, are there any additional workplace character traits you think should be highlighted—either as traits to be avoided or traits to be celebrated and promoted?

8

Light

Share Some Helpful Biblical Insights about Work at Work

Now we get to one of the most exciting and important—and overlooked—aspects of faithful workplace discipleship: lighting up our workplace with some great ideas and insights that come out of our biblical faith. Putting these ideas on the table at work can sometimes be like flipping a switch and lighting up a darkening room. As the previous chapter emphasized, some basic work habits and a good example already send a message. But there are also some amazing insights we can articulate about work, management, money, communication, team-building, and ethics. There are many specific biblical insights about the work of caring for and educating children, about law and justice, about healing and health care, about science and technology, about wine-making and almost all other professions and fields.

Think about this: Who knows more about business than any businessperson in the world? God! How about law and justice? God! Parenting and education? God! Farming? Music? Putting it this way, we can easily see why we need a chapter on bringing some divinely inspired ideas and wisdom to our place of work now and then. We can't just sit quietly at the table and deprive our workplaces of these ideas and insights. As I mentioned earlier, my own workplace discipleship quest began when I became consumed with a passion to understand how my biblical Christian faith could or should provide insights and perhaps alternative practices in the fields of history and teaching in which I was working.

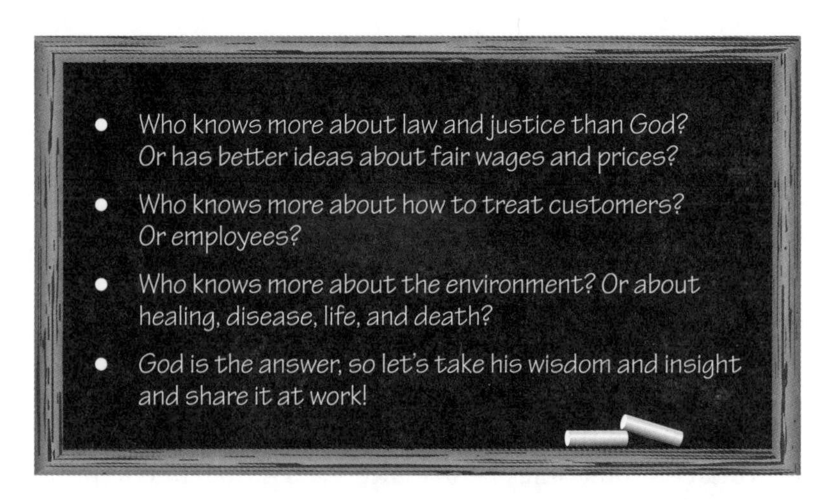

In the following chapter, we will talk about evangelism in the workplace: sharing our faith with others. I really believe in this, but the simplified evangelistic message about how to be born again is not the only thing we have to say. We know that because the Bible doesn't confine itself to messages about how to repent and convert. Also, just as our sharing of our faith is best founded on a steady presence of good, constructive character (which we saw in the last chapter), it is also vastly strengthened if it is associated with other good ideas we share in the workplace (which we will see in this chapter). If we establish a reputation for good ideas about our workplace issues, then our colleagues will be prepared to think we might have some good insights about God and faith. It all works together, but the evangelistic piece works best if it *follows* rather than precedes (cold turkey) a good example and some good ideas for the work itself. My long experience is that my audiences of MBA students or workplace folk will often follow up my presentations by asking me, "Where and how did you come up with these ideas?" Then I tell them and include the faith piece. They ask me first. Then I talk about it, and they are ready and eager to listen.

Have Something to Say

Imagine that we are sitting around a table with our fellow workers. Somebody is chairing a discussion of our organization—maybe looking back and evaluating our performance, or looking ahead and considering our plan going forward. Maybe we are discussing our team, our training, our marketing, our communication, or our budget. Maybe our discussion is focused on some threat or opportunity or challenge. Maybe it is about a specific initiative or problem that has come up. Maybe we are stuck—or maybe we seem to be thriving but we are concerned that rapid growth could have some dangers. Imagine this as either a top management gathering or a smaller team meeting. Question: Do we workplace disciples have anything to put on the table—any observations, ideas, suggestions, or responses that could help the discussion and decision-making?

In particular, do we have anything to share that comes out of our biblical faith? We do not want to share any half-baked, inappropriate comments just to be talking. We are looking for insightful thoughts and ideas that bring flashes of light and wisdom. Our colleagues (some of them anyway!) have a lot of good insights and ideas from their experience and study, but we have access to God's truths and insights in Scripture. This could be helpful! This could be a unique contribution. This is where the earlier chapters on listening (to Scripture) and learning (from others who have some expertise and experience) are important and foundational. Have something to say! Don't be silent when the team is sitting around the table. Don't avoid walking into the boss's office with a great idea. Put something brilliant and helpful on the table. Be articulate and clear in saying it. Before trying it out with the boss or at a team meeting, however, share it first with your posse, small group, or work buddies.

Say It with Humility as Well as Enthusiasm

How can we most effectively share these biblical ideas and insights? After many years of working with business students, in consulting relationships with businesses, and even in talks to Rotary Clubs, chambers of commerce, and professional organizations, I am convinced that we do not need to present these workplace ideas with religious announcements and qualifiers, such as "the Bible says" or "God says." In fact, if we use "Bible-speak" or "religion-speak," ears and minds may slam shut immediately. My approach is to begin with something like this: "I have a theory about this . . ." or "Let me try this out on you" . . . (or "put this on the table"). "I think this could help us," I say. Then I add, "Tell me what you think." "Does it make sense?" "Am I missing anything?"

Notice that the language I recommend is humble and tentative: "Could I try this out on you?" "Tell me what you think." This is part of successful communication. Have something brilliant to say (since the Bible is the most brilliant book ever written, we have a source smarter than us). Be humble about it, but at the same time don't conceal your own passion, enthusiasm, and excitement about what it might do for the company or team. If we are not enthusiastic about our ideas, we can be sure no one else will be. Truth with passion is infectious! Explain how this could solve a vexing problem or really help us move forward on our mission and goals. Always invite comments, suggestions, and improvements. Offer to lead a feasibility or study project or committee to explore the idea or proposal.

Point to Supportive Expertise and Practical Applications

Another move of strategic importance is to find support for our biblical insights in management or professional literature—and in the actual practices of other workplaces. The wisdom and insight that come from Scripture are often unknown or overlooked by the mainstream. But truth often wins its own hearing. The insights we share have power and will often make room for themselves. Nevertheless, it is often helpful if we can augment or support our suggestions with quotations from experts who agree with the particular point we are making—or with examples from the trenches of a competitor or other relevant organization. When I promote the first Beatitude (poor in spirit, humility, openness, teachability) in management education or consulting, I don't refer to Jesus as the author (I will get to that when appropriate), but I do mention that this is the first characteristic that Jim Collins identified in all "Level Five" leaders of his *Good to Great* companies.[1] I also give examples of successful organizations that practice this kind of humility, openness, and teachability and demonstrate it in everything from their architecture and office design to open door management policies, frequent "all comers" discussions, and multiple channels for submitting ideas and suggestions.

The reality is that Christians don't have all the wisdom and good ideas. The truths we learn from the Bible actu-

---

1. Jim Collins, *Good to Great: Why Some Companies Make the Leap . . . and Others Don't* (New York: HarperBusiness, 2001), 17–40.

ally do fit with both our common sense and our common experience and aspiration, at least most of the time. What the Bible does is bring these truths into stark clarity, and it brings the uncomfortable truths as well—there is no peace without justice, no peace without forgiveness and mercy, and so on. We workplace disciples are never any better or smarter in and of ourselves. It is only the grace of God that has opened our hearts, our eyes, and our minds so that we can be channels of some otherwise forgotten or undiscovered workplace truths. Thoughtful people learn from creation, from human nature, from study and experience. Invoking their support for our biblically inspired ideas is a good thing to do.

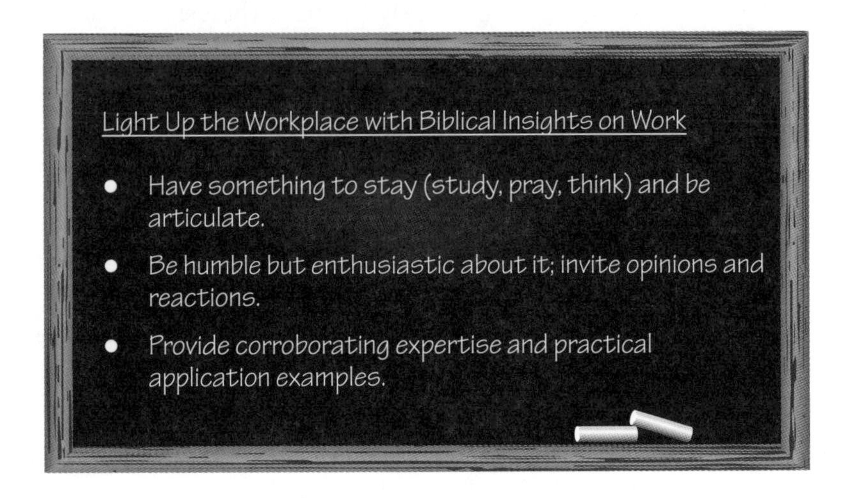

Biblical Insights Almost All Workers Can Share

What topics are we talking about? My bookshelves are groaning from the weight of so many Christian books on leadership. I have a growing collection of Christian reflections on money, economics, wealth, and poverty. I have books on Christian views of technology, science, medicine, nursing, law, and the arts. There are, of course, lots of Christian books about raising and educating children as a parent or other caregiver. I can't emphasize enough how important it is both to search the Scriptures for work insights *and* to search other resources (books, articles, interviews, conferences, etc.) that will stimulate and help shape our thinking about our field and help us discover insights to share at work. Following are just a few examples of biblical insights all workers could share.

1. Openness, Teachability, and Humility Are Keys to Healthy Workplaces

This seems so obvious. Some individual leaders in politics and business (and other fields) tend to think, "I am so smart that I don't need to listen or learn from you." But *smarter* leaders say, "I am so smart, and we are the best—but teach me what you know, and we'll be even better." It's about workers who learn and an organization that learns. It is common sense and is advocated by many management writers. Proverbs hammers away at fools who think they know everything. The first Beatitude says, "Blessed are the poor in spirit, for theirs is the kingdom of heaven." If you are not humble, teachable, and aware of your poverty, then you have no room for God to be your king, and you deeply undermine your capacity to see and achieve any kind of justice and righteousness (the fourth Beatitude) or build successful, peaceful teams (the seventh Beatitude). I urge individuals and organizations to be open and receptive, not just to the voices of everyone in the company but to competitors, customers, everyone. Remember that this point was emphasized in *Good to Great* by Jim Collins. Believe me, I reference that book when I make this point to classes and companies.

2. Mission and Purpose Are the Best Drivers of Good Work

I have heard that ancient rabbinic commentators on the Ten Commandments sometimes said that there are not ten commandments—but just one command and nine corollaries. In other words, if we worship Yahweh as God and allow no rivals (the first commandment), then all the other guidelines follow (rest, honor parents, don't murder, etc.). I really believe this. What we worship will drive the rest of our life and work. If you worship money, worship yourself, worship your race or nation, then watch out. In the ultimate sense, this is about God. In a more modest sense, it is about mission and purpose—both for individual workers and for organizations. A clear, positive, inspiring, shared mission and purpose will bring out the best in people. This is what will get people out of bed in the morning to bring their best selves to work. The previous chapter on "alignment" describes three basic themes in a good work mission (create, sustain, redeem). In almost any organization, workplace disciples can urge that the organization clarify its mission and purpose and ensure that it is well known, understood, and practiced.[2]

3. Work Is Best in Teams

We live in an age of runaway individualism and even isolation. Notice the people around us, almost anywhere, looking only at their little screens and listening only to their earbuds. The insight we can share is that more collaboration and teams

---

2. My book *It's About Excellence* is all about mission-driven organizations. Other helpful studies are Christine Arena, *The High Purpose Company: The Truly Responsible (and Highly Profitable) Firms That Are Changing Business Now* (New York: HarperBusiness, 2006); Richard R. Ellsworth, *Leading with Purpose: The New Corporate Realities* (Stanford: Stanford University Press, 2002); and Nikos Mourkogiannis, *Purpose: The Starting Point of Great Companies* (London: Palgrave Macmillan, 2006).

can strengthen our workplace. Remember the biblical (and management) case for partnership made above in chapter 4. Teams bring more experience, talent, and perspective to our work tasks. Since technical problems often resist individual solutions, we need to work as a team. Temptation and corruption are less likely when we are not working alone. Mistakes can be caught by another set of eyes looking at our work. Of course, there are plenty of occasions when work is best done by individuals; but as a general rule, "it is not good that the man should be alone—we need a helper" ("helper" in that full biblical sense of partner). Wherever we work, we can try to find ways to suggest more teamwork and less individualism.

4. Diversity Strengthens Workplaces

If anything is clear about God's Creation it is that there are animals and plants "of all kinds." If anything is true about the final shape of God's redemption, it is that "many will come from east and west and will eat with Abraham and Isaac and Jacob in the kingdom of heaven" (Matt. 8:11). The tower of Babel drove people apart; Pentecost brought people together from all over the earth. In the church, Paul taught that we all have different gifts, no one has them all, and we need each other (Rom. 12:3–8). I heard of a study once in which a team of brilliant male mathematicians from the same elite university could not solve some difficult equations as rapidly as a diverse team of men and women with varied backgrounds. This proves that we need to promote diversity in our workplaces.

5. All Stakeholders Matter

Modern capitalism sometimes has a bad habit of thinking that owners and shareholders are ultimately the (only) people we serve at work. Not even the godfather of capitalism,

Adam Smith, believed that.[3] Everyone who has a "stake" in our work has value and should be treated with respect. Whoever is impacted by our work (including the communities in which our work takes place) should have an appropriate say insofar as our operations affect their lives. It all goes back to our conviction that every man, woman, and child in the world has been created by and in the image of God and has intrinsic (not just instrumental) value. We Christians should be the first to speak up for anyone (our colleagues, customers, business partners, family members, community residents) whose interests are ignored as we carry out our work.

6. Good Leadership Is Serving, Not Dominating, Others

Here is another famous point made by Jesus: The true leader serves others. A true leader does not exploit, bully, or ruthlessly domineer those being led. Remember Jesus' emphatic teaching about how his leadership was about serving others, not "lording it over them" or abusing and exploiting them. Remember Jesus humbly washing the feet of his followers. Likewise, let's practice and encourage servant leadership. Let's expect that we might have some insights to offer about how to influence and mobilize our people and organization in the right direction. My sister, Kit Faria, told me about a big bank where she served as executive assistant to the CEO that was having a hard time integrating a smaller bank they had recently acquired. Leadership attitudes were terrible, and the cultural conflict was intense. She suggested to her boss that the executive team leave headquarters for a few weeks and spread out to work in the branches of the newly acquired bank. Although some grumbled at the begin-

---

3. Kenneth J. Barnes, *Redeeming Capitalism* (Grand Rapids: Eerdmans, 2018), clearly demonstrates this in his book.

ning, those who went "down" to serve and learn came back personally transformed and they achieved a remarkable cultural integration and uplift for the whole, enlarged company. This was a biblical idea about leading through servanthood in action.

7. Always Ask How We Would Like to Experience Something

Finally, in his Sermon on the Mount, Jesus describes the "Golden Rule" as the summary of the law and the prophets (Matt. 7:12). That alone should give it a prominent place in our thinking about life. It also turns out that Confucius and Immanuel Kant, among many others, advocated versions of this principle: "Do to others as you would want them to do to you." How do we treat our children or students or customers or neighbors? We how would we personally (and our loved ones) want to be treated in the same circumstances? Workplace disciples can always urge that we consider how we would like to be treated, as we consider various aspects of our work. What kind of data privacy would we want? What kind of safety or respect would we want or insist on for our families? How would we want to be communicated with? Most people can intuitively understand and value this kind of challenge. It is a core concept in our faith. Find ways to bring it up.

Organizational Ethics as a Specific Field

In every field or type of work, we can expect that Jesus and Scripture will provide us with some helpful insights for that particular work. Since my own field is organizational ethics, I want to give some specific examples of what this "sharing biblical insights" challenge has meant for me. Although I think these examples should stimulate your own thinking about your field of work, I also think that these ethics examples are relevant because *ethics cuts across all parts, all personnel, all processes in an organization.* My proposed "insights" can be adopted and advocated by anyone in just about any organization, not just by other business ethics teachers and consultants.

I have often given speeches with titles such as "Eight Biblical Insights You Can Take Straight to the Workplace." There are actually *hundreds* of such biblical insights. The seven examples reviewed in the previous section of this chapter all have direct and powerful application in organizational ethics, so I will not repeat them. But here are four that have loomed large in my work as an MBA ethics professor and as an organizational ethics consultant and presenter.

1. Good Character and Culture Are More Significant Than Good Rules and Decision-Making Formulas

Often, we think ethics is fundamentally about rules, codes, and the logic or method for coming to a decision. But real life and work are more like sports or music than law. In sports, while we can design great plays, on-field performance requires the players to be capable and motivated to actually perform them well. I might be able to understand a football or basketball play, but I can't perform them very well because I lack the conditioning and (especially in my seventies!) the capacity to perform what I know I should. The analogy in the workplace is that we must pay attention to the character (not just the business skills) of our individuals and the organizational culture (systems, policies, values, practices). Ethics is not just (or primarily) about the ethical rules and the decision-making method.

Management literature often pays attention to the character and culture aspect (though less so in its thinking about ethics).[4] Think about how Jesus told Nicodemus, "You must be born again" (John 3:7 NIV)—not "You need to know the rules better." We need a "new Nicodemus," not just some new rules. The Sermon on the Mount, the most systematic and comprehensive statement of kingdom of God ethics, begins with the Beatitudes (Matt. 5:3–16), an account of character and community, and only then moves on to reflect on the meaning of rules and guidelines from the Ten Commandments and elsewhere (Matt. 5:17–48).

This means that we need to promote the insight that our organization should *hire* for character, not just for business skills, and *evaluate* job performance in reference to company core values, not just quantifiable production. It also requires raising critical questions about whether company policies and structures recognize, enable, and reward the implantation and practice of these values (they often do not, getting lost exclusively in valuing quantifiable production goals).

---

4. Some helpful studies of the importance of culture are James C. Collins and Jerry Porras, *Built to Last: Successful Habits of Visionary Companies* (New York: HarperBusiness, 1994), esp. "Cult-like Cultures," 115–39; Terrance E. Deal and Allan A. Kennedy, *Corporate Cultures: The Rites and Rituals of Corporate Life* (Cambridge, MA: Basic Books, 1982); Edgar H. Schein's classic *Organizational Culture and Leadership* (Hoboken, NJ: Wiley & Sons, 2004); and Patrick Lencioni's *The Advantage: Why Organizational Health Trumps Everything Else in Business* (San Francisco: Jossey-Bass, 2012).

2. Ethics and Excellence Are Inextricably Linked

The biblical concept of *righteousness* includes both doing the right thing and doing things right. The insight here is that you can't truly be excellent unless you are ethical. And you can't be adequately ethical if you do shoddy work. It's not right to do less than the best you can at your work. You also can't make brilliant products, and then treat your customers and workmates with disrespect or other terrible behavior. For example, it is not okay to be a high performer on your work tasks or in your management while engaging in sexual harassment. And it is not okay to be sexually pure and appropriate, and then be self-righteous while doing a bad job at work. I believe this connection between ethics and excellence is a powerful insight that good organizations embrace. I lobby for it as an ethics trainer and a consultant.

3. Practitioners Should Play Large in Any Ethics Design and Implementation

I have always resisted invitations to come into a company and write a code of ethics for them. It happens too often that employees are merely presented with a statement of values and ethics brought in from the outside. It's almost as bad if the values and ethics are decided at the top without input from the people. It is infinitely better to invite and enable all the members of an organization to help design an ethics statement. There are practical reasons. First of all, involving the people utilizes their *expertise*. No one knows the ethical challenges (and appropriate guidance) for sales operations like the salespeople. No one understands the hazards and opportunities of quality control like the people working in that area. We need to challenge them to write guidelines that will safeguard the company's activities in those areas of their experience and expertise. Second, people feel a sense of *ownership* when they create it. It is not an alien intrusion, but something they created and are more likely to protect and value.

In addition to the commonsense arguments, there is a theological reason: This is a biblical insight! Paul said that even people without God's law nevertheless have a conscience and a law "written on their hearts" (Rom. 2:15). I have sometimes called the implications of this a "wiki-ethics" strategy. It is grounded in a high view of people's common sense, conscience, and responsibility. It leads with trust instead of suspicion, and people often rise to the expectations. There is still plenty of opportunity to catch and correct any isolated cases of corruption or incompetence in this approach, just like Wikipedia is self-correcting. Believe me, though, the impact of this insight on organizational culture and performance is significant.

4. Good Ethics Usually Benefits Its Practitioners

The final insight, or good idea, I will share is that the results of practicing good ethics will usually be positive for practitioners and organizations. Sometimes we hear the convenient, self-justifying myth that the winners are all cheating. Therefore, the logic goes, we have no choice but to play as dirty as necessary. For sure, some "winners" have cheated. Think about all the big banks. For a while after 2008, I thought Wells Fargo was the exception, an ethical big bank. They turned out to be one of the worst. We hope, anyway, that the victories of cheaters don't last too long and that they are exposed and punished appropriately by markets and government overseers.

But I want to argue the other side: Good ethics usually pays off. Too often, people think we have to sacrifice and suffer by choosing to pay all of our taxes and stand behind all of our promises. Think about this though: If we cheat our customers, then they will take their business elsewhere. If we cheat and exploit our workers, then they will not put out maximum effort for us, and they will be on the lookout for a more worthy employer. Good business needs repeat customers and productive employees. If we trash the environment or the surrounding community, they both (sooner or later) will strike back. This logic is especially true over the longer haul. "Short-term-ism" is the enemy of good ethics, because one can get in and get out before suffering the consequences of misdeeds (this is why we need some government oversight and can't "trust the market" alone).

My point is to get over the myth that high ethics leads to less successful business. Christians have sometimes reasoned that the most ethical human being ever ended up unjustly nailed to a cross. For sure, there is some unavoidable cross-bearing in life, perhaps especially by the faithful and ethical. But the cross wasn't the end for Jesus; there was resurrection, and there will be victory in the final end. That same person, Jesus, taught that if we practice the virtues of the Beatitudes, then we and our community will be "blessed" (Greek *makarios*, objectively good). The world around us will benefit from our "salt" and "light." The proverbs are full of promises that virtuous and ethical conduct usually benefits its practitioners. The Ten Commandments, rigorous as they may sound, are accompanied by the repeated promise: "Do what is right and good in the sight of the LORD, so that it may go well" with us and "for our lasting good, so as to keep us alive" (Deut. 6:18, 24).

The insight is to emphasize the *benefits* of high ethics in our organization and not just beat the warning drums about what might happen if we get out of line. This approach lifts up our people and our culture. It is positive and inspiring. It is commonsense, but it comes right out of biblical faith in its most profound foundation.

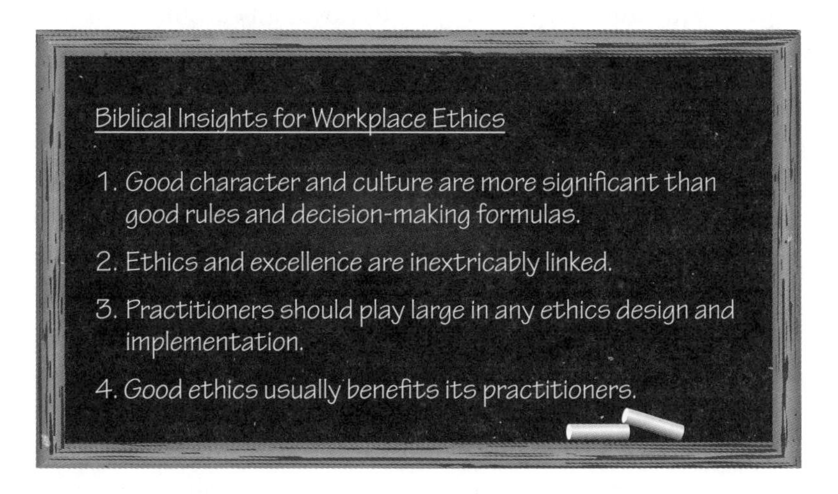

Insights for Other Work Arenas

I am convinced that in every work specialty we can find biblical insights that could brilliantly light up our workplace. Here are two examples. Dr. Raymond Downing (1949–2020) practiced and taught medicine in Kenya. Ray was well trained and experienced in Western, technological medicine, but he also paid careful and appreciative attention to the indigenous disease and healing traditions and cultures of Native Americans and Africans—with whom he spent most of his career—and to the biblical accounts of healing, disease, and death. These insights deeply illuminated and salted his thought and practice. Among the best of his books are *Death and Life in America: Biblical Healing and Biomedicine* and *Global Health Means Listening*.[5]

5. Raymond Downing, *Death and Life in America: Biblical Healing and Biomedicine* (Harrisonburg, VA: Herald Press, 2008); and *Global Health Means Listening* (Nairobi: Manqa Books, 2018).

I also recently picked up Gisela Kreglinger's book *The Spirituality of Wine*, mostly for fun. I was soon, however, totally enthralled by her deep and thorough command of biblical teaching, cover-to-cover, about vines, grapes, and wine, and their God-intended place not just in our worship and remembrance but in our feasting and in our relationships to farm, field, creation, and the creator.[6] A daughter of German winemakers and a trained biblical scholar and theologian, she illuminates powerful insights from Scripture about winemaking, vines and branches, and the winepress and suffering. These insights are not just for a pious spirituality, but are a critical and constructive qualifier to modern industrial, mass-market wine-making.

Every arena of work, every workplace, can be lit up by our bringing in biblically grounded and inspired work insights and ideas. We acquire these insights by our prayerful study of Scripture, our regular efforts at reading the work of others who share insight from God for our work, and lots of conversation and debate with our posse and other thoughtful workplace Christians.

---

6. Gisela Kreglinger, *The Spirituality of Wine* (Grand Rapids: Eerdmans, 2016).

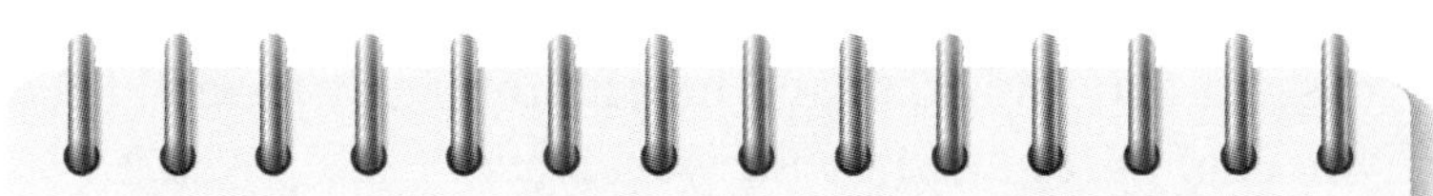

To Do

- ✓ Start making a list of insights from your Bible study that might be communicable in your workplace.
- ✓ Make a second list of good workplace ideas and insights that you glean from your "continuing education" reading of Christian veterans or experts in your field of work.
- ✓ Bring out your two lists and then discuss and pray over them with your posse or small group.
- ✓ Be bold and try out your ideas at work with your boss or workmates.

For Reflection & Discussion

1. Do you have any examples of general workplace insights (applicable to all work environments) that you received from Scripture and then shared at work? How did it turn out?

2. At a very simple level, what might be a couple of basic, easy-to-communicate and helpful biblically based ideas you could promote in your workplace?

3. At a more applied, field-specific level, what kind of insights do you think the Bible might bring to today's practices of law, criminology, and justice? How about schooling, teaching, and education? Medicine and health care? Design, engineering, and technology? Music and the arts? Child care? Other fields you are familiar with?

9

Share

Find Appropriate Ways to Talk about Jesus at Work

What about sharing our faith in the workplace—whether with our colleagues, customers, or business partners? We call this "evangelism," from the New Testament Greek word for "good news" ("gospel" in older English). Bear with me if you know all this by heart: the essence of this good news is that people who are lost, imperfect, and sinful (which means everyone) are invited back into full participation in the family and presence of God. To get there, we need to repent and confess our sin and neediness before God—and then open up our hearts and minds to receive God's gift of salvation, eternal life, and full membership as children of God our Father. All this is possible because God sent his Son into the world, Jesus Christ, who lived and died and rose again as our mediator and now lives as our Lord. While the message is surrounded and undergirded by ideas and facts, in its essence, the gospel is about a person, Jesus Christ, and our evangelism is about introducing this person to others who do not yet know him. It is about making the introduction and hoping and praying that it leads to a relationship in which Jesus becomes not just an acquaintance of that person but also their Savior, Lord, and God.

This is a pretty wild and astonishing story, especially for people who didn't grow up hearing it all the time. But, honestly, it makes so much sense of the mystery of our human history—and our own lives—with all its ups and downs. Yes, it takes a step of faith to accept this story: we have to trust without being able to verify all the claims in a lab. We have no video recording of the life of Christ. Even if we did, many would refuse to believe what they see. This kind of skepticism happens all the time today. The polar ice caps are melting, but some refuse, against all scientific testimony and visual evidence, to believe the globe is getting dangerously warmer. Although not all theories and philosophies are worthy of serious consideration, this one really is! When I compare it with the popular theory that human history is all just a meaningless chance happening over billions of years where a bunch of slime quivered its evolutionary way toward being Shakespeare or Jesus or Aretha Franklin . . . don't tell me that only "religious believers" take a leap of faith! So, we have a great story to tell—in fact, it's the greatest story ever told! It's also a great alternative way of thinking about life (and work).

Many people are really lost—not just spiritually but also relationally and psychologically. We look at them and know that they could be so much better off if they knew Jesus. Our attempts to share our faith are motivated by caring for these lost folks. We were lost just like them, and somebody brought us the good news. We want to pass it on. Frankly, I often am also motivated to want to share the New Testament gospel because so many people are so confused (if not repelled) by the appalling misrepresentation of Christianity by some in our political, business, media, and educational worlds. I want to correct this misunderstanding, defend the true Jesus, and apologize for the misrepresentation.

Although compassion for lost souls may be enough to stir us to share the gospel, it is Jesus' Great Commission that is always our main motivation. Whether we feel up to it or not, it is our responsibility, our mandate, to share our faith in Jesus Christ with other people. Christianity is not a tribal religion—it is for everybody. Jesus put it this way:

> "Go therefore and make disciples of all nations, baptizing them in the name of the Father and of the Son and of the Holy Spirit, and teaching them to obey everything that I have commanded you." (Matt. 28:19–20)

And Paul put it this way:

> We are ambassadors for Christ, since God is making his appeal through us; we entreat you on behalf of Christ, be reconciled to God. (2 Cor. 5:20)

"Ambassador" is a great way of describing our role in the world. Wherever we are, we are there to represent our homeland—what the Bible calls "the kingdom of God" or "the kingdom of heaven."

We often act as though people need to visit a church to hear this gospel, but there is nothing in the Bible to suggest that church is the preferred or best location. After all, Jesus himself went to Peter and Andrew's fishing business to call his first disciples, and very little of his "evangelism" was centered at the temple. Our message is not really about "getting religious" and joining a church. It is about reorienting our whole life around a person, Jesus Christ, as our Lord and leader.

On a practical level, think of how many more contacts we have with seekers and unbelievers at work than at church. Where there may be a handful of non-Christian visitors to our church services each week, at work we often have significant relationships with three or four, if not ten or fifteen, people who are not yet believers. While the potential audience for the gospel may be ten on Sunday for a church of two hundred, there are a thousand or more in that "audience" during the workweek! Workplace evangelism should therefore be a strategic priority.[1]

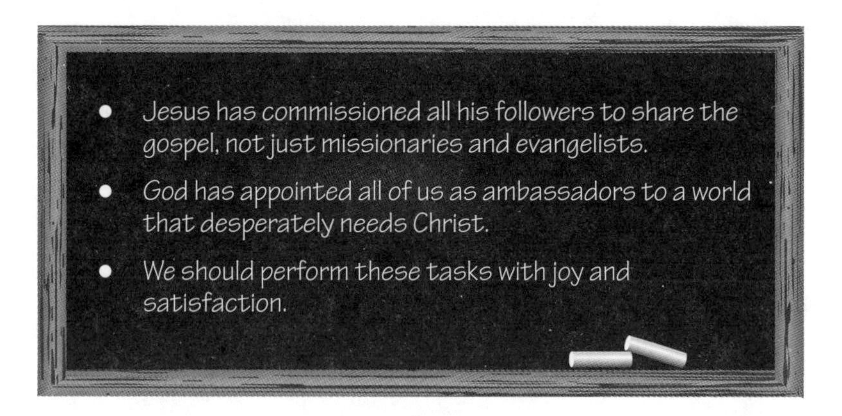

Of course, we need to be respectful of others, who may be a sort of captive audience at work. It is not right to "buttonhole" someone and "get in their face" aggressively. That's just rude and counterproductive. While we may be cheered back at church for our courage, what we did hardly comes across as welcome or good news. In fact, we may well have hardened that person's resistance to the gospel. Furthermore, it is also usually against company rules for people to proselytize on the job. We are trying to bring good news in a loving, caring way that respects our employment agreement and our work colleagues' space. We must be winsome, not antagonistic. It is just not ethical (or faithful) to abuse our freedom in the workplace by overzealous evangelism.

"Cold calls" by sales representatives and "robocalls" by telemarketers are not our models here. The best evange-

1. The very best book on workplace evangelism, by a wide margin, is *Workplace Grace: Becoming a Spiritual Influence at Work* by Bill Peel and Walt Larrimore (Longview, TX: LeTourneau University, 2014). Great ideas, beautifully written, totally biblical and practical.

lism builds on good relationships, and those take time and patience to develop. The process of coming to faith usually involves the impact of several voices on different occasions. Paul writes in 1 Corinthians 3:7–9 that one person plants a seed, another waters it, and another does the final harvesting—it is not our brilliance but God who gives the increase. Although our physical birth typically happens after nine months of development in the womb, our "new birth" as Christians can often take a lot longer!

The Context and Content of our Gospel

We are introducing a person, Jesus, and sharing the way one can enter into a lifelong relationship with him. Remember this: People are a lot more interested in meeting or hearing about my family if they know me as a good guy, a respectable fellow-worker, somebody who cares about them, and someone with helpful and wise input on our common work. This is the fertile context we look to create. The content of what we share is an introduction to Jesus. One of the best ways to share that content is with our personal story (our "testimony"). Personally, when the time is right, I never hesitate to say something like the following:

> I grew up in a church-going Christian family and committed to following Jesus when I was just a kid. I started reading the Bible on my own when I was about ten or twelve years old and have always loved that book. I went to public schools and then on to university at Berkeley, which means I was never in any kind of protected religious environment. I loved the interaction with people of all religions (or no religion). While I have learned a lot from them and respect the truth and faith I have seen, I have always kept my passion to understand and follow the way of Jesus and the Bible. I am far from perfect, and I acknowledge the

> ultimate mystery of life and the great questions about God and faith—so I'm not trying to give some heroic or perfect picture—but I still find Christianity the best way to live and think about life. I still see Jesus as Savior, Lord, and God.

As you can see, I don't have a story of getting saved out of a life of drugs or crime or of any miraculous healing of my body or relationships. Nonetheless, people are usually interested in my story—that is, remaining a Christian in the Berkeley of the Sixties and through all my academic study over the years. You, like every Christian, have a story of your own to tell. Get comfortable about it. How did you become a Christian? Why do you stay a Christian in an often pagan world where some find it old-fashioned and think it is too restrictive?

Our conversation partners will often push back against us with "why" questions. I love how the apostle Peter deals with that: "Always be ready to make your defense to anyone who demands from you an accounting for the hope that is in you; yet do it with gentleness and reverence" (1 Pet. 3:15–16). Be ready! That means anticipating what others might ask and figuring out how best to answer them. Read some books on apologetics (that is, the defense of the faith), such as Lee Strobel's *The Case for Christ* and Tim Keller's *The Reason for God.*[2] Don't be discouraged if you can't answer every question and criticism. It is just fine to respond, "I just don't know how to answer that. Maybe I can get back to you." Remember what Peter says: "Do it with gentleness." We are not trying to browbeat or bully anyone into Christian faith.

---

2. Lee Strobel, *The Case for Christ: A Journalist's Personal Investigation of the Evidence for Jesus* (Grand Rapids: Zondervan, 1998); Timothy Keller, *The Reason for God: Belief in an Age of Skepticism* (New York: Riverhead, 2008).

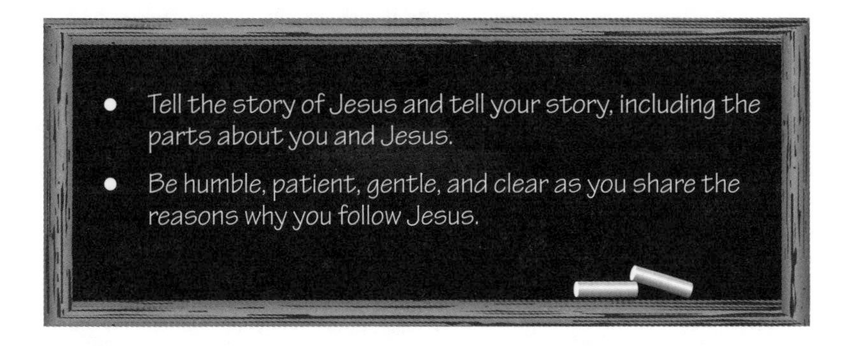

One important clarification I often make is to say that I am not a "Davidian" or "Paulian." I am a Christian, a follower of Christ. The Bible says that Jesus is the one and only perfect representation of God in our history. I am not here to defend everything that King David or the apostle Paul or other figures in the Bible did or said. For example, what does God think about children or other races or war or other subjects? I will go to the mat for Jesus, but not for some strange story in the Old Testament. Those other stories and passages are included in the Bible as important, even inspired, lessons for us; but those lessons are not always clear—and sometimes they are lessons on what *not* to do. I love the Bible, but I always read it with Jesus at the center.

The best evangelism is a humble but genuine introduction to Jesus—not to a philosophy, not to the weirdest parts of the Bible. And the best context is our good relationship with the other person and our humble, friendly manner. One final bit of advice is to spend at least as much time asking the other person for their story and their opinion (about religion, philosophy, Jesus, etc.) as we take in giving our own. We can be talking too much and listening far too little. We need to be genuinely interested in other people's stories and opinions. We are also picking up on where the soil is most fertile in their life for us to plant a gospel seed!

Five Sharing Strategies

Here are five approaches I have learned and practiced in sharing my faith with workplace colleagues and contacts.

1. Caring and Sharing

Many of our best and most important opportunities to share Jesus with others will be in the context of coming alongside a hurting or troubled colleague. All of this begins with, and depends on, our actually caring about others. It is not in our job description to be a pastor, chaplain, or counselor to our colleagues. But it is in our "job description" as an everyday disciple of Jesus to care about those around us, to love our neighbor as ourselves. We all have different gifts and personalities, but when we see a colleague who is upset or downcast, is there a chance we could say a word of encouragement? Is there an opportunity to ask them if everything is okay, to invite them to lean on us just a bit? The other side is also true of course. When they come to work unusually jubilant, do we say to them, "Hey, you are really happy today! Did you just win the lottery?" It's all about paying attention and caring about others—not just treating them like robots assigned to the workstation next to ours. Paul says that we should "rejoice with those who rejoice, weep with those who weep" (Rom. 12:15).

This is not about disrupting our work assignments or missing deadlines or standing around gossiping. It is about the caring look in the eyes as someone passes by, a brief question, a kind expression of concern. I'm not going to risk being too aggressive or intrusive; but if I sense some pain and some openness, I might ask if they would like to get coffee or lunch and talk about what's up. I would always say, "I don't want to be intrusive, and I'm not a trained counselor, but I think I am a pretty good listener and friend and maybe a shoulder to lean on" . . . or something like that. It is amazing how many people today really don't have any nearby or even good family, friend, or church relationships. It's all about being available, genuinely caring for others, listening and paying attention, and coming alongside.

If we can get some time together with a person like this, we might ask, "What's going on in your life that is weighing you down?" We don't need to say much. We need to listen a lot. After listening, commiseration is the next gift we give. Maybe it is relationship trouble with a spouse, parent, or child. Could be about finances or job issues. Could be a big health challenge. In this day and age, it could just be the overall and overwhelming sorrows and anxieties of this uncertain world!

At some point after lots of listening and caring and (we hope and pray) understanding, we may get a chance to speak. Understanding, empathy, compassion, and comfort are the first and most important things to communicate. Sometimes we can also share resources and strategies from our own experience that have helped us navigate life's struggles, such as book recommendations. Once in a while, it might be appropriate to share our testimony about how our faith (and maybe the community of faith) helped us make it through. Telling our story of how walking with God has worked out and helped us could be just the right message. Sometimes, I will ask the other person if they had ever tried to pray or seek God's help. I listen some more. If I sense that it would be appropriate, I may even ask if they would like me to pray for them at that moment. In any case, I tell them that I will pray for them on my own (and then I do). I invite them to call or contact me whenever they feel the need, and I tell them I will check back to see how they are doing (and then I do!).

It all begins with a caring relationship. It's wonderful if it leads to an opportunity to speak about Jesus . . . but even if it doesn't (yet anyway), we have still brought the love of God to someone, which is part of God's process of drawing them to himself.

2. Invitation to an Outside Event

Recently, my former church put on a performance of Handel's *Messiah* with a full orchestra and choir. It was nothing short of spectacular. Another one of my former churches locally puts on a jazz concert/jam session one Monday night each month (led by church members who are professional jazz artists). My friend, Al Erisman, used to post an invitation to the annual Christmas concert at his church on the bulletin board at Boeing where he was director of the IT research group, supervising about three hundred techies. Since he was in charge, he created a policy that anyone could post an announcement of any religious, cultural, or other gathering that might interest colleagues; he did not privilege Christianity above other interest groups. Al and his wife, Nancy, would invite colleagues to stop by their house for a low-key reception before or after the Christmas concert. Likewise, we could invite our workplace colleagues to an actual Christmas, Easter, or Thanksgiving service. This could be, if nothing more, an interesting cultural experience for them, especially for international colleagues. There are sometimes movies, plays, lectures, or discussions that could be helpful in exposing our colleagues to aspects of faith and the gospel. Be imaginative and creative. Be hospitable.

3. Attending, Hosting, or Sponsoring an Event at or Near Work

Another way to put some gospel on the table is to invite colleagues to a work-related event at or near our workplace. Maybe this could be a professional group of Christians in the workplace or in our specific vocation or industry. There are actually a lot of groups like this, and some of them are visitor-friendly and not just clubs of "insiders" speaking a religious jargon. Again, my friend Al in Seattle has been a leader in a monthly breakfast group called *Kiros* (from the Greek word for a decisive moment or time). After an enjoyable networking breakfast, there is a speaker (once in a while it's a well-known person, but it's always someone thoughtful and interesting) with some brief discussion afterward. This is an outstanding way to expose a colleague to a thoughtful, positive illustration of the faith. Some Christian groups more aggressively aim at converting all visitors at every meeting, so choose carefully; we don't want to bring our guest into the wrong situation and turn them completely against the gospel! There may be a Bible study at or near our workplace—or a Christian fellowship of some sort—that we could invite a colleague to visit with us. If not, maybe we could start one.

Here is another idea I implemented at the theological seminary where I taught (though I could imagine this kind of event at a hospital, a school, a big law firm, a financial or investment management group, a business office, or even a manufacturing center). I organized a multifaith panel discussion titled "Good Business Ideas from the World's Great Religions." I recruited a Sikh, a Jew, a Catholic, a Greek Orthodox, a Muslim, and a Protestant (me) with an assignment to speak for just fifteen minutes on the topic of "insights from my religious tradition on how to run a good, ethical business." I also arranged for four diverse "respondents" (managers, consultants, educators) to listen carefully and then comment on the implications and applications they saw for business in our global and diverse era. Each of the panelists and all of the attendees thought it was an extraordinary event. The panelists stayed on point and focused on positive workplace ideas from their tradition. The audience got a real sense of an important aspect of what these religions were about. We talked about work and business; and as part of that, they heard about a Jesus who cares about our work and who is a core part of our gospel. Other multifaith discussions like this could easily be imagined regarding technology, health and healing, teaching and learning, wealth and poverty, and so on. These kinds of events create opportunities for discussion and sharing of faith.

4. Provocative, Intriguing Discussion-Starters

I remember reading about a Christian business leader who kept a big black Bible in plain view on his desk as a statement of his biblical faith. I love the Bible, but I'm not sure if having a big one on my work desk would open—or close off—conversation! Maybe my French Bible would be more provocative. But even in that case ("Why do you have this French book on your desk?"), it may fail to communicate, because the word *Bible* is the same in French! This fourth strategy, then, is about displaying messages or symbols that might create discussion or questioning that leads to an opportunity to share our faith. If having a Bible in full view is not getting the message across, we could try leaving another book out on display such as Tim Keller's *Reason for God*, C. S. Lewis's *Screwtape Letters*, Jacques Ellul's *Subversion of Christianity*, or Bertrand Russell's *Why I Am Not a Christian*. We can see how this strategy might invite conversation, and then we can share our faith.

Back in Boston, I created a bunch of coffee mugs with the message *313 Club* in big letters with *Transforming Work* underneath in smaller letters. These were good-sized, nice-looking tan coffee mugs that most people would enjoy drinking out of (as we know, not all cups are created equal!). The point was to provoke work colleagues into asking, "What the heck is the 313 Club?" Our answer, then, was something like this:

> Oh, it's actually a symbol for the 313 days, Monday through Saturday, each year. Many people, including too many Christians, think Christian faith and values are only about church activities on church turf 52 Sundays each year. I am part of a movement of Christians who think that our values and faith ought to be practiced not just on 52 Sundays at church, but also on the 313 days including our work throughout the year. We are just not "52 Club" Christians but "313 Club" Christians![3]

Do you see how this works? We could wear a cross or a fish pin or a *WWJD* wristband, and maybe someone will ask us about it. Great! But let's not limit our creativity. Especially at work, the 313 Club or something like it could be an easy avenue to share our faith. In fact, maybe we should call our new workplace Bible study/fellowship group the "313 Club" just to make that point. It could be much more intriguing than just "Bible study" or "Christian fellowship."

5. Casual Conversation

The fifth and final strategy is actually my favorite one. We could call it the "make them ask you about your faith" strategy. In Berkeley thirty years ago, I used to work out at Gold's Gym in the early morning. I noticed that another guy who had started working out at that time looked an awful lot like a recently retired star player for the Oakland A's baseball team. Being a fan, I slowly worked my way along the dumbbell rack to where he was pumping iron. When I knew I wouldn't disrupt his workout, I introduced myself and told him briefly

---

3. The "313" message continues today in the nonprofit "Workplace 313" with its website (www.wp313.org), a free monthly e-zine, and a menu of educational and discussion forums.

how much I admired his career as a player. Life went on, and before too long he and his workout partner invited me to work out with them. (Just to let you know, I had to drop out of the series after doing my heaviest inclined presses with the 95 pound dbs; these two guys went up to the 130s; I may hold the record for middle-aged ethics professors but am no competition for Hall of Fame professional athletes!)

During the chitchat between sets every workout, I would ask the superstar his views on this subject or that. I began to find out a bit about what interested him, not just in sports but in business and culture. I honestly cared about him. I never asked him for his autograph or help getting tickets. After a few weeks, one day he turned and said to me, "David, tell me about you. What do you do anyway?" Bingo. "I am a teacher and writer, a professor of Christian ethics." His response: "I'm not surprised. I thought maybe you must be a minister or something like that, because you are always concerned about me and not about yourself, and you never ask me for anything." Months later, he asked if I could give him some personal counseling because he found himself depressed at times. I told him I was not a professional counselor, but I was a pastor and most of all I could be a brother. Soon we started meeting for some Bible study and prayer once a week. This went on for maybe three years, until we both took jobs in other parts of the country. But do you see how we got from nowhere to a Bible study and prayer together?

I have had many experiences where I asked questions of a colleague or neighbor, wanting to know what they thought about the scandals in the Catholic priesthood, for example, or the horrible talk and behavior of some Protestant pastor or political leader. Here are some questions you can use: Did you see or read about this story? What did you think? Did you ever go to a church in your youth, or any other time in your life? Did you see any leaders behaving like the ones we've been reading about? What do you think about Muslim terrorism? Do you know any Muslims? Do you think religion usually leads people to be narrow-minded or even hostile toward other religions and people?[4] Why do you think that anti-Semitism is still thriving today? What about racism? What can we do about it?

These are just a few examples of the kinds of questions I care about, often provoked by the daily news. I rarely lead with my opinion, though of course I have opinions on these questions. But it is so much better for me to hold back and humbly learn from my colleague until they turn at last and say, "You are always asking me. But what about you? What is your faith or religion, and what do you think about this or that issue?" Then I share my faith, values, and thoughts with them. I usually get to tell them a little about Jesus, though I don't "firehose" them with too much, too fast. But since they asked me, I tell them. That's why I say that the best time to share the gospel is when someone asks you about it and wants to hear your answer. Try it out!

---

4. For an interesting discussion from a Christian theological perspective on the debate over the relationship between religion and violence, see Peter D. Anders, "Nonviolence and the Immanent Logic of Christian Trinitarian Monotheism," in *Violence in Civil Society: Monotheism Guilty?* edited by Alejandra Vanney, vol. 6, Religion and Civil Society (Hildesheim, Germany: Georg Olms Verlag, 2013), https://d1ok7k7mywg42z.cloudfront.net/assets/5373edd8d6af687e7600000d/Anders___Nonviolence_and_Trinitarianism.pdf.

Promoting Faith-Friendly Workplaces

David Miller of Princeton University has argued for the legitimacy and importance of today's workplaces becoming "faith-friendly."[5] Just as many or most workplaces today seek to be woman-friendly, racial minority-friendly, disability-friendly, and LGBTQ-sexual-orientation-friendly (hey, don't forget old guy, geezer-friendly) . . . isn't it important that our workplaces become "faith-friendly"? Of course, our workplace-related skills and performance must be the criteria for hiring, promotion, and compensation decisions. Employee faith and religious commitments (just like our sexuality, appearance, nationality, musical preference, etc.) should normally not matter significantly, except insofar as diversity itself is a positive characteristic in most working organizations. But "faith-friendly" makes sense.

---

5. David W. Miller, *God at Work: The History and Promise of the Faith at Work Movement* (Oxford: Oxford University Press, 2007), 150.

Faith-friendly at the minimum means no discrimination. But there are two other more positive aspects to the issue. First of all, faith or religion is often a critical, central part and a shaper of a worker's identity. Just as being a certain race or gender is a vital part of who people are, so too is being Jewish, Buddhist, Hindu, Muslim, or Roman Catholic, and so on. While our business missions and agendas are to work—not religious enlightenment or propagation—we still want to see and respect the religious aspect to each person's character. Not just toleration, but respect. Not agreement, but respect. That has to do with how we talk—no religious jokes, no stereotypes. But it could also mean providing a space for Jewish or Muslim prayers, a Christian Bible study, or Buddhist meditation.[6]

The second potentially positive aspect of a religiously diverse workforce has to do with insights that might be shared from different religious traditions on how to resolve conflict or misunderstanding, how to market to this or that community, and what constitutes fair wages and just prices. While we are not seeking a religious decision-maker for our issues, we are inviting good ideas from all sources, including the religious traditions of our workers.

Some Christians (and many other religious groups, especially those who have been marginalized or persecuted) can be suspicious, wary, or negative about a religiously diverse conversation. Some people worry about the potentially negative impact of false ideas or gods, while others may be concerned that those they consider "weak" might become confused or converted or lose their faith. Speaking strictly here regarding the Christian faith, we certainly don't want to get overconfident in ourselves or be reckless about exposing

---

6. For an eye-opening and helpful exploration on promoting interfaith communication and understanding between Christians and Jews, see Anthony Le Donne and Larry Behrendt, *Sacred Dissonance: The Blessing of Difference in Jewish-Christian Dialogue* (Peabody, MA: Hendrickson, 2017).

newer and weaker believers to assault or seduction by falsehood. There is a point, however, at which we must trust God, have courage, and strongly urge Christians to step outside their comfort zone while staying in close relationships with other Christians—and then jump into the fray! Resistance is absolutely essential in developing physical strength, intellectual and psychological strength, and spiritual strength as well. To have other religions or philosophies push back on Christian truth-claims is or should be a good experience, a strengthening experience. I became a vastly stronger, more committed Christian by the time I graduated from Berkeley.

In November 1644, the great Puritan writer John Milton gave a long speech to the English Parliament on behalf of freedom of the press. It was called "Areopagitica," a name inspired by the speech of Paul in the book of Acts on Mars Hill (that is, the Areopagus). In this speech, Milton argued against tighter regulation on printing businesses and in favor of freedom of press and speech. Listen to his eloquent defense:

> I cannot praise a fugitive and cloistered virtue, unexercised and unbreathed, that never sallies out and sees her adversary, but slinks out of the race where that immortal garland is to be run for, not without dust and heat.
>
> Let her [Truth] and Falsehood grapple; who ever knew Truth put to the worse in a free and open encounter?
>
> Give me the liberty to know, to utter, and to argue freely according to conscience, above all liberties.

Milton's confidence in truth echoes Saint Augustine from twelve centuries earlier: "The truth is like a lion; you don't have to defend it. Let it loose; it will defend itself." We see this also in a similar comment made by famous nineteenth-century London preacher Charles Spurgeon: "Defend the Bible? I would as soon defend a lion! Unchain it and it will defend itself."

I confess that I am a radical free speech-er. It's because I love truth. I hate lies, denials, excuses, and cover-ups. I loved the Free Speech Movement that started at Berkeley in 1964 when I entered as a freshman. That Free Speech Movement opened up the university to us radical Christian types, just as it did to the Black Panthers, Socialist Workers, Vietnam War opponents, marijuana advocates, and everybody else. The truth of the Christian gospel can stand on its own without fear.

I therefore urge us workplace disciples to advocate for faith-friendly workplaces. When appropriate, let's create spaces for Christian prayers and meetings as well as prayers and meetings of other faiths, arrange meetings where people can share the origin of their values (including their religious roots as appropriate), and share the positive insights about work and workplaces that come from our various religions and philosophies. In the freedom of others, we will find our own freedom. Truth has nothing to fear in a free and open encounter.

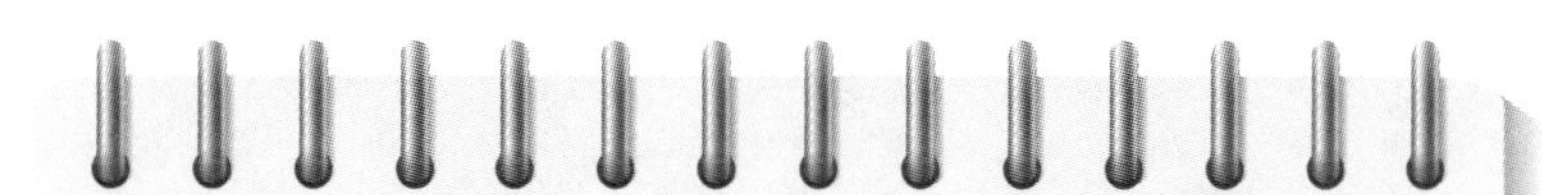

To Do

- ✓ Ask a few Christian friends (adult converts if possible) how they came to know the Lord, how they were "born again" and committed to being Christian.
- ✓ Read a book or two on Christian apologetics and reasons for the faith.

For Reflection & Discussion

1. What have been your experiences in sharing your faith with your coworkers? How about your customers, clients, or patients? Describe your evangelistic "methods" and results. Did any business or boss or colleague try to shut down your efforts to share your faith?

2. Have you ever been "evangelized/proselytized" by other Christians or someone from another religion? Describe it.

3. What do you think are the appropriate and inappropriate times and ways to share one's faith?

10

Overcome

Deal Well with Conflict and Wrongdoing at Work

Up to now, we have mostly been thinking proactively: How can we work in alignment with the creator, sustainer, and redeemer? How can we personally be a positive example? How can we contribute some helpful workplace insights? And how can we share our faith appropriately? Now we must think about how to respond to bad things that happen. The reality, Jesus said, is that "in this world you will have trouble"—not just positive opportunities and experiences (John 16:33 NIV). Thankfully, he went on immediately to say, "But take heart! I have overcome the world." Step ten in faithful and wise workplace discipleship is to face up to (not deny!) the evil and nastiness we see in our workplaces—and try to overcome that evil with good. We must not close our eyes or walk away or paper over the bad stuff. Evil offends God, but it also harms people and the planet. Even if it doesn't harm us personally, immediately, and directly, it will eventually corrupt and diminish our character and our reputation if we choose to wash our hands and look away.

How does good work go bad? In the third chapter of Genesis, the emphasis is placed squarely on the desire to decide on our own what is good or evil, what is ethical or unethical. In the two Creation accounts of Genesis 1 and 2, it is God (the God of all the earth) who pronounces things "good" or "not good." This is "Ethics Plan A." Ask God to clarify and name what is good or not good. In the fall, Adam and Eve seize that power to name good and evil for themselves *outside* and *against* the God of all the earth. By the end of the book of Judges (21:25), we see that "all the people did what was right in their own eyes"—and truly, all hell broke loose! Right after Adam and Eve's fateful choice, we see shame and hiding, accusation, blame, and alienation: "She did it—the woman you gave me!" "The snake did it!" And that leads to isolation, relational breakdown, pain, suffering, toil, and soon enough murder (Cain and Abel).

The long human saga of doing what's right in our own eyes (instead of what's right in the eyes of the God of all the earth) leads ultimately to the judgment of Babylon. Here is a sampling of some of the rejoicing over her condemnation at the end of history (Rev. 18:2–3, 7, 11–13, 23–24):

> "Fallen! Fallen is Babylon the Great! . . . [T]he merchants of the earth have grown rich from the power of her luxury. . . . As she glorified herself and lived luxuriously so give her a like measure of torment and grief." . . . [T]he merchants of the earth weep and mourn for her since no one buys their cargo anymore, cargo of gold, silver, jewels and pearls . . . cattle and sheep, horses and chariots, slaves—and human lives. . . . "Your merchants were the magnates of the earth, and all nations were deceived by your sorcery. And in you was found the blood of prophets and of saints, and of all who have been slaughtered on earth."

Excessive luxury, glory for the self, enslaving and selling human beings in various ways, leading people astray, repressing prophets who tried to speak truth, engaging in violence, and death. It all goes back to "doing what's right in our own eyes" and seizing the fruit of "the tree of the knowledge of good and evil" (the ethics tree). Wanting to "be like God," knowing good and evil without relying on God. Instead of wanting to know what would be good from the perspective of the creator, sustainer, and redeemer of the whole earth and all of its people, we choose what we think is right for our tribe, our nation, our clan, our race, our company, our family, or, ultimately, Me. Out of that selfish, narrow concern comes all the other horrible consequences of bad politics, bad relationships . . . bad and wrong workplace behavior. "In this workplace you shall have tribulation and trouble. You shall see conflict and wrongdoing."

The Basic Overcomer Stance

Before looking at any specific situations, there are some crucial preliminaries. First of all, we need to be humble. Nobody likes a self-righteous, judgmental accuser and finger-pointer. In fact, the devil himself is at his core the "accuser of our comrades . . . who accuses them day and night before our God" (Rev. 12:10). Let's not be like that. I like to think that most of the time, rather than *accusation*—a face-to-face confrontation—we should use *exhortation*, which is more side-by-side, like sharing a concern with a brother/sister or friend. In any case, we need to honestly and clearly bring up the problem, which takes not just humility but also courage and wisdom. I love the wisdom we find in the book of Proverbs: "Better is open rebuke than hidden love. Well meant are the wounds a friend inflicts" (27:5–6). We are no friend to our organization or to a wrongdoer if we keep silent. And let's remember from earlier chapters that our wisdom, courage, and humility require us to pray and partner—to ask for the help of God and others. But there is no arrogance allowed: we need to think and act humbly. We need to remember, "But for the grace of God, there go I."

Second, our strategy, especially as Christians, is never just to crush evil and punish the guilty, but to correct and redeem situations and persons. Paul puts it this way, "Do not repay anyone evil for evil, but take thought for what is noble in the sight of all. . . . Never avenge yourselves. . . . Do not be overcome by evil, but overcome evil with good" (Rom. 12:17, 19, 21). We may need to act decisively and immediately to stop the evil and damage and prevent the wrongdoing from continuing. This, however, is only the beginning of our overcomer response. Our goal is not just condemnation but also redemption. We want to follow through, to heal the victims, to reform the wrongdoer, and to improve the institutions and processes that allowed the wrongdoing to occur. While there is no perfection or true permanence in these matters, our mantra is always to find the good and use it to overcome the bad.

Third, even though individuals must stand accountable for their behavior, they don't fully act alone without other influences on them. As part of our overcomer process, we need to step back and look at our organizational culture in its multiple aspects. Do our systems and processes enable or even encourage employees or executives to get off track in weak moments? If there is little transparency—lots of individualism and lots of closed doors (physically, financially, etc.)—then don't be surprised to discover some yielding to temptation. Does our organizational culture allow or perpetuate racist or sexist joking and behavior? Don't be surprised then when lines get crossed and the chickens come home to roost. Do our compensation systems get so twisted in favor of the top executive tier that "grab for all you can get" becomes an unstated core value embraced by everyone in the company?

One aspect of a systems weakness is a failure to interview and hire for good character, not just for educational pedigree and technical skills. "Hitler got the trains to run on time," people said. But that administrative success came at the price of putting the devil in charge of Germany and led to unimaginable death and destruction. When will we ever learn? Workplace disciples also recall what Paul said, "Our struggle is not against enemies of blood and flesh, but against . . . the cosmic powers of this present darkness, against the spiritual forces of evil in the heavenly places" (Eph. 6:12). All of this is to say that workplace disciples must not just deal with the immediate, highly visible, personnel and situation, but insist on a broader, deeper, longer understanding of what happened—and then respond and follow through accordingly.

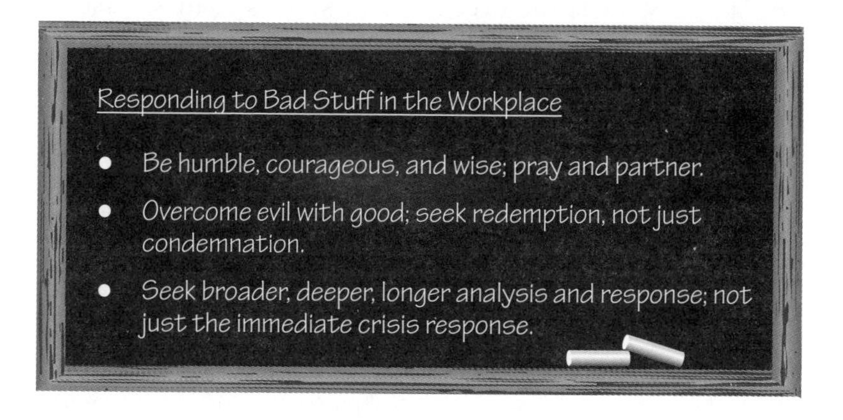

Overcoming Conflict

Let's begin by thinking about conflicts in the workplace. This includes colleagues who don't get along and can't seem to work together, conflicts between managers and employees, and between people in our organization and customers, business partners, and neighbors. Some of these conflicts are because of specific events where someone was insulted or mistreated. Sometimes it is impatience or a personality conflict. And sometimes it is flat-out racism, sexism, or other prejudice. But Christians are followers of a reconciling, peacemaking God, breaking down barriers between Jew and Gentile, male and female, slave and free. We have been given the "ministry of reconciliation." "Blessed are the peacemakers, for they will be called the children of God" (Matt. 5:9; the seventh

Beatitude). We are never more recognizably, visibly, the children of God than when we bring peace and reconciliation.

Conflict of a certain kind can be productive and healthy, if it is constructive competition and we are "playing by the rules," not cheating, disrespecting, or harming one another. The kind of conflict we must address here, however, is the destructive kind that undermines teamwork, harms people, and actually hurts the organization and its clients (customers, patients, students, et al.). Before exploring how we might intervene as peacemakers, we need to acknowledge that we, personally, should not necessarily get involved in every conflict we see, at least not right away.

If we are new employees or young or timid, we may be well-advised not to "stick our nose" into a conflict among our colleagues or bosses. We don't have enough clout or experience or respect quite yet. What we might do, rather than intervening directly, is discuss what we have observed with a trusted colleague. We might pray about it and ask our posse what they would advise. Get to know the adversaries and become a positive, encouraging part of their experience, even if it is not the right time to bring up their conflict. It is easy to imagine situations where we are just not in a position to get involved and help. It is not in our job description, and our efforts could be distracting or counterproductive. The conflict may be unfortunate and sad, but not totally debilitating to the organization—which may tolerate such conflict because of upside payoffs in other ways.

But sometimes we are "the one." Sometimes we can sit down with adversaries (who should be, or used to be, good teammates) with an agenda to try to improve a bad situation. Here is what I have learned (again, from the Beatitudes) about being a reconciler and peacemaker.[1] (By the way, this

1. In chapter 7 above on the character traits and habits we want to model in the workplace, we viewed the Beatitudes as habits; here we are

pattern works in cases of marital conflict, parent/child conflict, and faction conflict. I actually think it is the best model even for resolving international conflicts.).

The first step is to be sure that those involved in the conflict want to see things improve. The goal is *shalom*—peace, harmony, flourishing together. This is actually the seventh of the eight Beatitudes Jesus taught (the eighth is about carrying on, persisting even when our pursuit of righteousness is rejected). The seventh, "Blessed are the peacemakers," is the ultimate goal—and the preceding six Beatitudes outline the way to get to this peace and harmony. So, in order to make progress, in order to get people's attention to those first six Beatitudes, we first have to sell our conflicted colleagues on the value of overcoming their conflict and arriving at harmony. Here is the argument we may need to make: The team and the organization will function better if we can work together without unnecessary conflict. There may be a financial payoff if we work more effectively together. And on a personal level, wouldn't we prefer to get rid of these bad feelings and work experiences? Maybe we won't all be "best buddies," but wouldn't it be nice if we could get past our conflicts and work in greater harmony and respect? Wouldn't it be desirable to overcome our disagreements and actually enjoy coming to work together?

Assuming that the conflicted parties want to resolve things (a critical prerequisite), the Beatitudes teach us that we must begin in a "poverty of spirit" and in "mourning" (the first and second Beatitudes). In other words, we need to acknowledge that we are (all parties to the conflict) in some way broken, weak, and messed up. If we are arrogant, full of ourselves, and think we know everything, then we will never establish peace. It is essential not just to acknowledge our

---

looking at how this model of character can guide our response to conflict around us.

brokenness (the first Beatitude) but also to "mourn it," to lament it, to regret where our relational breakdown has left us (the second Beatitude). We mourn rather than just naming it and then blaming others. The next critical step (the third Beatitude) is to "let go" of attempts to control the conversation and outcome. This is what "meekness" (sometimes translated as "gentleness") means. Be gentle rather than controlling. All parties to the conflict need to back off and not insist on taking over and personally managing and fixing the problem. These first three Beatitudes are steps that are essential if we are to move forward, and our overcomer strategy is to nudge (or persuade) the combatants toward these attitudes.

We could call these first three Beatitude steps the "preparation" phase. The next three steps are then the "action" phase. This begins with "hungering for justice/righteousness" (the fourth Beatitude). You may have seen the bumper sticker that says, "If you want peace, work for justice." If there is no justice, then there will be no peace (the seventh Beatitude). This is where the parties to the conflict need to take turns articulating what they see as the problem, the truth and reality, that underlies or caused the breakdown of a good relationship.

People need to be allowed to speak without interruption and put their cards on the table honestly and fully. "You did this." "This is what messed us up." "This is how you talk (or act) and tick me off." Each one of the parties needs to be heard fully. Only after fully being heard is it time to listen to the other side's point of view. We ask each party, "Do you hear what the other person is saying?" There will probably be differences of opinion. The tendency is to be defensive. The mediator/overcomer needs to help people say, "This is how it comes across to me"—and not just "This is how it is." To say instead, "This is how it is *in my experience*" helps make room for possible acceptance or at least understanding of what seems "righteous" and true to the other party.

There has to be some basic acceptance of the truth of what has been causing the conflict. We need to try to pull back from blame, accusation, and negatively interpreting the other person's motives. We need to try to acknowledge the other person's perspective, pain, feelings, and concerns. We need to acknowledge our own faults and failures and weaknesses. This is all about hungering for righteousness and justice.

Next in the Beatitudes are "mercy" (the fifth Beatitude) and "purity of heart" (the sixth Beatitude). There can never be perfect justice in the world. We can never heal all the wounds, pay back all the debts, or achieve perfect fairness. We can do our best to name the injustice, the issues, the facts, and the values. But we can't go back and change what happened. Justice by itself is paralyzing. That's why once we identify the justice issues and make some acknowledgment of our part in the problem, we need to show some mercy toward one another. We need to forgive one another—rise above the demand for retribution and then let it go. And we must do it all with a "pure heart"—with integrity, not harboring revenge in our attitude, but truly meaning what we say. Justice is basic, but it must be accompanied by some mercy and by a good-faith effort to mean what we say and move on with no hidden agenda.

This process gives us our best chance to live and work in renewed peace and harmony with our team. The Hebrew term *shalom* suggests that this peace is not just détente or a cessation of conflict, but rather a positive "flourishing" as we resume our common tasks together. To use a basketball analogy, *shalom* is not just avoiding stepping on each other; it is finding ways to set a screen for one another or to make an assist and feed one another a pass leading to a score. Again, we are not suggesting that we are now ready to move into the same house together and live happily ever after. But the peace we seek needs to play out in some positive ways, not just in conflict avoidance (though that is a piece of it).

As I have described it, this peacemaking strategy looks like some kind of simple formula. Life is complicated, and simple formulas provide no guarantees. But for workplace disciples to absorb the wisdom of the Beatitudes and deeply commit to Beatitude-shaped lives, in the workplace and everywhere else, offers real promise of being peacemakers who can help colleagues to overcome their conflicts. As I said earlier, the Beatitudes are both a description of a good personal example and a working agenda for conflict resolution and peacemaking.

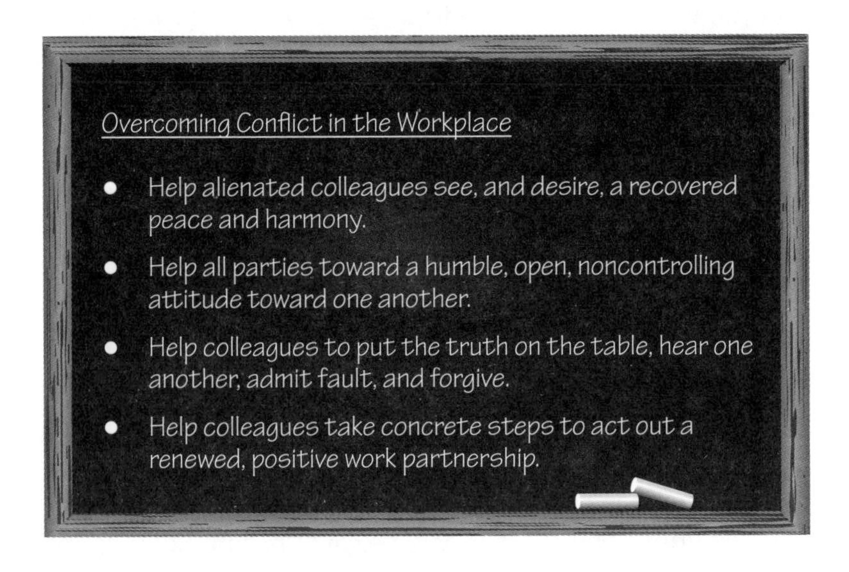

Overcoming Wrongdoing

The kind of conflict in the workplace we have been discussing is certainly undesirable. But sometimes conflict is accidental or inadvertent—not really a matter of intentional evil. Things get even more serious when workplace disciples come up against behavior that violates our standards of right and wrong. Sometimes, we are just the observers of wrongful activities. Other times, we could find ourselves participating in these wrongful activities. We may even be ordered to do something wrong. What do we do in these kinds of cases? How do we overcome this kind of evil with good? When do we raise our voices and object? When do we walk away—either quitting our job in protest or just staying quiet (and trusting God or others)?

How do we know something is wrong and not just offensive? The yellow and red lights start flashing when something (1) violates the law, (2) violates company or professional ethics, (3) violates our conscience and our understanding of biblical right and wrong, (4) violates the Golden Rule (i.e., we wouldn't want it done to us), (5) wouldn't be done if outsiders knew what was going on, or (6) might result in serious harm to others.

Here are some examples. Our company is distributing shoddy or dangerous products or services. It is engaging in deceptive communications, marketing, and sales. Lies are covering up the fact that our diesel automobiles are polluting the environment (hello, Volkswagen). People are cooking the books, misstating financials and taxes owed, filing false expense reimbursements, or overcharging business partners and customers. Racist and sexist attitudes are discriminating against job applicants and employee evaluations. Women are being sexually harassed. Bosses or colleagues are taking credit for ideas and efforts that others actually created or performed. Managers or employees are not pulling their weight, are showing up late, are skipping out early, or are unprepared for their responsibilities.

Recognizing Serious Wrongdoing in the Workplace

1. It violates the law.
2. It violates company or professional ethics.
3. It violates our conscience and understanding of biblical right and wrong.
4. It violates the Golden Rule (we wouldn't want it done to us).
5. It wouldn't be done if outsiders knew what was going on.
6. It could result in serious harm to others.

If we are witnesses to these various forms of wrongdoing, what should we do? If we are asked to assist in wrongdoing or stay silent and help the cover-up, what should we do? If we ourselves are the ones being harassed or exploited or ripped off, what should we do? How can we be overcomers in these situations? Walking away, looking away, is not an option for a workplace disciple. But if we speak up, there could be serious retaliation that could affect not just us personally but our families. We could be fired or falsely accused. How do we overcome evil with good?

The kind of response we make will depend in a significant way on our position in the organization. If we are the manager responsible for wrongdoing by our own staff, then we have a direct and immediate responsibility to intervene and stop what is going on. If we are veteran employees with some job security and respect, then we have greater responsibility and potential to speak up than a younger or newer employee. If we have established a good reputation and been a model employee with a clearly positive impact on the organization, then this gives us a stronger voice that might be listened to. If we are newer, weaker, and in a more vulnerable position, however, then we may be best advised to first confide in a trusted colleague (or two) at work. Raising the issues as a twosome or threesome could be more effective and safer for us. Obviously, a workplace disciple should pray for God's help and guidance. Sharing the challenge (at least in general outline, if identities and specifics at work need to be protected) with our workplace Christian posse or support group could give us a lot of insight and wise counsel.

We need to be careful to get the facts of the case straight. Keep notes, texts, and emails. If possible, ask a trusted colleague to witness what we are witnessing. Be careful to know what guidelines are being violated (laws, regulations, company codes). Think about the reasons why this should not be tolerated: for example, we might get sued, we might lose customers and our public reputation, we might lose trust with our business partners, we might get fired, and so on. Business requires trust, but there will be no trust if we are not trustworthy. Wrongdoing requires lying and cover-ups, which require time and effort that could better be directed to constructive activities.

In addition to these "damage-control" reasons, we need to raise other questions: What kind of people do we want to be? Don't we want to have a great reputation in our industry and community and have a positive impact? Do we really want to cheat our way forward, or do we want to succeed because we are the best? How can we inspire our employees to bring their best, most creative and ethical selves to work every day? Sometimes we need to bring in some news stories of badly behaving organizations that get caught or ruined—and just as many news stories of companies that succeed and have great reputations for ethics and how they treat people.

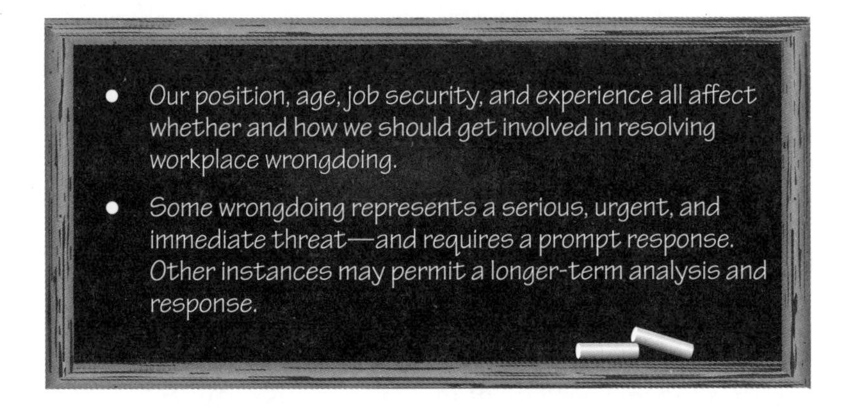

We may be in a delicate position where we need to report the wrongdoing anonymously. Some companies provide confidential hotlines for such reports. The drawback with such anonymous reporting channels is that those receiving the reports can't contact us for more information, and we may not know whether they follow through on the problem. Alternatively, we may be able to report the problem to our boss or the HR director or another manager. In this case, our identity may be more exposed. Of course, if the offender is our boss, then the difficulties can mount. Again, pray and consult before taking action. I would never advise someone being harassed or abused to go alone to confront the perpetrator.

Jesus' counsel applies to many cases of wrongdoing:

> "If your brother or sister sins, go and point out their fault, just between the two of you. If they listen to you, you have won them over. But if they will not listen, take one or two others along, so that every matter may be established by the testimony of two or three witnesses. If they still refuse to listen, tell it to the church; and if they refuse to listen even to the church, treat them as you would a pagan or a tax collector." (Matt. 18:15–17 NIV)

Whenever it is possible, it is good if the victim or observer can approach the wrongdoer and urge them to straighten up. It's better for the wrongdoer to step up, acknowledge responsibility, and pledge to correct the situation. That goes for individuals and for organizations. Don't deny, excuse, obfuscate, and wait until others come after us in public. Take responsibility. But if the perpetrator won't straighten up, take another colleague or two (and maybe an attorney!), and confront the wrongdoer again. If they continue to deny and reject, then we make it a public issue. This is when we blow the whistle.

So much depends on the specifics. We might be in a position where we can speak up and tell someone their flirtatious or insulting comments or behavior are hurtful and not welcome. Their unethical or illegal actions could get them and the organization in trouble. My wife had to put a couple guys in their place to stop their flirtation when she was in the business world. But her job was not in any danger, and her maturity and identity were strong (they quickly backed off!). There are cases where a racist comment or hiring practice needs to be confronted, and we don't want to leave the victims of this behavior to be the only protesters. We need to speak up and come alongside anyone being attacked or disrespected. What Paul writes has some relevance here, "If anyone is detected in a transgression, you who have received the Spirit should restore such a one in a spirit of gentleness" (Gal. 6:1). The message is that the strong need to go to the wrongdoer, gently but firmly, to help them get back on track and (most of all) to stand by those attacked.

As disciples of Jesus, our purpose is to *protect people from harm*—and actually to *do them some good*. We need to protect the weak—those with fewer resources, less strength, and more critical need. We want justice and peace to reign. One final point must also be added: We want the wrongdoer to be redeemed and reformed.

When I was teaching business ethics to MBA students, I had to turn in a student who had plagiarized a report for class. Dismissal from the program was an ironclad rule, and he suffered that fate. But I couldn't just say good-bye to this young man, and so I asked him if I could meet with him. I knew he must be totally devastated and shamed in front of his family and friends. I talked to him about how to better manage his time and studies and deal with deadlines and crises of not enough time, which had led him to cut corners and plagiarize. I told him that I had seen his potential and would be happy to write him a reference letter to get into another MBA program when the timing was right for him. The "plagiarizer" took me seriously and appreciated my caring for him—and he reformed his ways. Wrongdoing was not just punished but was overcome with good.

It is also important to reform structures, processes, and cultures that may be inviting and enabling wrongdoing. This is an important step in our overcoming agenda. While individual managers may not be consciously racist or sexist in their hiring and promotion decisions, organizational processes may be recruiting and promoting only through channels that have yielded white guys for years. We may need to reform the advertising and recruiting process to add channels that are likely to bring applications from talented women and minorities. If some male-only clubs or activities are the primary venues where informal relationships and mentoring happens, you can see why women are at a procedural disadvantage. If we keep bringing in the same old list of mostly white male consultants and speakers, then we are perhaps inadvertently reinforcing a culture that privileges white males. As Christians in the global body of Christ that unifies men and women and all nations, tribes, and languages in Jesus Christ, we must be voices and actors for the blessings of diversity.

Overcoming Wrongdoing

- Be clear about the facts, the standards, and the guidelines.
- Bring in God along with your posse (pray and consult).
- Be clear about why this wrongdoing must be stopped/corrected.
- Confront (gently) the perpetrator(s) if possible, maybe with a couple colleagues.
- Make it a public issue (whistle-blowing) as a last resort.
- Try to follow through and reform the wrongdoer if possible.
- Reform the processes, structures, and culture as needed.

Of course, not all wrongdoing can be corrected. The bad activity we address may not be completely or permanently reformed. We may be labelled a trouble-maker or a whistle-blower, and our career could be negatively affected (although we may be viewed as heroes by others). We may, in other words, suffer for doing the right thing. Remember again what Paul wrote:

> Whatever your task, put yourselves into it, as done for the Lord and not for your masters, since you know that from the Lord you will receive the inheritance as your reward; you serve the Lord Christ. For the wrong-doer will be paid back for whatever wrong has been done, and there is no partiality. Masters, treat your slaves justly and fairly, for you know that you also have a Master in heaven. (Col. 3:23–4:1)

Perfect justice is rarely possible in this world. We always need to trust that God will take care of us, as well as the wrongdoers in our workplaces. But we simply cannot walk away from injustice or harm to others. Our call is to overcome evil with good.

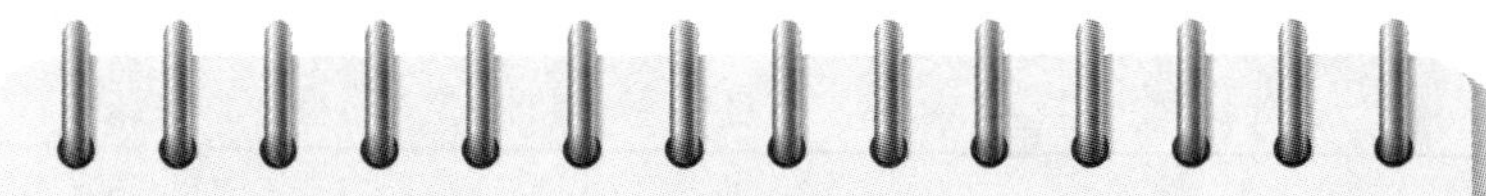

To Do

- ✓ Read up on some of the corporate scandals that brought down Enron, Arthur Andersen, and other organizations. What were the causes of the downfall of these companies and leaders?
- ✓ Interview a couple of veteran workers at your church or in your Christian network, and ask them how they responded to wrongdoing they saw during their work careers.

For Reflection & Discussion

1. Can you share a story of dealing with a difficult colleague or situation in the workplace? What did you do? What did you learn?

2. In your experience and opinion, what are the major examples of wrongdoing in your line of work?

3. In your various workplaces, were you given guidance on how to report or respond to wrongdoing on the job?

PART THREE

MOVING BEYOND OUR WORKPLACE

In this book, we have emphasized over and over that God values, commands, and models good work. We have lamented the lack of attention to workplace discipleship in our churches and parachurch groups. We have emphasized that our work is our ministry in service of God. It is a form of worship—the Hebrew word *avodah* means both work and worship! But the time has come to insist that the workplace is not the *only* place. First of all, we want to make time to bring back our workplace skills and experience to contribute to our church, neighborhood, and community. Second, we must cease our work every week (every day also) and get some rest, as well as worship God and play with friends and family.

11

Contribute

Bring Your Work Skills and Resources Back to Your Church and Community

We first looked at five essential steps to get ready for faithful workplace discipleship. Then we looked at a second group of five steps that describe our presence and activity in the workplace. Obviously, this is not about a strict time sequence of the ten steps. These preparation steps all mingle and interact together, and we return to them constantly, daily, as we carry out the agenda described in the second series of five. The second series of five is interdependent in itself: our model, or example, is intimately related to our capacity to share our faith or help overcome conflict and bad ethics. This is an ambitious but doable program with God's help, the support of our brothers and sisters, and a determined commitment on our part. It creates a shining light in the darkest work environment.

But now we look outside the workplace. Of course, there is more to life than working at our job. Although I have been writing as though we work six days a week, most of us work five days a week, Monday to Friday. For many of us, much of Saturday is also a work day, though for a different kind of work—maybe chores around the house or yard. We need to remember that our churches, neighborhoods, and communities also need us to step up and help out, usually as a volunteer. Did you ever hear the old analogy of church and a big football game? There are twenty-two players on the field desperately in need of rest, and sixty thousand people in the stands desperately needing exercise! Sometimes we need to get out of the stands and go down on the field to help our churches—not just watch the hired staff do it all. Same for our neighborhoods!

Let's think about four ways we workplace disciples might contribute to the important work outside of our normal workplace.

Contributing Money Made at Work

Just about every Christian knows the importance of tithing to God—of giving 10 percent of our income to charity, the chief of which is our home church. Just as one day out of seven is to be dedicated to God as a Sabbath day of rest (more on that in the next chapter), one-tenth—the first tenth—of our "crops and herds" and income are to be contributed to the Lord for his work. Tithing was part of the Israelite law, just like the Sabbath day. To be sure, God already owns 100 percent, not just 10 percent, of what we have and gain—just as he is also Lord of all seven days, not just the Sabbath.

The Old Testament required the people of God to give 10 percent of the production from their crops and herds to the Lord. Here is one of several accounts:

> Set apart a tithe of all the yield of your seed that is brought in yearly from the field. In the presence of the LORD your God, in the place that he will choose as a dwelling for his name. . . . But if, when the LORD your God has blessed you, the distance is so great that you are unable to transport it . . . then you may turn it into money. With the money secure in hand, go to the place that the LORD your God will choose. . . . As for the Levites resident in your towns, do not neglect them, because they have no allotment or inheritance with you. . . . [T]he resident aliens, the orphans,

> and the widows in your towns, may come and eat their fill so that the LORD your God may bless you in all the work that you undertake. (Deut. 14:22–29)

You can see how this practice is easily transferable from Israel to our churches where our gifts support the staff, our church activities, and our benevolences help those in need in the church and the community. The New Testament does not specifically direct Christians to give 10 percent as in the Old Testament, and some justify not doing so by saying we are now "free from the law." But are we set free to do less than the law? Or are we free to do more? Does the generosity of Jesus in giving his whole life for us not inspire us toward a generosity to others that goes way beyond a 10 percent minimum? We rarely, if ever, deny ourselves the luxuries we crave beyond our basic subsistence. Since, however, there is so much true need around us in the world, should we not give as much as we possibly can? Paul wrote to the Corinthians, "Each of you must give as you have made up your mind, not reluctantly or under compulsion, for God loves a cheerful giver" (2 Cor. 9:7).

The New Testament talks about the importance and blessings of giving, and it warns against selfish, faithless greed and hoarding. We should give generously as we are able. Sometimes that means giving more than 10 percent; sometimes that may mean giving less. It all depends on our ability and the needs of the church and world. We should diligently, prayerfully seek God's wisdom, and then give with pure motives and an attitude of worship to God and service to others. In both the Old and New Testaments, there are examples not just of "ordinary" giving but also offerings for special projects and needs. Think about Joseph of Arimathea donating the use of his tomb to the crucified Jesus, Jesus' teaching that if someone asks for our shirt we should give him our coat as well, Paul's reference to a special collection taken for the poor in Jerusalem, or how Paul offered to pay off any debts owed by the returning runaway Onesimus to owner Philemon.

Our work is usually the source of our ability to contribute money. Proverbs is full of references to God's approval of those who are generous to the poor—and his disapproval of the exploitative and tightfisted. In addition to giving a portion of our income, we need to think seriously about giving away a portion of our assets, perhaps especially upon our death. All of us should carefully consider giving at least 10 percent of our assets, and maybe a whole lot more, to charitable causes upon our death, such as our church. For most of us, our assets have appreciated in a huge way over our lifetime, not just because of our "sweat equity" but because of inflation, economic growth, and other factors. Shouldn't we think about giving a big chunk of this back to God and various charitable causes?

Two of my personal thoughts and practices have been, first, to try to give more to God and charity than to the government in taxes. Maybe it is just my personal preference, but I like the idea of giving more to God than to Uncle Sam (I am not an anti-tax person; I am happy to contribute to governmental programs and the common good—even though I don't like government waste and corruption any better than for-profit, or nonprofit, business waste and corruption).

Second, I have usually given about half my tithes and offerings to my home church and the other half to a range of worthy causes we care about. I have friends who think the whole tithe should go to their church. Since churches usually give a significant part of their budgets to outside causes, so our church donations participate in that support. But my wife and I also want to support the programs that help the poor in our town and in various places around the world. We want to support various nonprofits engaged in missions, education, job development, and the arts. Some of these causes would not be visible and adequately supported if it was left up to church budgets alone to support them. As I wrote above, my way is certainly not the only way. Each of us has to figure out before God how to be a generous and cheerful giver.

What do we do when we don't make much (or any) money? Maybe our work is unpaid, or maybe every cent is needed to keep food on the table and the lights on. According to surveys, poor people actually tend to be the most generous of all givers. Many economies have not been fully monetized. Old Testament folk usually gave 10 percent of their crops, herds, or manufactures. In our present-day context, if someone is cash-strapped, it is completely legitimate for their "tithing" to be in the form of labor or materials donated. When my wife and kids and I were living on $375 per month and our rent was $235 per month (during graduate school), we still donated a few shekels each month. But even more, we donated time at a preschool and entertained folk with simple fare at our table or at picnics. I also donated hours of teaching to my church (that hasn't changed!).

Contributing Money

- Donate at least 10 percent of your *gross* income to church (and other charities) is a great product of your paid work.
- If monetary income is absent, or nearly so, think about "in kind" contributions of labor or materials.
- Be generous, be faithful, be cheerful when you give.

Contributing Skills and Knowledge Acquired at Work

Beyond money, a second way workplace disciples contribute to church and community is with our work skills and knowledge. Most of this kind of contribution will be (and should be) volunteer work. In my opinion, it is sometimes appropriate for the church (or a local nonprofit) to provide some financial compensation to its workplace people for services rendered (i.e., outside of the normal pastoral job descriptions for which we usually pay salaries). "Starving artists" in music and in other artistic arenas often really suffer financially, and I think the church should help out—even if they are paid at a discounted rate. The same could go for technological support, childcare services, and other functions. If the workplace service providers are in need of income, I don't think we should fail to give it.

For most of us, if we have adequate outside income, our contribution of workplace skills should be freely given within reasonable time constraints. A trained bookkeeper or accountant can help the church (or local nonprofit) with some pro bono service. Carpenters, painters, electricians, and landscapers can donate some of their services to church and community. Tech-savvy people can help us set up, maintain, and operate our websites and sound systems. Chefs and restaurant workers can bring quality food to our events. Human resources people can help us with our personnel files, recruiting and hiring, and team-building systems and processes. Pastors rarely, if ever, study these kinds of things before or during seminary or have natural gifts in these areas. Contributing our expertise can therefore be a huge gift. Pastors aren't usually trained in how to write job descriptions, run meetings, or create and manage budgets and financial transactions. While we don't want to simply transfer secular business management techniques from marketplace to church, we certainly want to learn from best management practices and adopt sanctified versions of them.

Historically—and in New Testament practice—health care was inextricably linked to the proclamation of the gospel of the kingdom. While we should pray for our private as well as public/governmental health-care programs to succeed in helping and healing the sick, our churches need to recover their mission in this arena. Health screening and information, dental, eye, and basic physical exams, diet, exercise and nutrition counseling and support, and even some primary care, could be given through church-based programs led by volunteer nurses, doctors, and other medical professionals in our fellowship.

People often cannot afford basic legal advice and help on any number of issues. Some Christian lawyers, however, are reticent to offer pro bono consulting at church. This is sad when they could be of great help in providing even basic legal information and counsel to those who need their expertise but cannot afford them. Perhaps even more frustrating for people today is grappling with information technology options, breakdowns, and vulnerabilities. This is another huge opportunity for our workplace techies to offer some pro bono courses and consulting.

Many public and private schools today no longer offer music, art, cooking, or basic shop courses. Our churches could step into this void and soon become community leaders. Sliding scale fees could make this kind of education available in our church and community. We might also offer some language courses or sports activities, which are also disappearing from our communities.

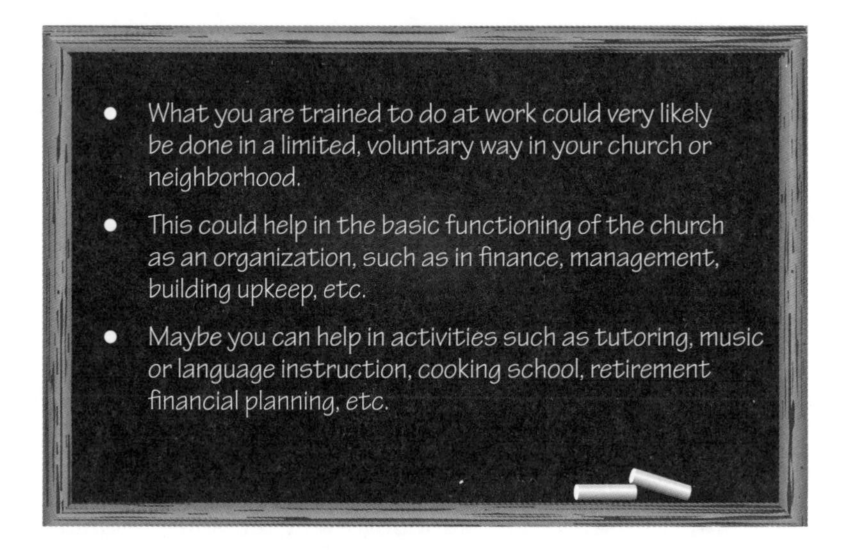

Coaching and Encouraging Workplace Disciples and Neighbors

A third avenue of contribution is to coach, encourage, or mentor other workplace disciples through the twelve steps discussed in this book. Coming alongside other workplace disciples in our church and community can be most helpful. We could reach out to younger folk while they are in school or at their start of their careers. Maybe there are some mid-career folk who could use a prayer and support mentor or partner. Or maybe we can reach out to late career or "re-tired" folk.

Maybe the neediest population of workers in our church and community are those who can't find good work. They may have no job and been searching for months or years. They may be trapped in a low-wage, abusive, dead-end job. Their needs may be financial survival or even homelessness. This is a desperate time. Their self-respect and self-image may be totally destroyed by their lack of a decent job. I want to urge us workplace disciples to watch for people in this difficult situation. Come alongside with a listening ear, an encouraging word, and some concrete help.

Much of my life's work has been to encourage Christian workers to integrate their faith and values with their work. It didn't take me long, however, to realize that there was a significant group of people who could say, "David, I'd like to do that. I have lots of faith—but no work to take it to!" This is so important: We are here to love, appreciate, value, and serve the whole body of Christ, not just its fully, happily employed members, not just its executives and professionals. There are people in our church and community who badly want to work but don't know how to find or create a job, while there are others in our church and community who know how to create or find jobs. Let's work together on this challenge. Let's pray that the economy will expand and create more jobs; let's hope that government jobs programs will also succeed. But neither government nor business by themselves will ever be able to get the whole job done (it's the same with health care and education). We need the church to be a true third force. That's what I'm talking about.

One approach is to help those without work to upgrade their résumé preparation and job search and application skills. Not far from where I live, a big Presbyterian church created a monthly job search fair with not only job search and application training but also job opening information. This program lasted for a decade and became a go-to resource for people all over the region. Wouldn't it be wonderful if many churches took on this task in their locales?

Helping Those without Work to Find or Create It

Maybe we could even provide some entrepreneurship training. For three years in inner-city Boston, Pastor Larry Ward and I co-led an annual spring training course we called "Entrepreneurship in Church and Community."[1] Our forty-five students (fifteen each year) succeeded in launching forty small businesses (the other five were quickly abandoned because they ran into insurmountable legal permit or financial obstacles just out of the gate). First, each year we recruited fifteen pastors or lay leaders to join our program as entrepreneurship coaches. Their first assignment was to find a high potential "wannabe" entrepreneur in their church or neighborhood. We provided them with application forms and some criteria to help make good candidate evaluations. The coach and entrepreneur together would then attend our Saturday morning course for the next ten weeks. Each week my co-teacher and I started with a biblical lesson related to that week's topic. Then we (sometimes with guest speakers) taught them skills, such as how to identify the best business to launch based on their skills and on market needs (product, location, name, etc.), how to create a business start-up plan, how to set up a business bank account and financial system, how to do inexpensive sales and marketing, how to create a website, build a database and network, and use basic information technology, how to deal with HR and personnel issues, how to deal with city government, legal, and permit requirements . . . all the basics of starting a small business.

Each Saturday (and a couple hours in between), our entrepreneurs sat with their coaches and worked on (and prayed about) these matters. When their business start-up plan and financial/banking framework were in place and ap-

1. Larry Ward was a successful midcareer urban pastor who I discovered had been doing entrepreneurship training with inner-city youth for a few years, getting them inspired about business instead of gangs! We quickly became a teaching team.

proved, we deposited a $500 start-up grant (from a foundation grant we received) into their business account. On our final Saturday, we asked each entrepreneur (not their coach) to make a ten-minute launch presentation, describing their new business and why we should be a customer or send customers their way. Most of our entrepreneurs had never spoken in public before, and most of them told us that no one had ever believed in them before like we did. They created some wonderful businesses, most of which are still operating several years later.

If we can encourage entrepreneurship on a larger scale, that would be great. But small-scale, even individual, enterprise is often the clearest, most direct path from poverty and unemployment to survival and self-worth. Here are some examples of the small businesses our people started:

- Julie Phillips developed “Jesignz Graphix,” a now-booming graphic design business focusing on website design, event promotion, and hip-hop culture.
- Victor Cubi turned his random, odd-job career into a more organized and profitable “Victor for Hire” landscaping and handyman business.
- Jennifer Dhanjee founded her vocal training school, “Lift Up Your Voice.”
- Pamela Cazeau created an event-planning business (weddings, parties, etc.), “Expressions of You.”
- Huegens Alexis turned his carpentry skills into “1sq Inch Custom Storage Solutions,” a custom cabinetry and remodeling business.
- Veronique Francois turned her Haitian cooking talents and gifts into “Anointed Catering Services,”

providing catered meals to church groups, small business events, and various celebrations.

- Izetta Jackson was able to move from a minimum-wage hotel worker to proprietor of her own "Mama Boney by Faith Cleaning Service" where she doubled her hourly pay and controls her working hours so she can get to church regularly.
- Eva Clark created "L.A.S.T." (Love All Skin Tones), a cosmetic business with a message about rejecting tanning and bleaching and learning to love the colors God made us in a healthy way.
- Christine Paige built her personal talent into "Bliss Salon," a thriving beauty and hair salon which now employs multiple coworkers.
- Neal Samudre used his IT background to create "JesusHacks," an online discipleship training resource.
- Shannon Lankford turned her hobby into "Real Life Photography."
- Sokhan Prak developed "Straight Ahead Silkscreen," a T-shirt operation in the middle of the gang neighborhood where he previously hung out.
- Devin Marks turned his event planning and speaker coaching into "myTEDtalk," now a thriving presentation training program.

The key to our success included our spiritual-biblical foundation. We were all on "a mission from God" to use our creativity to serve him and the people. We were constantly "fired up and ready to go" because of this. We had simple, clear teaching on the basic, common-sense tasks in creating and running a small business—with lots of concrete examples. Just as the leaders of the course were two teammates, each entrepreneur had a personal coach/mentor/teammate. Teams bring strength. We figured out the best business start-up option based on the individual's gifts and the neighborhood market's needs and wants. And clearly, it helped that we had a seed fund of $500 per entrepreneur to help them get it off the ground.

Many of these small business entrepreneurs and their coaches still gather together every couple of months for mutual support, learning, and encouragement. There is every reason to think that a group of neighboring churches—anywhere—could collaborate in an entrepreneurship program such as this.

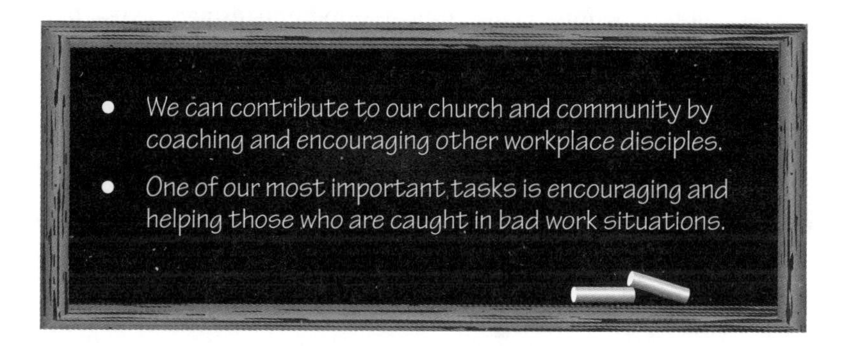

Awakening and Using Our Other Gifts

Finally, it must be said that all workplace disciples have gifts and abilities beyond what they use in their official careers and workplaces. Although you may be a carpenter professionally, you are able to contribute more than just carpentry. You might have gifts of singing and worship leadership, cooking or childcare, or adult or small group teaching. You might be a stay-at-home parent raising a family, but you are also a gifted writer and editor who could use those gifts at church or in the neighborhood. You might be a big business executive, but you are also gifted as a prayer ministry leader. I am a longtime teacher, writer, and organizer and use those skills in my church and neighborhood. But I also love to cook, I love to garden and pull weeds and make it all look beautiful, and I actually enjoy the physical grunt work of putting chairs and tables away after events. There are many gifts that we can consider spiritual gifts, as seen in the following list from the apostle Paul:

> For as in one body we have many members, and not all the members have the same function, so we, who are many, are one body in Christ, and individually we are members one of another. We have gifts that differ according to the grace given to us: prophecy, in proportion to faith; ministry, in ministering; the teacher, in teaching; the exhorter, in exhortation; the giver, in generosity; the leader, in diligence; the compassionate, in cheerfulness. (Rom. 12:4–8)

And here is a second list from Paul:

> Now there are varieties of gifts, but the same Spirit; and there are varieties of services, but the same Lord; and there are varieties of activities, but it is the same God who activates all of them in everyone. To each is given the manifestation of the Spirit for the common good. To one is given through the Spirit the utterance of wisdom, and to another the utterance of knowledge according to the same Spirit, to another faith by the same Spirit, to another gifts of healing by the one Spirit, to another the working of miracles, to another prophecy, to another the discernment of spirits, to another various kinds of tongues, to another the interpretation of tongues. All these are activated by one and the same Spirit, who allots to each one individually just as the Spirit chooses. (1 Cor. 12:4–11)

The fact that these lists of spiritual gifts are not all identical suggests that the boundaries are somewhat fluid. I think it is best to say with James that "every perfect gift is from above, coming down from the Father" (James 1:17). Some may seem more "spiritual" (such as prophecy or faith), while others are more mundane (such as giving or being diligent). We may have gifts and abilities for which there is no possible expression in our "regular" work, and our church or community may be a place to exercise them. The point is that the church and community are not just places for us to bring our obvious work skills and experiences. They could also be places where our other gifts can be developed and expressed.

- *Sometimes we are not able to exercise our God-given gifts and abilities in our workplaces.*
- *Our churches and communities may instead provide us with the opportunity to develop and exercise those gifts and abilities.*

While the main message of *Workplace Discipleship 101* is that Jesus wants to be Lord of our Monday-to-Saturday work lives, this does not diminish the value and importance of the work that needs to be done in our churches and communities, whether on Sunday or any other time. Our workplace efforts make it possible for us to contribute back to our church and community a generous portion of our money, and to apply our workplace skills and knowledge on a volunteer basis. We can also coach and mentor other workplace disciples, perhaps even help those trying to find or create good work for themselves.

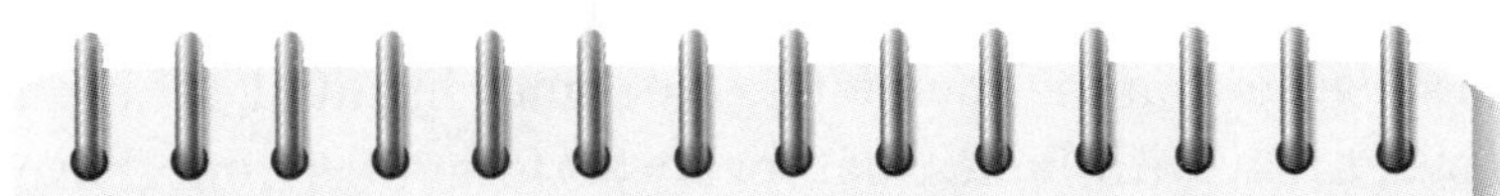

To Do

- ✓ Study what the Bible teaches about generosity, tithing, and giving in general.
- ✓ Ask your church and neighborhood leaders if they have any projects with which you may assist by volunteering some hours in your field of expertise.
- ✓ Do some research and maybe an exercise to help identify your spiritual gift(s).

For Reflection & Discussion

1. What has been your view of tithing and charitable giving? What do you think about the idea of a "graduated tithe," where people who make more should normally contribute a higher percentage than 10 percent?

2. Have you had any experiences of donating your workplace skills and expertise to a church? To a community or neighborhood?

3. Have you done work for church or community where you developed and used gifts and abilities that are not part of your "regular" profession, career, or work?

12

Rest

Say No to Workaholism and Idolatry—Rest, Worship, and Play

It is one of the great curses of human existence when we can't find good work. We were made for good work in the image and likeness of our creator, sustainer, and redeemer. An equal curse, ironically, is when we can't get free of work, whether imposed by the necessities of survival or by a vicious system like slavery or by our own compulsion, which we sometimes call "workaholism." Of course, it is not just work that results in our being "crazy busy," the title of a book by pastor Kevin DeYoung.[1] Our communication technologies and social media often keep us constantly connected and distracted. Our hobbies, our church, and our kids can keep us on the run. But our topic here is the critical importance of getting time off from work.

There was a time when predictions were made that technology would shorten our work hours. In fact, even today there are predictions that technologies such as automation, robotics, and artificial intelligence will lead to massive unemployment. Workers will be replaced by machines and idled. Some of this has happened. Companies have downsized, and

1. Kevin DeYoung, *Crazy Busy: A (Mercifully) Short Book about a (Really) Big Problem* (Wheaton, IL: Crossway, 2013).

people have lost their jobs. The quality of many of today's remaining or new jobs can be low, with people working harder than ever, with longer hours, and with often delayed "retirement" because of financial needs. The future of work is very much up in the air.

We must not minimize for a moment that many men and women are forced to work long, stressful hours, and that any call to enjoy some regular rest will seem like a distant dream to them. Nevertheless, to the extent that we can choose to take a break from our work, and to the extent that managers can encourage and enable rest for their workers, we need to value it and promote it. A few years ago, I participated in an interview of Cisco Systems executive vice president Gary Daichendt, whose Silicon Valley giant was widely known for its workforce putting in sixty or seventy hours per week. First of all, Daichendt told us that those long hours included a certain amount of goofing off and camaraderie in the hallways. More importantly, he said that when he found someone laboring at their computer long into the evening, he would often tell that person to go home and get some rest. He told them that they could complete whatever project they were working on at a higher quality and in half the time the next day after getting adequate rest. One of the other questions raised by this interview was: If our people are working these kinds of hours, who in our communities is left to work with our kids or on neighborhood or church projects? Excessive hours may result in lower-quality work, a lower quality of life and health for the worker—but also lower-quality experiences for our families, churches, neighborhoods, schools, and communities.

Reacting to the madness he saw and experienced in Silicon Valley, consultant Alex Soojung-Kim Pang decided to study the relationship between work and rest. He discovered that many (if not most) of the great scientists, writers, and political leaders of history did not work excessive, long, frantic hours but got regular and daily rest.[2] Many of them rose in the morning and worked hard for four hours or so. But then they enjoyed a good lunch, took a nap and then a long walk, before spending a pleasant evening of reading or relaxing with friends. While Britain's prime minister during the Second World War (unless bombs were actually dropping on London), Winston Churchill always took a shower followed by a nice nap in the afternoon in his silk pajamas! To these biographical examples, Pang adds an interesting report from science on the way our creativity is unleashed in our brains while we are sleeping.

Both Kevin DeYoung and Pang point to the beneficial effects on our work that come from rest, but they also argue that rest has its own intrinsic rewards. We should not take a purely utilitarian approach that values rest only for what it does for our work. The equation should be reversed or at least balanced: our work points toward and enables our rest. Our work is valuable in all kinds of ways, but so is our rest. There can be no faithful workplace discipleship unless we learn how to rest, worship, and play. This is the final step in workplace discipleship 101.

Biblical Rest: *God Makes Me Lie Down*

We need to pay attention to the sequence of thought in the most famous of all the psalms, Psalm 23:

> The LORD is my shepherd, I shall not want.
> He makes me lie down in green pastures;
> he leads me beside still waters;
> he restores my soul.

2. Alex Soojung-Kim Pang, *Rest: Why You Get More Done When You Work Less* (New York: Basic Books, 2016).

> He leads me in right paths
> for his name's sake. (vv. 1–3)

Before we pursue paths of doing the right thing (vocationally, politically, or otherwise), God makes us lie down, be still, and restores our souls. The active life on "right paths" grows out of the "green pasture" and "still waters" of the contemplative life. The same pattern is seen in the Beatitudes: first, we embrace our weakness (poverty of spirit), mourn it, and let go of fretting and control (meekness). Only then are we ready to hunger and thirst for righteousness and justice (Matt. 5:3–6).

Going back to the beginning, remember the story of Creation:

> Thus the heavens and the earth were finished, and all their multitude. And on the seventh day God finished the work that he had done, and he rested on the seventh day from all the work that he had done. So God blessed the seventh day and hallowed it, because on it God rested from all the work that he had done in creation. (Gen. 2:1–3)

Already in the story of Creation, we should note the description of each day: the evening and the morning were the first day. The Jewish day begins in the evening, the time of rest and reflection—not in the morning as we begin our work. By itself, this teaches us something about rest and work and our priorities. While there is nothing in that Creation story yet about a command to take a day off, we see that God takes a day off and rests from his work. God blesses and hallows (makes holy, sets apart) the seventh day. As we have already stressed, men and women are made in the image and likeness of God. It is in our DNA, therefore, both to creatively work six days and blessedly rest on a seventh.

Later on, the Decalogue (the Ten Commandments) makes it official. It is now a command, not just a suggestion:

> Remember the sabbath day, and keep it holy. Six days you shall labor and do all your work. But the seventh day is a sabbath to the LORD your God; you shall not do any work—you, your son or your daughter, your male or female slave, your livestock, or the alien resident in your towns. For in six days the LORD made heaven and earth, the sea, and all that is in them, but rested the seventh day; therefore the LORD blessed the sabbath day and consecrated it. (Exod. 20:8–11)

The second giving of the Decalogue repeats the first but modifies the rationale:

> Observe the sabbath day and keep it holy, as the LORD your God commanded you. Six days you shall labor and do all your work. But the seventh day is a sabbath to the LORD your God; you shall not do any work—you, or your son or your daughter, or your male or female slave, or your ox or your donkey, or any of your livestock, or the resident alien in your towns, so that your male and female slave may rest as well as you. Remember that you were a slave in the land of Egypt, and the LORD your God brought you out from there with a mighty hand and an outstretched arm; therefore the LORD your God commanded you to keep the sabbath day. (Deut. 5:12–15)

In the first case we are commanded to "remember," and in the second to "observe." In the first case in Exodus, the rationale is the importance of ceasing even from good, creative work. In the second case in Deuteronomy, the rationale is to get a break from bad, slave-like work. This is a beautiful illustration of the "dialectic" of both Scripture and life experience. Our work is sometimes a joyful exercise in creativity, and other times more like painful toil. Often it has elements of both at the same time. The message is to be intentional about it (remember and observe). Whether our work feels like creativity in the garden—or slavery under a hard taskmaster—we must get free for a day of rest. And it isn't just about us. It is about our family members, our workers, any strangers we meet, and even our animals. It is about our rest, but it is also about God, "a sabbath to the LORD your God."

In addition to the weekly Sabbath, there were several *annual* festival breaks (celebrating the Passover, the Day of Atonement, the Feast of Tabernacles, etc.) and even the *passage of the years* had a rhythm of work and rest: "Six years you shall sow your field, and six years you shall prune your vineyard, and gather in their yield; but in the seventh year there shall be a Sabbath of complete rest for the land, a Sabbath for the LORD" (Lev. 25:3–4). And there was a *rhythm of the decades*: "You shall hallow the fiftieth year and you shall proclaim liberty throughout the land to all its inhabitants. It shall be a jubilee for you. . . . [Y]ou shall not sow, or reap the aftergrowth, or harvest the unpruned vines. For it is a jubilee; it shall be holy to you" (Lev. 25:10–12).

In this book, we have been hammering away about the value and importance of our workplace discipleship. God works and so do we. The fourth command is therefore emphatic: "Six days you shall labor and do all your work." But we must not become workaholics who are obsessed or addicted or enslaved to our work. We must take a break.

We need to be careful, however, to observe the spirit and intent of the Sabbath and not get caught up in legalism. Jesus defended his hungry disciples for gathering food to eat when they were hungry on a Sabbath day. And amid howls of protest from the Pharisees, he defended his own actions of healing a man with a withered hand and later a crippled woman on the Sabbath (Luke 13:10–17). Bottom line from Jesus: "The sabbath was made for humankind, and not humankind for the sabbath; so the Son of Man is lord even of the Sabbath" (Mark 2:27–28). This is about promoting life and about living under God's leadership. Paul later had to correct some Sabbath legalists: "Some judge one day to be better than another, while others judge all days to be alike. Let all be fully convinced in their own minds. Those who observe the day, observe it in honor of the Lord" (Rom. 14:5–6).

My friend, Pastor Earl Palmer, made a wise observation many years ago. He pointed out that God tells us to work on our weekly schedule first: to schedule Sabbath rest each week, whether it is all day Sunday or parts of two or three days. Trying to manage our life by controlling our hours and minutes day-to-day is in practice too narrow as a foundational framework. Managing our months or seasons or year is important but too elongated. We need to focus first on scheduling our week: block out some real, quality Sabbath—and then work inward to our daily schedule and outward to our months, seasons, years, and decade. Wise counsel, and totally in harmony with what God prescribes!

- A weekly Sabbath rest follows God's own model in creation; we are made in God's image.
- A weekly Sabbath is God's commandment, not just a suggestion.
- The Sabbath is "holy"—pure, different, not ordinary time.
- The Sabbath is not just for God and us, but for everyone and everything touched by our life.
- The weekly break should be accompanied by longer breaks.

A Day of Ceasing and Resisting

Marva Dawn's outstanding book *Keeping the Sabbath Wholly*, emphasizes that the Sabbath is first about *ceasing*—stopping from our work, from productivity and accomplishment.[3] It is about *trusting* that God will take care of the world and our work while we let go for a time. Of course, we need to plan our work responsibilities with an upcoming Sabbath rest in mind and not leave things to disintegrate in our absence. This is partly what it means to *remember* the Sabbath: not just recall past Sabbaths, but remember to plan ahead for the time off. But no matter how much we plan ahead, we can never control all things. We must trust others and, above all, trust God with our work as we unplug and step away. This means not just ceasing from our work but also ceasing from anxiety, worry, and tension. While Sabbath rest is physical, Dawn writes, it is also spiritual, emotional, intellectual, and social.

Alex Pang, writing from a secular perspective, captures the necessity of *choosing* to take time off from work:

> Rest is not something that the world gives us. It's never been a gift. It's never been something you do when you've finished everything else. If you want rest, you have to take it. You have to resist the lure of busyness, make time for rest, take it seriously, and protect it from a world that is intent on stealing it.[4]

Walter Brueggemann's brilliant little book *Sabbath as Resistance* argues that the fourth commandment is about resisting our culture of anxiety, coercion, multitasking, commodification, materialism, and workaholism. The Sabbath command is the central hinge on which the Decalogue turns, linking our relationships to God and to others. It ensures

---

3. Marva Dawn, *Keeping the Sabbath Wholly: Ceasing, Resting, Embracing, Feasting* (Grand Rapids: Eerdmans, 1989).

4. Pang, *Rest*, 10.

that God is not replaced by work ("no other gods before me," the first commandment) and it resists the covetousness temptation which drives much of our work (the tenth commandment).[5]

Abraham John Heschel's classic *The Sabbath* is a deep, beautifully written, classic meditation on the Sabbath.[6] In this book, Heschel explains that the primary accent in the Hebrew Bible is on *time* rather than *space*.

> Technical civilization is man's conquest of space. It is a triumph frequently achieved by sacrificing an essential ingredient of existence, namely time.
>
> The emphasis on time is a predominant feature of prophetic thinking. "The day of the Lord" is more important to the prophets than "the house of the Lord." . . . There is no mention of a sacred place in the Ten Commandments.
>
> Time is man's greatest challenge. . . . Space is exposed to our will; we may shape and change the things in space as we please. Time, however, is beyond our reach, beyond our power. It is both near and far, intrinsic to all experience and transcending all experience. It belongs exclusively to God.

Heschel writes that "the Sabbath is not for the sake of the weekdays; the weekdays are for the sake of Sabbath. It is not an interlude but the climax of living." It is not an escape but a companion of the weekdays: "It needs the companionship of all other days. All days of the week must be spiritually consistent with the Day of Days."[7] The days of the week are partly a

---

5. Walter Brueggemann, *Sabbath as Resistance: Saying No to the Culture of Now* (Louisville, KY: Westminster John Knox, 2014).

6. Abraham John Heschel, *The Sabbath* (New York: Farrar, Straus & Giroux, 1951). Quotations from 3, 79, and 99.

7. Heschel, *The Sabbath*, 14, 89.

remembrance of the past Sabbath and partly an anticipation of the coming Sabbath.

There have been times in history that civil as well as religious laws prohibited work, commerce, or some other activities on the Sabbath (often observed on Sundays in predominantly Christian cultures). Even without legal strictures, some businesses have chosen to be closed on Sundays. Sometimes church traditions and disciplines virtually enforced the Sabbath (or the "Lord's Day," as Sunday was always called in the church of my youth). But such laws and traditions have largely disappeared in today's world. If we are to recover a Sabbath day in our lives, we almost certainly need to actively choose to do so. It will take an intentional act of resistance to our culture. But even in the past when there were laws or traditions mandating a Sabbath day, it still took a choice to experience its intended reality.

Embracing a Day of Holy Delight

The reality of the Sabbath is that it is a *holy* day. Abraham Heschel points out that the first time anything is declared to be holy (Hebrew, *qadosh*), it is applied to time: "God blessed the seventh day and hallowed it" (Gen. 2:3). It was not a holy mountain or temple but a holy day.

> When history began, there was only one holiness in the world, holiness in time. When at Sinai the word of God was about to be voiced, a holiness in man was proclaimed: "Thou shalt be unto me a holy people." It was only after the people had succumbed to the temptation of worshipping a thing, a golden calf, that the erection of a Tabernacle, of holiness in *space* was commanded. The sanctity of time came first, the sanctity of man came second, and the sanctity of space came last.[8]

8. Heschel, *The Sabbath*, 9–10.

Holiness meant "purity" or "separation from sin." But it also and equally meant "set apart" or "different." The Sabbath was a day to be different, other than the ordinary, free from the ordinary. Heschel writes that even the word *rest* (Hebrew, *menuha*) means much more than withdrawal from labor and exertion, more than freedom from toil, strain, or activity of any kind. "*Menuha* is not a negative concept but something real and intrinsically positive. . . . What was created on the seventh day? *Tranquility, serenity, peace* and *repose*."[9]

The first and primary purpose of the holy day is to worship God. Josef Pieper's classic *Leisure: The Basis of Culture* emphasizes this point at great length.

> The soul of leisure, it can be said, lies in "celebration." . . . But if celebration is the core of leisure, then leisure can only be made possible and justifiable on the same basis as the celebration of a festival. *That basis is divine worship.*
>
> The meaning of celebration, we have said, is man's affirmation of the universe and his experiencing the world in an aspect other than its everyday one. Now we cannot conceive of a more intense affirmation of the world than "praise of God," praise of the Creator of this very world.[10]

Every day, of course, not just one day each week, we workplace disciples need to make time for prayer and praise of God. But the core of our special Sabbath day needs to be worship and celebration of God. It is a time to gather together with the church. The "Holiness Code" in Leviticus reminds us that part of its purpose is a "holy convocation"—a time to

9. Heschel, *The Sabbath*, 22–23.

10. Josef Pieper, *Leisure: The Basis of Culture* (New York: Pantheon, 1952), 56.

come together (Lev. 23:1–3). Our work lives involve some distance from both God and our brothers and sisters. Certainly, God is alongside and within us as we work—and our brothers and sisters are with us in prayer, and our lives may remain in contact even if they're not immediately by our side. But the holy day is when we come together more visibly and consciously, leaving distractions behind as much as possible, to focus on God together, to celebrate and worship together.

In our worship together, we can raise our voices in song and prayer, unimpeded by the noise and the protocols of our workplace. We can focus on listening to God's word as it is read and preached. We can share in the bread and the wine. We can kneel in prayer and lift our hands in praise. We can eat and drink in love feasts together, setting aside our work worries and our portable phones. Focusing on God reminds us of our purpose and mission in the world, including in our workplace. We receive exhortation and comfort, challenge and forgiveness.

> I was glad when they said to me,
> "Let us go to the house of the LORD!" (Ps. 122:1)

Marva Dawn describes the Sabbath as a time not just of ceasing but also of embracing and feasting. She writes about embracing time instead of space (Heschel's great theme), embracing giving instead of requiring, embracing community and the world as well, embracing *shalom*—peace and flourishing. She encourages feasting with music, beauty, food, and festival.

No author has done a better job of inspiring Sabbath celebration than Dan Allender in his *Sabbath*.[11] God intends the

11. Dan B. Allender, *Sabbath*, The Ancient Practices Series (Nashville: Thomas Nelson, 2009).

Sabbath to be the best day of our week, a day of delight and of beauty, an experience of the joy and love of God.

> Delight doesn't require a journey thousands of miles away to taste the presence of God, but it does require a separation from the mundane, an intentional choice to enter joy and follow God as he celebrates the glory of his creation and his faithfulness to keep his covenant to redeem the captives. . . . The Sabbath is a day of delight for humankind, animals, and the earth; it is not merely a pious day . . . [but] a feast day that remembers our leisure in Eden and anticipates our play in the new heavens and earth with family, friends, and strangers for the glory of God.[12]

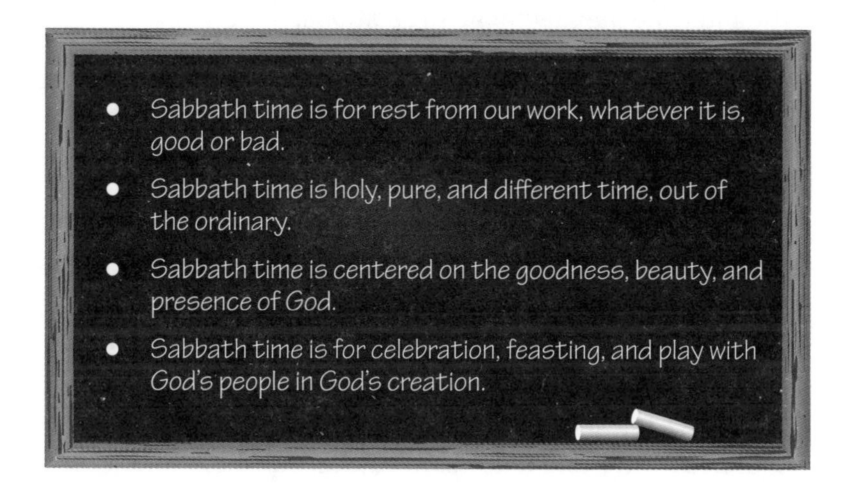

Proactive, Creative Scheduling

By now, I hope that we are convinced and inspired to aim for quality (and quantity) time away from our work. When I say "work," I don't just mean our employment but also our volunteer work commitments and even our household chores.

---

12. Allender, *Sabbath*, 4–5.

Cooking, entertaining, gardening, and house painting could be fun for us; but to the extent these kinds of things become toilsome, we need a break from them also. We need time for sufficient physical exercise and activity, time to talk and hang out with our family and friends, time to attend to personal needs such as the dentist, clothing store, or hair salon. We need time to answer emails, phone calls, and texts, and visit friends and family, especially when they may be struggling. Since some (or maybe most) of these activities can seem more like work than play, rest, or Sabbath, we need to find some Sabbath time from them as well.

From my experience, for what it's worth, here are six Sabbath and time management suggestions:

1. Make a conscious commitment to a weekly time of corporate worship and fellowship. That means joining a local church and participating every week in its gathered worship, where we go to praise the Lord, hear the word of God, celebrate the Lord's Supper, and cultivate and enjoy fellowship with fellow church members. No church (or pastor or preacher or music and worship leader or congregation) is anywhere near perfect, so this commitment can have its share of disappointment and pain. We may need to visit a few nearby churches to find one where the worship, learning, and fellowship sustain our soul—and where we can fruitfully contribute our own gifts and service to the congregation. But let's avoid church-hopping, which condemns us to a superficial and self-centered experience. Let's accept our church with its imperfections—just as God accepts us even with our imperfections!

2. If possible, dedicate not just Sunday worship hours but the whole day to being holy and different. There is no formula that fits everyone. Earl Palmer used to say that if our workweek is pretty sedentary, our Sabbath could or

should include some movement and activity—while if our workweek is physical and exhausting, our Sabbath could or should be more relaxed and physically subdued. I think it is important to try to get some family or community feasting into our Sabbaths. Inviting people to our table in our homes is becoming a lost art but it is such a wonderful gift to our guests and ourselves. Cater in a pizza or other food—or potluck it—or meet at a restaurant—or prepare a feast (maybe mostly a day ahead) that is relatively easy to bring to your table. While I try (with mixed results) to be consistently restrained in my eating and drinking habits during the week, I love to bring richer fare and better beverages to our table for our Sunday midday feasts.

Singing together, playing games, going for a walk or hike together, or just sitting around and sharing our life stories—these are wonderful ways to pass the Sabbath day. Going on an excursion can be a great thing. Find ways to delight in God and his creation and in people. Take a day off from the phone and computer—or at least make yourself wait until Sunday evening to check in. Protect as much of the whole day as a Sabbath as you can.

Reality-check: We may have a job that requires us to attend to our work for some hours on Sunday. We might have to closet ourselves Sunday evening to prepare for Monday morning work. Or we might be on the church staff, so our Sunday is to a significant extent a kind of work day and we are exhausted by it. I have been in these situations much of my career. For long stretches, I had to look at Sunday as a sort of half-Sabbath, but I was able to set aside Monday until about 1:00 or 2:00 p.m. as the other half of my weekly Sabbath. Jesus and Paul teach us not to be "Sabbath legalists" but to pursue the principle of a holy day each week. Early Christian church Sunday Sabbath observance got no help from the Roman Empire's pagan calendar. Many early Christians were domestic slaves or servants and had to have their gathered worship early in the morning before their (Sunday) work responsibilities began. Many Christians in non-Christian cultures still get no help from political or economic calendars in finding Sabbath. We are far from alone in having to be both creative and dedicated in finding Sabbath time each week.

3. On our calendars (you do maintain a weekly, monthly, and annual calendar, don't you?) work ahead and ink in church and other Sabbath day plans (and also a weekly date with your spouse, parent, child, best friend, or that workplace discipleship posse we talked about earlier). If I had waited and only spontaneously attempted to have quality time with my wife or kids over the decades, we would have been constantly foiled and frustrated. Sometimes we had to reschedule because of sudden emergencies, but most of the time I was able to plan work and meetings around the inked-in wife or kid time already in my schedule. Proactive is the way to do it. Same thing with my small support/posse group. Ink these commitments into the calendar and only change if forced.

4. Do the same kind of thing with longer term, annual planning. The Israelites celebrated several festivals during the year, including Passover to celebrate the liberation from Egypt and the fall Feast of Tabernacles where they all went out camping in makeshift huts to recall the journey through the wilderness. We all need to break up our year with some vacations and festivals—not just for Christmas, Easter, and Thanksgiving, though those are very important. Get them on the calendar and start making advance plans. Participate in any retreats your church organizes.

5. Think and dream about the rhythm of the years and decades. As a professor, I was able to take three sabbatical

study breaks during my forty-year career (not quite every seventh year as you can see!). The origin of the sabbatical year idea was, of course, ancient Israel. There is real value in arranging a year that is very different every seventh or tenth year or so. It is often a time of not just rest but special learning and reflection. I took my family and lived in Sweden, France, and central Pennsylvania during those years away from my ordinary work. They were not vacations but radical changes of workstyle, location, context, and sometimes even language and culture. I became just a writer and knocked out a book each sabbatical year. I was usually on half-salary, so we typically had to fund these sabbaticals by renting out our house and then living in less expensive, sometimes tight quarters during our time away. Some version of sabbatical leave is often possible even in many other professions and job specialties, but it will take creativity and maybe some sacrifice to make it happen, even if it is only a three-month sabbatical once a decade or so.

The sabbatical year concept is often appropriate in other ways. If you have been serving on a board of directors it could be good to take a year off every few years. If you are really maxed out in commitments to church or community activities and leadership, it could be very important and good for you (and them!) if you take a year off before resuming these busy tasks.

6. Finally, we need to come back to the daily schedule. Let me urge everyone to be dedicated to three one-hour habits every day. It is pretty critical to your physical (and mental) health to get *an hour of exercise* at least six days each week. It is, if anything, even more critical to spend *an hour a day with your family*, probably over a meal with all phones and the television turned off. And the most important thing is to spend *an hour with God*. Read and underline

your way through the whole Bible over time. Pray your way through your praises and thanksgivings, your confessions, and your requests for God's help in your work, your family, your church, and the world.

We have a lot of evidence and testimony from the Bible, from history and biography, and even from brain science and psychology that regular daily and weekly rest is a crucial part of life and companion to our work. We have multitudes of "how to" books on managing our time and getting our schedule under control. But we are involved in a real dog fight to actually succeed here in our frantic, workaholic, technological culture. We have to be pit-bull dedicated, and we need to find creative ways to move forward. We need God's help and the support of our posse and closest family and friends. And we need to avoid guilt-tripping ourselves or giving up when we fail or get knocked out of our preferred rhythm.

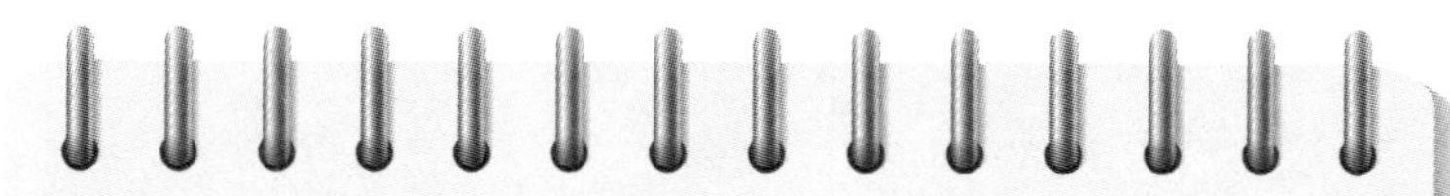

To Do

- ✓ Carefully study your calendar, short term and longer term, and make an ambitious but realistic plan and commitment to times of rest, worship, and play.
- ✓ Make sure you have a Bible you can study and write in each day—maybe one with study notes to help explain things.
- ✓ Think about getting a journal to use each day to jot down your best discoveries from the Bible and your list of people and things to pray for.

For Reflection & Discussion

1. What has been your thinking and your experience with trying to have a special "Sabbath" day each week?

2. How do you make daily time for physical exercise, family relationships, and quiet time with God? What has worked or not worked for you?

Conclusion

Ever since the curse of sin descended on the planet, the work of bearing and rearing children has been accompanied by great pain, and the work of tilling and harvesting the fields has been via the sweat of our faces and the exhaustion of our bodies in the midst of thorns and thistles. Even in the best of circumstances and health, our work has times of labor, difficulty, disappointment, and even defeat.

Despite all the advances of technology and so much progress against poverty, exclusion, and oppression, we find ourselves at the start of a new "Roaring Twenties." But not as "the years between 1920 and 1930, when society was returning to normal after the First World War and the general mood was positive."[1] As this book is going to press about halfway through 2020, we find instead that we are in a time of challenge and anguish. The global COVID-19 pandemic is not just a massive, unexpected threat to health and life; it also has disrupted human relationships (social distancing required!), businesses, workplaces, and economies. There is currently record unemployment, politically forced followed by economically forced closing of businesses, and then cascading impacts on government budgets and services. Who could have imagined? How will we ever recover?

---

1. From https://dictionary.cambridge.org/us/dictionary/english/roaring-twenties.

And if the health and economic crises owed to COVID-19 were not enough, the roof of society has been blown off by the brutal killing by policemen of a black man under arrest. Millions of citizens went to the streets in protest, not just of the death of George Floyd but also of a shameful, lengthening list of similar victims of racist violence. Unfortunately, the peacefully demonstrating millions were joined by many hundreds of anarchists and vandals who inflicted billions of dollars of further damage on our workplaces, large and small. How will we ever recover?

While these massive crises would be challenges in the best of times, it turns out that our climate has been also changing in ways that have brought increased extreme and severe weather—hurricanes, floods, wild fires, earthquakes . . . and in their wake, famine, population dislocation, and disease. As if that were not enough, the global political/diplomatic climate has itself been rocked by authoritarian, nationalistic, militaristic leaders of many nations—undermining alliances and peaceful cooperation, and fanning the flames of partisanship within and between nations. How will we ever recover?

When Jesus came on the scene two thousand or so years ago, the context at that time was also pretty grim. So, what did Jesus do? He called individuals into a small band of followers (disciples!) who would seek to live out the kingdom of God every day of the week. It was often rough, and there was pain and suffering along with joy and celebration. But they kept at it, loved one another as he said to do, welcomed strangers into their community, reached out to help others, and over the next couple of centuries grew to impact the whole of the Roman Empire.

The challenges we face often seem overwhelming. But how does change occur? How was Jim Crow segregation overcome? Not by the initiatives of the powerful in high political positions, but by the courageous acts and prayers of faithful Christians in small black churches in the South. How did hip-hop music and fashion come to such influence? From creative kids on street corners in the inner city—not from big players in the recording industry. Where did our coffee revolution come from? Not from the corporate headquarters of Hills Brothers or Folgers, but from little Peet's in Berkeley and then Starbucks in Seattle. Where did Hewlett-Packard come from? Not from IBM or General Electric headquarters, but a garage in Palo Alto.

Hear what I'm saying? In the face of massive problems, there are always opportunities. Start now; start where we are. By ourselves, we can't reform or resuscitate old businesses, much less the whole economy, today or maybe ever. What we can do, though, is work however and wherever we are. We can commit to following Jesus, not just in our Sunday worship and family life, but also in our work, whatever and wherever it may be. We can pray every day, and ask God for help, insight, strength, and success. We can read God's word and say, "Teach me! Teach me, Lord, how to follow you and work like you." We can find a couple of kindred spirits and form a reliable, enjoyable "posse" to help one another along the way. We can create a small business around our skill and the community's needs—or we can find employment with somebody else's business. Whatever we do, wherever we work, we can try to bring in some divine creativity, productivity, wisdom, righteousness, and redemption. We can do this! We can help calm some tensions and help people get along, as well as get right in their behavior.

I don't know about everybody else, but I am never going to be content with just being a Sunday *churchplace Christian*. I want the whole adventure. And that means I am a *workplace disciple*!

THE WORKPLACE DISCIPLESHIP PLEDGE

As God gives me strength and opportunity, and to the best of my ability, I pledge:

To pray about my work and seek God's guidance for it in Scripture.

To be in an accountability and support partnership with other Christians.

To be a good example of lifelong learning, diligence, integrity, and excellence.

To strive to work in alignment with the creator, sustainer, and redeemer.

To share my faith and the work insights of Scripture when appropriate.

To be a peacemaker and overcomer when work gets tough.

To share my workplace gifts in church and community.

And to guard some time for rest, worship, and play.

____

Signature   Date

"Whatever you do, in word or deed, do everything in the name of the Lord Jesus, giving thanks to God the Father through him. . . . Whatever your task, put yourselves into it, as done for the Lord and not for your masters. . . . [Y]ou serve the Lord Christ."

(Colossians 3:17, 23)

Postscript for Pastors

Dorothy Sayers, the literary colleague of C. S. Lewis and the other Oxford Inklings, wrote one of the most powerful indictments of the church regarding workplace discipleship:

> In nothing has the Church so lost her hold on reality as in her failure to understand and respect the secular vocation. She has allowed work and religion to become separate departments, and is astonished to find that, as result, the secular work of the world is turned to purely selfish and destructive ends, and that the greater part of the world's intelligent workers have become irreligious, or at least, uninterested in religion. But is it astonishing? How can anyone remain interested in a religion which seems to have no concern with nine-tenths of his life? The Church's approach to an intelligent carpenter is usually confined to exhorting him not to be drunk and disorderly in his leisure hours, and to come to church on Sundays. What the Church should be telling him is this: that the very first demand that his religion makes upon him is that he should make good tables.[1]

It is a rare pastor these days who has any trouble seeing the biblical mandate—and the practical importance—of connecting with the day-to-day, in-the-trenches lives of one's congregants. It is right there in front of us in Scripture and in the life challenges of our people. But it is also rare to

1. Dorothy Sayers, "Why Work?," *Letters to a Diminished Church: Passionate Arguments for the Relevance of Christian Doctrine* (Nashville: Thomas Nelson, 2004).

find workplace churchgoers who can say much about how their church helps or supports them in the workplace. It just doesn't happen much. No surprise though: the seminaries haven't been teaching it, and the pastoral guild hasn't been given much to pass on to workplace disciples.

As the first occupant of the Mockler-Phillips Professorship of Workplace Theology and Business Ethics at Gordon-Conwell Theological Seminary from 2010 to 2016, I came to know the story of Colman Mockler, the legendary CEO of the Gillette Corporation. Mockler was the leading exemplar of "Level Five" leadership in Jim Collins's best-selling management book *Good to Great*.[2] Colman's widow, Joanna, told me that he sometimes remarked that he had been attending church weekly for decades but had never heard even one word from the pulpit affirming the value of the work he had been doing. Church leaders loved his career when it came time to raise the annual church budget or building fund! But his work per se? It did not seem important to either the pastor or his church. The Mockler endowment (matched by Tom Phillips, longtime CEO of Raytheon) sought to change pastoral education by funding an endowed chair in the heart of an influential seminary.

I was a bit bowled over (with surprise and delight) when I heard Kansas City pastor Tom Nelson share at a conference of pastors that just a few years earlier he had been moved to stand in front of his congregation and say (if I may paraphrase) something like this: "Friends, I need to confess a serious sin to you this morning as your pastor." Tom described the predictable shock and worry immediately on the faces of his people! He went on: "I have let you down and failed as your pastor to bring to you what the Bible teaches about your

---

2. Collins, *Good to Great*, 23–25.

work during the week." In his book *Work Matters*, Tom puts it this way:

> For way too long, I did not see work as an essential component of a broader, robust theology of Christian calling, nor did I see how the gospel transforms work. I failed to grasp that a primary stewardship of my pastoral work was to assist and equip others to better connect the professions of their Sunday faith with the practices of their Monday work. As a pastor, I regret that I have often given minority attention to what most of us do the majority of our time.[3]

Tom Nelson continues to serve as lead pastor of Christ Community Church in Kansas City and as president of the Made to Flourish network of churches and pastors committed to supporting workplace discipleship (www.madetoflourish.org).

Can you relate to what Colman Mockler and Tom Nelson described? It certainly matches up with my seventy-year church-attending experience. Church is about a lot of great things, but our work (and often our education) is not usually on the list, even though we spend half or more of our waking hours at work during our life. Almost everything is centered on church turf, but very little speaks to work turf. I finally found help with my workplace discipleship *outside* the church—among Christians, of course, but the "scattered church," not the gathered church. What can we do about this?

At the most extreme end of the spectrum of options, I am impressed by the sort of radical restructuring of church described by Britisher Neil Hudson in *Imagine Church: Releasing Whole-Life Disciples*, and of worship by his friends Sam and Sara Hargreaves in *Whole Life Worship: Empowering*

3. Tom Nelson, *Work Matters: Connecting Sunday Worship to Monday Work* (Wheaton, IL: Crossway, 2011), 15.

Disciples for the Frontline.[4] In his book, Hudson invites us to join in a movement of churches to become more "missional" and outward directed, mobilizing the whole congregation to think and act "missionally" wherever they live and work (on the front lines, which for most people is their workplace). In their book, the Hargreaveses unpack and rebuild the "imagine church's" approach to worship, including its songs, prayers, sermons, liturgies, and other aspects. They provide a multitude of samples and examples.

It would be wonderful for church leaders (elders, pastors, worship and music leaders) to devote some hours or even weeks of careful study and prayer to the inspiring and convincing arguments of these writers. While all church leaders will not necessarily resonate with what they propose for music and liturgy, their expansive, ambitious theology, mission, and vision for renewal is right on target.

On a more modest and immediately achievable level, I have for several years been urging pastors to take six fairly simple steps that will connect them in positive ways with their workplace disciples. (You can get around to radical change when you and your people are ready!) But right now, this week, you personally can start with these six steps. These are not time-consuming additions to your workload. Any pastor can do it. Believe me: your workplace folk will be transformed in their attitudes toward church and toward you—and toward their work itself. You will likely see tired church dropouts return when the buzz spreads about what is going on. Your studies and sermons will take on a fresh, new vitality as they connect to your people's real lives.

4. Neil Hudson, *Imagine Church: Releasing Whole-Life Disciples* (Nottingham, UK: Inter-Varsity Press, 2012); Sam and Sara Hargreaves, *Whole Life Worship: Empowering Disciples for the Frontline* (London: Inter-Varsity Press, 2017).

Step 1: Study, preach, and teach the workplace lessons and implications of the Scriptures as you encounter and understand them in the texts before you.

Why?

Two reasons: The Bible itself demands that we pay attention to its teaching about work. For example, Jesus had more to say about money, property, and wealth than about heaven and hell or many other topics that tend to occupy our attention. We must be faithful and pay attention. Second, our workplace disciples, and our workplaces and marketplaces themselves, are in desperate need of creative insight on ethics, management, decision-making, work/life balance, respectful work relations, dispute mediation, and a host of other topics. Are we prepared to share the insights that come from our biblical faith? This is how our people are equipped to be the salt of the earth and light of the world!

How?

As a pastor, you spend time reading and studying the Scriptures every week, if not every day. Your sermons and lessons each week draw on the insight of God's word. The most basic way to carry out this step is simply to ask, as you study Scripture, no matter what the text, no matter how you have thought of it in the past: What insight might God be giving us here about our workplace activities?

There are explicit lessons on money and work in many texts, but even with a text like Romans 12:2—"Do not be conformed to this world, but be transformed by the renewing of your minds, so that you may discern what is the will of God—what is good and acceptable and perfect"—your sermon could remind your listeners that we must not simply roll over and conform to our work environment; we need to try to figure out how *God* wants us to work! See what I'm saying? People will perk up when you make that application. Make notes and integrate these insights into your sermons and lessons. Explicitly challenge your audiences to think about how to apply God's word to their workplace lives. Ask God to help you. It doesn't need to be complicated. Let the biblical text speak to our workplace reality.

Step 2: *Read at least one article per month and one book per year specifically focused on workplace, marketplace, or economics topics.*

Why?

Pastors need to do this in order to better understand the context in which our people live and work every day. We ask them to read the Bible and good Christian literature. Let's also read some of the literature from our people's work worlds so we can better understand their challenges and opportunities. Share insights and questions from this reading with your people. They will be delighted to help you understand it.

How?

You can go online if you wish, but think about going to the nearest magazine vendor and buying a copy of the *Wall Street Journal, The Financial Times, The Economist, Wired*, or any number of other newspapers or magazines dealing with business and economics. Buy an issue that looks interesting, get some coffee or tea, and read an article or two. Once a month! If you are really serious about it, subscribe to one of these publications and read it or browse it regularly. Browse the business section of your newspaper every day.

And at least once a year, actually read a whole book on business and work. Read the history of a company . . . or an analysis of the recent financial disaster in the banking industry . . . or a CEO's memoir or management theories. Go to a big bookstore, look through the business and management section, and find something interesting. All the business newspapers and magazines mentioned earlier have book reviews and sometimes lists of business best-sellers that can help you decide. I think it is good to read some Christian reflections on business and economics, but pastors need to push outside of that and listen to the voices and stories of the workplace itself. And believe me, your workplace people will perk up when they find out you are reading material from their world.

Step 3: *Visit at least one of your congregation's workplace disciples per month in his or her workplace environment, asking about their work experiences, challenges, and opportunities—and offer them encouragement and prayer.*

Why?

This simple step can have truly revolutionary consequences for your church and for you as pastor. All too often, our parishioners must come to us, on our turf, to our office. If we show up at their workplace, it sends a powerful message that we care, and it also informs and educates us in an important way. The people we visit in their workplaces will come to church with a different attitude. They will listen differently—and more closely. You will speak to them more knowingly. You may illustrate your sermons with vignettes from your visits. This experience will change you, and it will change your congregation. Those who are at the church service will tell others, and the buzz will be positive.

How?

Say, "Hey Joe/Jane, I would love to visit you where you work some time. Any chance I could do that? I don't want to get in the way, but I'd just love to see where you spend your workweek, and have you show and tell me how you spend your time. I'd love to take you to coffee or lunch also if that works out." (Note: If the person works in a no-visitor, high-security environment, suggest at least meeting somewhere nearby. Don't give up! The symbolism of getting close to his or her turf is powerful.)

When you arrive, ask questions: (1) "Tell me how you spend your time here." (2) "How did you get into this kind of work and this company?" (3) "What do you like best about your job and your career?" (4) "Are there any ways I could pray for you especially or support you in your work here?" (5) "Could I just say a short prayer here before I go?" (Don't embarrass them; do this only if you have a quiet, private moment; thank God for them and ask God to bless and strengthen them. NO SERMONS! You are there to learn and to ask them questions.)

Larry Peabody's blog *Called into Work* recently recalled Richard C. Halverson, who pastored churches in Hollywood and Washington, DC, and who served thirteen years as US Senate Chaplain. In his book *How I Changed My Thinking about the Church*, Halverson mentions how he began what he calls a "ministry of listening."

> I devoted several days a week simply to moving from office to office, shop to shop, and out on the oil leases and large farms which surround the city—just being visible and available. Men became used to my presence where they were putting in their daily work and I was soon able to visit with them on their jobs.[5]

---

5. Richard C. Halverson, *How I Changed My Thinking about the Church* (Grand Rapids: Zondervan, 1972).

Peabody comments that "Halverson's change of thinking about the church resulted in several insights we need perhaps even more today than when he wrote them." Here are some sample quotes:

- I began to realize there is a real distinction between church work and the work of the church.
- The real work of the church is what is done between Sundays when the church is scattered all over the metropolitan area where it is located—in homes, and schools, and offices, on construction jobs, and marketplaces.
- Many Christians have become so busy in church work they have not had time to do the work of the church.
- In the minds of many there is absolutely no connection between what occurs in the church on Sunday and what goes on in the community the rest of the week.
- Most of the week the church is not at the address where she worships; she is scattered all over the community, in hundreds of homes, schools, offices and markets, etc.
- All the programs within the church are for the purpose of enabling the church to do the work of the ministry between Sundays when she is invisible as a congregation.

We need to remember that our Lord didn't just hang out in the temple giving religious talks. He walked the city streets and surrounding hills, and visited people's homes. He visited Peter, Andrew, James, and John in their fishing business toward the beginning of his public ministry and after his resurrection. From our contemporary perspective, we need to realize *God already is in our workplaces* of all kinds by his Spirit, who indwells and accompanies believers. So, our task is not just to go to the workplaces of our congregants, carrying the gospel. Pastors need to go there to receive, to listen, and to observe what God is already doing in those workplaces in the lives of our people. It does not take a seminary degree to figure this out. Once a month (or even better, once a week), take the initiative to set up a visit to the workplace turf of one of the men or women in your congregation.

Step 4: Pray for the workplace disciples under your care, and for their workplace opportunities and challenges, at least once each week in your personal prayers and at least once per month in your congregational worship.

Why?

Emergency and crisis prayers are good when needed. We all do them: "We ask for your special help for Joe, who just lost his job" . . . and so on. But we really must get beyond the emergencies and become more holistic and positive.

How?

At least once a week (maybe on Mondays, the first day of the typical workweek), spend some time in your personal prayers praising and thanking God for the work your people are doing, paid or volunteer, asking God to bless them, guide them, protect them, and use them as his instruments in our needy world.

And at least once per month, let's remember our workplace folk, their needs and opportunities, in our public, congregational prayers. Let's not just pray about our "religious" concerns, not just about political and diplomatic crises or natural disasters, or even missionary efforts—which is all great—but let's also mention our workers and their needs and opportunities to the Lord. My colleague, Al Erisman, has often urged that we not just pray for those in difficult work situations, but call up those who have been promoted to more responsibility and pray that God will protect and guide them. Success brings its own vulnerabilities and challenges along with the opportunities!

Step 5: Recognize and commission at least once each year (with a charge and a prayer in the context of congregational worship) our workplace disciples (in general or in a particular specialization such as health care, management, technology, arts, finance, education, etc.) for faithful service representing Christ in their work.

Why?

The fifth step is to recognize and actually commission some of our workplace disciples to serve the Lord in their work. Already, we call forward our missions teams, short term and otherwise, for commissioning and prayer. We call forward and commission our deacons and elders. And, of course, our pastoral installations are often powerful occasions of commissioning and joint prayer. Our marriage and baptismal ceremonies include a commissioning, commitment, and prayer. Joining a local church often is accompanied by a ceremony of the same kind. Away from church, graduation exercises (commencement) is where we give congratulations and also a challenge and a prayer. Clubs, service organizations, and fraternities/sororities provide other examples. These are all widespread human traditions, sometimes only a common ritual but other times a major life passage.

Recognizing and commissioning our parishioners for the work they do during the week is a powerful message that their work matters, not just to them but to their brothers and sisters and, above all, to God himself. They are called to serve the Lord in and through their work, to be an ambassador of another way of life and work. It is too easy to slip back into an attitude that their work doesn't really matter except maybe for their paycheck and tithes to enable God's *real* work. But this is bad, unbiblical theology. Our work *does* matter to God. It is our arena of service and love to God and our neighbors. It is not just about money.

Recognizing and commissioning our parishioners for their workplace discipleship changes *them* first of all. It is a powerful affirmation from the church leadership and the congregation, and hard to forget when they go off to work the next day. It is also a powerful message to our younger people as they think about the meaning and direction of their own education and future work. It can be a powerful message to onlookers in the neighborhood or those at work who hear about it: "These people worship a God who cares about their work! What an amazing and unusual thing." Finally, it is a powerful message to pastors and church staffs: we are not the only ones doing God's work full time. Introducing this kind of commissioning into your church life and worship is not some kind of "magic bullet" or automatic formula for renewal. But I am convinced that it really can have a renewing effect on congregations and their pastors.

How?

My suggestion is that maybe one Sunday worship every three months, we carve out fifteen minutes during the congregational prayer time to include this commissioning.

At Trinitarian Congregational Church in Wayland, Massachusetts, where I served as interim pastor for a year, I alerted the congregation two weeks in advance (by newsletter and announcements in the service) that we were going to call our health-care workers forward and pray for them during the service. Few if any were surprised, then, when I walked to the front of our platform during our congregational prayer time on an October morning, and said the following:

> This morning we would like to recognize, commission, and pray for the health-care providers in our congregation. Would all of you who work in this field in any capacity, and all of you students preparing for such vocations, come up and stand in front of the congregation this morning so we can pray for you? If you are a doctor or nurse, a chiropractor or massage therapist, dentist, dietician, hospital administrator or orderly, pharmaceutical researcher or manager—if you work in any capacity in health care, would you come up here now? In fact, if you are between jobs but health care is what you believe God has called you to do, please come forward also. *[Thirty people came forward; I had no idea it would be so many.]*
>
> I am going to pass around this portable mic. Please quickly say your name, where you work, and what you do in health care. *[This took a few minutes but it worked well: "I'm Joe Smith, pediatrician at Mass General." "Eleanor Mays, orderly at Lahey Clinic." "Joanne Adams, CEO of Cancer Research Pharmaceuticals." "Eddie Ibanez, medical student at Harvard."[6] And so on. What an amazing and diverse group. What a team!]*

I then continued:

> This morning, my friends, we want first of all to thank you. Thank you for hearing God's call and being willing to serve our

6. Names and companies changed here.

Lord in health care. Thank you for studying and preparing for your work in health care. We are so grateful for your service in the footsteps of Jesus Christ. We all want to remember clearly that our God is a healer. The mission of our Lord was to heal as well as to proclaim the gospel. The apostles were sent out to heal as well as preach. Throughout the history of the church, our greatest missionaries brought medicine and health care, as well as the gospel, to the ends of the earth. Health care is at the very heart of the way of Jesus Christ. So, thank you for being our health-care team out there in a needy world.

Second, we want to challenge and encourage you to carry on, to be the hands of Jesus Christ reaching out with a healing touch to those who suffer. We don't want to do our work just like everyone else, but to find the redemptive difference Jesus and Scripture can provide. We want to bring some "salt" and "light" to health care today. We want to challenge you to anchor your health-care thinking and practice in the values and insights of Jesus and Scripture.

This morning, I want to ask if you will pledge, to the best of your ability, to deepen your approach to health care in the perspective of Jesus and Scripture. If you will make that pledge, please say "I will." *[They then responded with "I will."]* And those of you in the congregation, would you pledge to pray for our health-care team as God brings them to mind, that God would bless, strengthen, protect, and use them in their work? Please say, "We will." *[Congregation: "We will."]*

And third, we want to join together in prayer for you this morning. I'd like to invite our elders and any others who would like to join them to step up to the front here and lay a hand on one of our health-care workers as a sign of solidarity as we pray. *[Dozens of people came forward and surrounded our health-care team.]* "Our Father, we thank you for each of these your servants. We pray that you will work your healing and caring purposes through their hands, their minds, their skills, and their efforts, wherever they are working on the health-care team. Lord, please give them strength. Please protect them from danger and harm. Please provide for them and supply them with the resources they need for their work. Please keep them from temptation and discouragement. Work through them, O God, just as you worked in Jesus Christ our Lord. Help their colleagues and their patients to see Jesus Christ in them each day. Bless these dear servants of yours, our brothers and sisters. We pray in Jesus' name. Amen."

There was one interesting follow-up to this Sunday. A week later two immigrants, who were working as orderlies in a big hospital, came up to me after the service looking concerned. They said, "Pastor Gill, we couldn't be here last week because we have to work every other week and can't attend church on those days. But we don't want to miss the blessing! Could we have the blessing?" I was only too happy to share the challenge with them and get a nearby elder to join me as we laid hands on these two dear brothers and prayed for them.

Three months later, I called up all the congregants who worked in the finance field. At the service, I followed the same three-part approach: (1) Thank you for going into this line of work; tell us who you are and what you do; this is God's work you are doing. (2) We want to challenge you to deepen your understanding of how Jesus and Scripture can bring a difference to the way you do your work out there; your profession needs this salt and light; will you pledge to try? And will the rest of you congregants here pledge to pray for our financial team out there? (3) We want to lay hands on you and pray.

Here is the introduction for people in finance for the service:

This morning, I want to invite all of our financial workers to come forward and let us pray for you. If you are a CFO, financial advisor, accountant, or treasurer; if you work at a bank or

> insurance company; if you are a tax preparer or bookkeeper for a home business; if you work in any way managing money or are studying for one of these professions, please come forward. If you believe God has called you to this work arena but you are between jobs, you come forward also. I am going to pass around this portable mic. Please quickly say your name, where you work, and what you do in the financial world.
>
> First of all, this morning we want to thank you for going into this profession, for studying and learning, for all your hard work in an industry that is full of temptation and scandal. Despite this, you are providing people with an essential service and help. Our Lord had more to say about money, property, and wealth than heaven and hell or most other subjects. He really cared about your field. So, this morning we want to challenge you to deepen your knowledge and understanding of what Jesus and Scripture have to say about money, debt, loans, and all those related subjects. If you will pledge to do this, then [insert prayer from above].

Three months later, I called up all the engineers, techies, and builders. It went something like this:

> This morning, I want to invite all of our engineers and techies and builders to come forward and let us pray for you. If you are in any kind of engineering or technology or work for such a company, if you are an architect, a contractor or builder, if you work in the building trades or are a handyman, if you are an apprentice or hope to get work in this arena, please come forward. I am going to pass around this portable mic. Please quickly say your name, where you work, and what you do in the technology and building professions.
>
> First of all, this morning we want to thank you for going into this field of work, for all of your study and your hard work. You know the Bible doesn't begin by saying, "In the beginning God preached a sermon!" No, in the beginning God designed and

> built a beautiful, amazing world. And that's what you do! It is God's work to design, build, and support useful and beautiful things. So, thank you for going into this field. There is a lot of corruption and temptation and challenge in your work area, and we are so glad we have you out there to represent the Lord and his way of building.
>
> In addition to thanking you for going into your line of work, we want to challenge you to make a real effort to deepen your understanding of how to honor God and follow Jesus and Scripture in your work so you will be true salt and light. If you are willing to pledge to work on this, please say, "I will."

Another three months later, I called up all the teachers. You can easily imagine how to affirm teachers (college professors, public and private school teachers, administrators, coaches, homeschoolers, online educators, the whole team!) in light of Jesus' role as a teacher.

I then finished off my one-year interim term and the new pastor arrived. I am not sure whether he continued what I started (interim pastors must not meddle!). Had I continued, I certainly would have had all the arts folk (painters, writers, singers, poets, thespians, dancers, etc.) come forward. I would have loved to call forward the food service folk (grocery store employees, farmers, chefs, waiters, etc.). Infant and childcare providers and parents could easily have their day (recognizing the true labor of bringing children into the world and caring for them!). Whenever I did these commissionings, I tried to be inclusive so that students and apprentices and those out of work were part of it. It might make sense some time to invite all those who are unemployed or underemployed to come forward for special prayer.

In a small congregation, there may be only three healthcare workers, one attorney, and five engineers/builders. I would still do the commissioning, but I would have these folk come up on the platform to be briefly interviewed by me before the commissioning and prayer. In a very large church, the list of folk might need to be in the church newsletter (with their permission and not announced live on the spot), and the people might need to stand in place around the sanctuary and be touched on the shoulder by those seated around them during the prayer. I don't see any reason why any church couldn't always do this prayer and commissioning every three months, eventually repeating and renewing the vocational focus from two or three years earlier.

Step 6: Educate—work with others in the church to offer at least six hours each year of Christian education with practical biblical perspectives on workplace topics such as calling, stewardship, money, leadership, character, honesty, and ethics.

Why?

We have Sunday school classes and retreats on all manner of topics, especially on straight-ahead Bible study. Most churches have classes on parenting, marriage, prayer, evangelism, and the defense of the faith. This is all great, but if we want to get serious about a 24/7 approach to discipleship, then we need to make sure we have some Christian education about work for all age groups.

How?

This could be during Sunday school, a small group, or a Saturday or weekend retreat. It could be structured around a series of topics or biblical passages. It could be organized around a particular book, such as the following: *Working in the Presence of God: Spiritual Practices for Everyday Work* by Denise Daniels and Sharon Vandewarker (Hendrickson, 2019), *Where's God on Monday?* by Alistair Mackenzie and Wayne Kirkland (Hendrickson, 2015), *Kingdom Calling: Vocational Stewardship for the Common Good* by Amy Sherman (InterVarsity, 2011), *Every Good Endeavor: Connecting Your Work to God's Work* by Timothy Keller and Katherine Leary Alsdforf (Dutton, 2012), *Work Matters: Connecting Sunday Worship to Monday Work* by Tom Nelson (Crossway, 2011), *Work: A Kingdom Perspective on Labor* by Ben Witherington (Eerdmans, 2011), *Your Work Matters to God* by Doug Sherman and William Hendricks (NavPress, 1990), *Mastering Monday: A Guide to Integrating Faith and Work* by John D. Beckett (InterVarsity Press, 2006), or one of the other good books mentioned earlier in this book. There are also some excellent video programs, such as Regent College's "Reframe" (https://www.reframecourse.com/).

If someone has the time, motivation, and ability, they could create an adult education course for their church. I have created and taught many adult education courses and seminars in churches on a biblical theology and philosophy of work. Like my forthcoming book, I often call it "The God of Good Work." I organize it around God's work example and instruction, with sessions ranging across the canon on creative work, bad/fallen work, sustaining work, wise work, just work, redemptive work, finished work, and after work. That is the "theory," the ideal, the mission, and the vision. I also do courses and seminars on the practical aspects of workplace discipleship, following the outline of this book. Here I address commitment, prayer, study, partnership, and the other steps covered in previous chapters of this book. I am now (in my retirement) the volunteer, part-time "Workplace Discipleship Coach" at my home church.

There actually are no panaceas or ironclad formulas for revival or renewal in the Christian church. But hopefully, you can begin to see that committing yourself to these six specific steps has real and understandable potential to positively impact peoples' lives and your ministry. This is not about more money in a stretched-to-the-limit budget. It is not about your taking a course or earning another degree. It is about reordering your schedule and priorities, though not in an extreme or disruptive way. It is common sense. These are simple steps. Take them!

Acknowledgments

My debts are too many to list here. My seminary, business school, and university students and colleagues over a long career have walked with me through a great learning adventure and I thank them all. I am especially grateful to Scott Thomas, Lauri Stott, Ken Morris, Don Tinder, Chris Sillerud, Amy Brannon Keltner, Fred Vann, Jay Boone, and Bonnie Johnston at New College Berkeley, to Greg Clark, Karl Soderstrom, and Steve Bouma-Prediger at North Park University, and to Yuna Oh, Rachel Tang, Chloe Wu, David Horn, Joanna Mockler, Tom Phillips, Mike Garry, Andrew James, and Ed Keazirian at Gordon-Conwell. I have also road-tested and shared my ideas and questions with countless church groups, student fellowships, professional groups, and conference participants. I have also learned so much from the authors of books and articles I devour; some of the most influential are listed throughout this book.

I have been blessed to have students, colleagues, and friends who sometimes push back and critique my ideas. Among the most important of those who have helped shape my understanding of the integration of faith and work are Jacques Ellul, Os Guinness, Ward and Laurel Gasque, Doug and Joan Anderson, Paul Stevens, Jim Sire, Virginia Viola, Katherine Leary Alsdorf, Amy Sherman, Tom Nelson, Larry Ward, J. Alfred Smith Sr., Robert Banks, Dave Evans, Bill Peel, Patrick Lencioni, Bill Pollard, John Beckett, Raymond Downing, Bernard Adeney, Earl Palmer, and Walt Hearn—and I am sure I have left some deserving names off this list, for which I apologize. For their encouragement and suggestions on this book in particular, I am especially grateful to Catherine Blake, Gina Casey, Buddy Childress, Clay Collins, Tom Cowley, Kim Daus, Al Erisman, Ginny Halstead, Susan White, Jewel Hyun, Chuck Proudfit, Mark Roberts, Missy Wallace, Rachel Tang, and Mark Washington. This is my ninth published book, and I consider myself an experienced wordsmith, but I have to express my deep appreciation and gratitude to Patricia Anders, whose detailed editorial attention to this book has been nothing short of spectacular. Best editor ever!

I am grateful to my home church, First Covenant Church of Oakland, and our pastor Marco Ambriz, for welcoming me as their "Workplace Discipleship Coach" in my post-professor stage of life. Of course, my list would never be complete without acknowledging the support and insight of my wife Lucia, with whom I have walked closely since our first date in November 1963.

I am dedicating this book to two of my brothers and their wives. No, we are not blood brothers, but our parents and our grandparents were good friends in the Plymouth Brethren movement they helped lead across North America. I grew up with three sisters and no brothers—but in my late teens and early twenties, first John and then Al Erisman became my lifetime brothers, friends, and colleagues. We never actually lived in the same town, though John and Marj were just an hour away for about ten years. John and Marj bonded with Lucia and me over music-making, jazz, good wine, and a shared commitment to "thinking Christianly," renewing our church communities, and positively impacting our world. John reviewed several of my book manuscripts before publication and often got me speaking gigs to share my ideas. He never hesitated to kick my butt when I needed it, or encourage me (even more frequently!).

On my way to Vancouver to teach a 1993 Regent College Summer course on "Jacques Ellul and the World of Technology," I stopped at Al and Nancy Erisman's house in Seattle and realized that my longtime friend Al was not just a mathematician working at Boeing, but was now their director of technology, managing three hundred R&D techies. Yikes! I quickly realized that he (a technology creator) should be co-teaching this course with me (a technology critic). Three years later, our co-taught course in a Regent College Summer School on "Business, Technology, and Christian Ethics" was a huge hit with a big class of techies as well as theology students. By 1998, we co-founded the "Institute for Business, Technology, and Ethics" with a bimonthly journal called *Ethix* (www.ethix.org). Since then, Al and I have co-taught dozens of courses and co-presented to technology and business audiences around North America. Our shared faith, mission, ethical values, and mutual respect are ironclad—while our very different perspectives on some aspects of both business and technology are appreciated by audiences that like both heat and light! Nancy also has inspired me (and many others) by her local initiatives for women in the workplace.

In chapter 4, I urged the importance of having a posse with whom to navigate the challenges and opportunities of workplace discipleship. In a critical way, John and Al have been not just my posse serving that purpose, but also my beloved brothers for more than fifty years. The fact that our friendship includes our wives and goes far beyond just an interest in workplace discipleship has been one of God's greatest gifts to me. To these two amazing brothers and their wives, I gratefully dedicate this book.

About the Author

David W. Gill has been a pioneer in the faith at work, marketplace ministry, workplace discipleship, theology, and ethics of work domains (www.davidwgill.org). It all began for him in the late 1960s as a history undergrad at Cal Berkeley, where he began a quest to integrate his faith with his university studies and vocational thinking. Finding little support or help from either church or seminary in those days, David earned his PhD in ethics at the University of Southern California, and then spearheaded the project to found a graduate school of theology and ethics for the laity close by his Berkeley alma mater. From its 1976 inception in his dreams to his retirement from the faculty and presidency in 1990, New College Berkeley was a one-of-a-kind think tank and study center oriented both to the academy and the marketplace, graduating about twenty master's degree recipients each year, and providing courses and conferences to literally thousands through the years. Unfortunately, this free-standing, degree-granting, graduate school became financially unsustainable over the long haul with its dependence on tuition-funded graduate-level lay education and had to close in 1994.

From 1990 to 1992, David served as Interim Senior Pastor at University Covenant Church in Davis, California; and from 2011 to 2012, he served as Interim for Trinitarian Congregational Church in Wayland, Massachusetts. From 1992 to 2001, he was the Carl I. Lindberg Professor of Applied Ethics at North Park University in Chicago; and from 1998 to 2003, with Albert M. Erisman, he founded and led the Institute for Business, Technology, and Ethics (and its bimonthly journal *Ethix*). From 2004 to 2010, David was full-time business ethics professor for virtually all MBA students in the St. Mary's College Graduate School of Business (Moraga, California). From 2010 to 2016, he served as the inaugural Mockler-Phillips Professor of Workplace Theology & Business Ethics and Director of the Mockler Center for Faith & Ethics in the Workplace at Gordon-Conwell Theological Seminary. He was the primary organizer of the historic 2014 Faith at Work Summit Conference in Boston.

He is now back home in Oakland, California, pursuing several writing projects, promoting workplace discipleship in his church and community, and leading WorkPlace 313, a workplace discipleship resource and training nonprofit based in Oakland (www.WP313.org).

David is the author of more than two hundred articles, chapters, and reviews in multiple journals, magazines, books, and other publications—and eight published books, including a two-volume introduction to Christian ethics. He is proud to say that he worked as a gas station attendant and mechanic during high school, as a factory laborer during his summers and academic breaks while in college, and as a public school teacher for three years, before finding his calling as a university, business school, and seminary professor of ethics.

Raised in the Plymouth Brethren, he was a licensed minister in the Evangelical Covenant Church and is ordained by Allen Temple Baptist Church (Oakland, California) in the Progressive National Baptist Convention. He has been a guest preacher, teacher, or conference speaker for countless churches and student groups across North America, Europe, and China. He has also lectured and given papers at many universities, seminaries, and professional meetings on business and technological ethics, Christian ethics, and on education. He has been an organizational ethics consultant and trainer for many firms, including Harris & Associates Construction and Project Management, Kaiser-Permanente Hospital, East Bay Municipal Utility District, Paradise Foods, Swedish Covenant Hospital, and Nikon Precision. In 1988, he cofounded the Jacques Ellul Forum, and since 2000 has served as the founding president of the International Jacques Ellul Society (www.ellul.org) and founding member of the board of the Association Internationale Jacques Ellul based in Bordeaux, France.

Born in Omaha, Nebraska in 1946, David has lived most of his life in Berkeley or Oakland, California. In 1967, he married Lucia Paulson, with whom he has two children (Jodie [Gill] Hoffman and Jonathan Gill) and six grandchildren.

About the Hendrickson Publishers/ Theology of Work Line of Books

There is an unprecedented interest today in the role of Christian faith in "ordinary" work, and Christians in every field are exploring what it means to work "as to the Lord" (Col. 3:22). Pastors and church leaders, and the scholars and teachers who support them, are asking what churches can do to equip their members in the workplace. There's a need for deep thinking, fresh perspectives, practical ideas, and mutual engagement between Christian faith and work in every sphere of human endeavor.

This Hendrickson Publishers/Theology of Work line of books seeks to bring significant new resources into this conversation. It began with Hendrickson's publication of the *Theology of Work Bible Commentary* and other Bible study materials written by the TOW Project. Soon we discovered a wealth of resources by other writers with a common heart for the meaning and value of everyday work. The HP/TOW line was formed to make the best of these resources available on the national and international stage.

Works in the HP/TOW line engage the practical issues of daily work through the lens of the Bible and the other resources of the Christian faith. They are biblically grounded, but their subjects are the work, workers, and workplaces of today. They employ contemporary arts and sciences, best practices, empirical research, and wisdom gained from experience, yet always in the service of Christ's redemptive work in the world, especially the world of work.

To a greater or lesser degree, all the books in this line make use of the scholarship of the *Theology of Work Bible Commentary*. The authors, however, are not limited to the TOW Project's perspectives, and they constantly expand the scope and application of the material. Publication of a book in the HP/TOW line does not necessarily imply endorsement by the Theology of Work Project, or that the author endorses the TOW Project. It does mean we recognize the work as an important contribution to the faith-work discussion, and we find a common footing that makes us glad to walk side-by-side in the dialogue.

We are proud to present the HP/TOW line together. We hope it helps readers expand their thinking, explore ideas worthy of deeper thought, and make sense of their own work in light of the Christian faith. We are grateful to the authors and all those whose labor has brought the HP/TOW line to life.

William Messenger, Executive Editor, Theology of Work Project
Sean McDonough, Biblical Editor, Theology of Work Project
Patricia Anders, Editorial Director, Hendrickson Publishers

www.theologyofwork.org
www.hendrickson.com